Dynamic Management of Growing Firms

Dynamic Management of Growing Firms

A Strategic Approach

SECOND EDITION

Lorraine Uhlaner Hendrickson

John Psarouthakis

Ann Arbor

THE UNIVERSITY OF MICHIGAN PRESS

This book is dedicated to our families,
to Professor Basil Georgopoulos,
and to the modern entrepreneur.

Chapters 1–15 and Appendixes A–C were originally published
as *Managing the Growing Firm* (Englewood Cliffs, NJ:
Prentice-Hall, 1992).

A CIP catalog record for this book is available
from the British Library.

Library of Congress Cataloging-in-Publication Data

Hendrickson, Lorraine Uhlaner.
    Dynamic management of growing firms : a strategic approach /
Lorraine Uhlaner Hendrickson, John Psarouthakis. — 2nd ed.
        p.   cm.
    Rev. ed. of: Managing the growing firm. 1992.
    Includes bibliographical references and index.
    ISBN 0-472-10927-8 (alk. paper)
    1. Small business — Management.   2. Industrial management.
I. Psarouthakis, John, 1932–   .   II. Hendrickson, Lorraine Uhlaner.
Managing the growing firm.   III. Title.
HD62.7.H457   1998
658.02′2 — dc21   98-15333
                                                                          CIP

Acknowledgments

We are grateful to the many individuals and organizations making this project possible — the original research as well as the two editions of this book.

Our research benefited from the ideas, advice, and encouragement of many individuals. We especially would like to thank Dr. Basil Georgopoulos, University of Michigan, Ann Arbor, Professor Emeritus, whose approach to organization effectiveness provided the foundation of the DSP Model. We are also indebted to Dr. Eric Flamholtz for his permission to use the "Growing Pains" index in our research. Others we would like to recognize include the following: Dr. Robert Brockhaus, Director, Jefferson Smurfit Center for Entrepreneurial Studies, St. Louis University; Neil Churchill, Director, Babson College Center for Entrepreneurship; Dr. Daniel M. Spitzer, Chairman of the George S. Aldhizer II Department of Economics and Business at Bridgewater College; Larry T. Eiler, President and founder, Eiler Communications; Dr. Jerry Katz, Research Director, Jefferson Smurfit Center for Entrepreneurial Studies, St. Louis University; Bernard Goldsmith, retired, formerly Associate Dean, Graduate School of Industrial Administration, Carnegie-Mellon University; Robert T. Uhlaner, corporate finance specialist at McKinsey Associates and a co-founder of Quantum Consulting; Tim Korzon, President, Lakeland Chair; Dennis DuBois, director of the Family Business Council, University of Illinois, Chicago; and Dr. Tom Lumpkin, assistant professor of management at University of Illinois, Chicago. We also appreciate the help of Dr. Ken Lacho, professor of management at the University of New Orleans, in updating the literature on growing firms. We are especially grateful to Reyn Hendrickson, former President and CEO of StarPak Energy Systems Corporations, and current Vice-President, Edgemere Enterprises, for his patient and exhaustive editing of the manuscripts for both editions for both content and style, greatly enhancing their readability. We also would like to thank Eric B. Hendrickson for the preparation of new figures for the second edition and Dawn Aziz, M.B.A. student at Eastern Michigan University, for her help in updating the research literature for the second edition.

We would also like to acknowledge funding support for the original study from several sources: initial funding from the State of Michigan Research Excellence Fund and Eastern Michigan University, as well as continuation grants received from the United States Small Business Administration and J. P. Industries. Beth Ann Welch provided valuable computer assistance. Further, we could not have completed the original research project without the cooperation of almost five hundred CEOs and managers from almost two hundred companies, who will remain anonymous. We would also like to thank Gary

Reed and Jim McAuliffe, both past JPI senior executives, as well as Leo Smith, former President of Coastal Chem, for the opportunity to interview them for the book. To complete the original research project, "Managing the Growing Firm," we received assistance from research project members Timothy F. Grainey, Vivian H. Watkins, Saad Shah, Rebecca Liksey, and other Center for Entrepreneurship staff, including Kathleen Ward, Gary Chuslo, Sandy Bambas Sakalauskas, Barbara Epstein, and Dr. Patricia Weber, past director of the center.

Finally, we are deeply grateful to Ellen McCarthy, Business and Economics acquisitions editor at the University of Michigan Press, for her enthusiasm, encouragement, and support throughout the preparation of the second edition.

Contents

Appendix

Preface

Dynamic Management of Growing Firms: A Strategic Approach is a unique addition to the literature on growing firms. First, it presents the Dynamic System Planning Model, an alternative approach to strategic planning for growing firms. The DSP Model is a validated approach: It is based on open-system theory as well as analysis of data from close to five hundred face-to-face interviews with CEOs and other executives from small and mid-sized companies. In addition to the basic research results, the book provides rich accounts of strategies used effectively by these small firms. Using the Dynamic System Planning Model as a base, the book also provides an insider's view of how automotive and plumbing supplier J. P. Industries (JPI) was catapulted to FORTUNE 500 status in only ten years during the 1980s.

The book is the product of a unique team effort. Co-authored by an academic, Dr. Lorraine Hendrickson of Eastern Michigan University, and an entrepreneur, Dr. John Psarouthakis, founder, president, and chairman of two successful companies, J. P. Industries, and JPE Inc., the book provides a practical yet research-based guide to managing small to mid-sized firms. *Dynamic Management of Growing Firms: A Strategic Approach* is actually the second edition of the book *Managing the Growing Firm*. For the second edition, we present a revised preface and completely new introductory chapter to clarify key points of the Dynamic System Planning Model and to update relevant research on our topic.[1] In addition, very minor revisions were made to Chapters 1–15 and the appendixes. We believe the book's message remains timely and important.

In the book, we present a new approach to strategic planning that will help to steer you away from crisis management toward more profitable growth. Our aim is to change your perception of strategic planning from an annual academic exercise lining your bookcase to a daily guide for running your growing business more profitably. We identify and analyze a comprehensive set of strategic management issues derived from organization theory, entrepreneurship and strategic management research, and practical experience, taking a broader perspective than the marketing and financial focus of strategic management dominant in the 1980s and early 1990s. Our approach recognizes the cross-functional, dynamic forces at work in today's organizations. It is consistent with the emerging view that the CEO needs to develop company strategy not only regarding external competitive pressure but also upon development of internal capabilities, or core competencies.[2]

Open-systems theory forms the cornerstone of our theoretical orientation. Validated by decades of research, open-systems theory identifies a relatively easy-to-learn set of basic management issues that, if attended to, should enhance a company's odds for short-term as well as long-term success — survival, growth, and profitability. We refer to this open-systems-based model as the Dynamic System Planning Model, or DSP Model, throughout the remainder of our book. In spite of its research base, the DSP Model can be used as a practical, analytical, and problem solving tool. The DSP Model identifies seven enduring system issues that you must manage strategically, operationally, and dynamically as your company and its environment change over time. These seven issues include the following: market strategy, resource acquisition, resource allocation, work flow, human relations, public relations, and technical mastery. We systematically examine the relationships among these issues, as well as their linkages to the eighth issue, the financial viability, or performance, of the company.

DON'T SKIP THE INTRODUCTION

We strongly advise readers to read the introduction before reading the rest of the book. In that chapter, we present new schema to explain the DSP Model — the central focus of our book. We also explain how the DSP Model can be used in more familiar strategic planning methodologies. The introduction describes more fully how the DSP Model can be used as a simple analytical tool at several intersection points in the strategic and action planning process — first to identify strengths and weaknesses, then to identify core competencies around which strategy can be developed or refined, and finally at the implementation stage, to explore the types of changes required to implement a new strategy. In the introduction, we also explain how our research fits in with other work in strategic management and entrepreneurship. For interested readers, the introductory chapter also provides an updated literature review on management strategy and sales growth.

WHO THIS BOOK IS FOR

For simplicity and improved readability, in the body of the text we frequently address the reader as if he or she is an entrepreneur/business owner. However, we would like to underscore that the book is useful to a much broader audience — anyone interested in improving an organization's effectiveness. Business owners and other organizational leaders will find the book helpful. We also recommend it to business planning advisors or others interested in mastering a new mental model for identifying a company's strengths, weaknesses, or potential competitive advantages. Scholars and students in entrepreneurship, organization theory, and strategic management may similarly find our perspective useful. The first edition of the book was used as a required text for the second year graduate program in Enterprise Management at Swinburne University of Technology, Center for Innovation and Enterprise in Melbourne, Australia. It is also on the recommended list in the course Managing the Growing Business, designed by Professor Ken Lacho at the University of New Orleans.

Those consultants, scholars, and business owners working with unconventionally structured businesses (i.e., those not divided by business function) may find the mental model presented in our book especially useful. Unlike traditional analysis approaches that focus on examination of the different functional areas, the systems-based issues that make up the DSP Model naturally cross different functions. Thus, the particular structure of the organization is not an obstacle to analysis of the seven issues, even if the company has no departmental structure at all (as is often the case with very young firms). You do not have to have a marketing department, production department, or other standard, functionally defined divisions of organization to find our model applicable.

Though the examples in our book are from the private sector, you can easily apply the analytical approach offered by Dynamic System Planning to the public and nonprofit sectors. You can use the seven DSP issues to assess hospitals, charter schools, public agencies, or nonprofit service providers. In fact, the roots of the model are derived from organization effectiveness research done by others on schools, hospitals, and government agencies. Managers in larger firms, whether functionally or nontraditionally structured, may also find that the DSP Model will provide a new perspective in problem identification and problem solving.

In short, anyone interested in more effective management of an organization, with an eye toward improved performance (whether with respect to sales, profits, or other parameters), may benefit from reading *Dynamic Management of Growing Firms: A Strategic Approach.*

SCOPE OF THE BOOK

In the first edition we described this as a "how-to" book for the CEO. Although many readers indicated that they benefited from reading the book, they did not agree that it is a "how-to" book in the traditional sense. Although our book provides practical benefits, its real purpose is to provide a new paradigm or mental model around which you can reorganize your thinking about your organization.[3] We outline the key issues you must track and plan for as you develop competitive strategies for your organization.

This book is not a business planning book per se. Nor is it aimed at providing information on how to start a business. There are many publications that outline the basic format that bankers and investors expect to see for the business plan — the overall vision of the company, the description of the business, the marketing plan, the operational plan, financial statements, and so forth, whether for start-up or the existing business.[4] But in developing or revising the strategic plan, almost any approach requires the clear identification of the company's strengths and weaknesses, its core competencies, its competitive advantages, and, in turn, its competitive strategy. Many strategic management texts tend to be somewhat vague as to the content of capabilities or weaknesses that you should review, typically listing the business functions (marketing, accounting, manufacturing) and perhaps a few other disconnected areas. As an analytical and planning tool, the DSP Model provides a cross-functional, open-systems-based alternative, an approach that is fundamental to effective system functioning, regardless of industry, age, or size. By examining these seven issues, you may identify strategies or tactics that you might otherwise have overlooked. The book also offers a set of categories more easily adapted to nonmanufacturing organizations than the value chain approach described in many strategic management texts.[5]

BASIS FOR THE BOOK

This book is the product of a unique team effort by the two authors, Dr. Lorraine Uhlaner Hendrickson and Dr. John Psarouthakis. Our book is primarily based on a research project conducted between 1985 and 1990 while we were both affiliated with the Center for Entrepreneurship at Eastern Michigan University (see appendix A for details). The research team interviewed 462 CEOs and managers face-to-face from a randomly drawn sample of 168 small and mid-sized firms. Our book is also based on other entrepreneurship research, other face-to-face interviews, and case materials developed for the book. We present data and illustrate each of the seven DSP organizational issues with case examples drawn from the research project and from interviews with former managers of J. P. Industries (JPI) as well as other resource materials. Founded by Dr. Psarouthakis, JPI was sold to P&N PLC, a large British industrial corporation, for $376 million 10 years after its founding.

FEEDBACK TO THE AUTHORS

We would very much appreciate hearing from you. We would like to receive your reactions to our ideas and want to know whether you have found our ideas useful. We are accumulating examples of how the DSP Model and our book are used in different companies and universities. We would also appreciate updates on any research being done on strategy and sales growth and any other comments you might have on the book. Please contact Dr. Hendrickson at Eastern Michigan University, Department of Management, Ypsilanti, MI 48197 or by e-mail at lorraine.hendrickson@emich.edu.

NOTES

[1]Lorraine Uhlaner Hendrickson and John Psarouthakis, *Managing the Growing Firm* (Englewood Cliffs, NJ: Prentice-Hall, 1992).

[2]C. K. Prahalad and Gary Hamel, "The Core Competence of the Corporation," *Harvard Business Review,* 68, no. 3 (1990), 79–91. See also Gary Hamel and C. K. Prahalad, *Competing for the Future* (Boston, MA: Harvard Business School Press, 1994).

[3]For discussion of mental models, see Peter Senge, *The Fifth Discipline: The Art and Practice of the Learning Organization* (New York: Doubleday/Currency, 1990).

[4]For a helpful business planning guide, refer to David H. Bangs, *The Business Planning Guide: Creating a Plan for Success in Your Own Business,* 7th ed. (Chicago: Upstart Publishing Co., 1997). Another good reference for the start-up venture is Kathleen Allen, *Launching New Ventures: An Entrepreneurial Approach* (Chicago: Upstart Publishing Co., 1995).

[5]The value chain approach was originally developed by Michael E. Porter, *Competitive Advantage* (New York: Free Press, 1985). See John A. Pearce and Richard B. Robinson, Jr., *Strategic Management: Formulation, Implementation, and Control,* 5th ed. (Burr Ridge, IL: Irwin, 1994), pp. 183–88, for an excellent description of the value chain approach and also for an introduction to strategic management.

Introduction

Based on comments we received from readers of the first edition, we sensed a need to provide a clearer presentation of the central focus of our book — the Dynamic System Planning (DSP) Model — and an explanation of how the model and our research relate to other work in strategic management and entrepreneurship, especially more recent research. To accomplish these ends, the introduction is organized as follows:

1. We restate our fundamental research question in the context of the overall entrepreneurship research literature.
2. We explain how strategic management and organization theory have begun to merge as disciplines.
3. We schematically present the DSP Model.
4. We clarify the cross-functional nature of the DSP Model.
5. We present ways you can use the DSP Model in more familiar strategic planning methodologies.
6. Finally, from a review of the current empirical literature on strategy and sales growth, we highlight key findings overlooked by or published since the first edition.

We urge you to review the first five sections of the introduction before reading the rest of the book. The last section, updating the literature since publication of the first book, may be read either now or later, depending upon your interests.

OUR FUNDAMENTAL RESEARCH QUESTION: WHICH STRATEGIC ACTIONS DETERMINE CONTINUED GROWTH AND PROFITABILITY IN THE SMALL TO MEDIUM-SIZED FIRM?

Once a company is in operation, which factors determine its growth and profitability? Entrepreneurship researchers have taken four main directions in answering this question. Some adopt a *population ecology* approach — a Social Darwinian view seeking to identify external environmental factors influencing the birth and growth of a cluster of organizations that share common industry or geographic characteristics.[1] Others seek to identify *owner-founder characteristics* to predict the birth or success of enterprises. A third cluster of researchers employs a corporate *life cycle* approach — a developmental view suggesting that firms go through inevitable stages from birth to maturity and eventual death, analogous to the life cycle of human beings. A fourth group focuses primarily on internal actions taken by the founder and other managers after a company has been established. This last group attempts to identify which strategies might be associated with growth and profitability (*strategic adaptation* perspective).[2]

Although all four approaches have merit, our research primarily reflects the fourth perspective. Our book provides a theoretical framework, strongly grounded in decades of open-system-based organization theory research, that helps to identify the categories of strategies you must consider in directing your company. These categories of strategies form the essence of the DSP Model and our book. Our book further emphasizes the open-system-theory perspective that multitiered social systems (at individual, company, and larger social levels) all interact dynamically to impact organizational outcomes. This perspective is quite consistent with recent research in the field of entrepreneurship and strategic management of growing firms, showing that interactions among individual, environmental, and strategy variables provide more accurate predictions of sales growth than any one set of variables alone.[3] We provide an update and interpretation of this research in the last section of this chapter.

STRATEGIC MANAGEMENT AND ORGANIZATION THEORY: A MERGING OF DISCIPLINES

Apart from its roots in the field of entrepreneurship, our research straddles two other disciplines: strategic management and organization theory. Until the late 1980s, the fields of strategic management and organization theory appeared quite distinct. Though both are interdisciplinary outgrowths of other disciplines, strategic management was more heavily influenced by the fields of marketing and finance, whereas organization theory was an outgrowth of social psychology and sociology. But it is logical and inevitable that researchers from each field would begin to pay attention to one another while searching for common truths. Both attempt to predict a common set of dependent variables — organizational success and effectiveness.

Strategic management has shifted since the 1950s from a focus on long-term corporate resource planning toward a focus on competitive advantage.[4] Through the 1980s, much of strategic management research looked outward from the organization for competitive advantage: A company's success depends upon its choice of industry, markets, and products. The three generic competitive strategies — cost leadership, differentiation, and focus — outlined by Michael Porter in his seminal work, *Competitive Strategy,* each define an aspect of a company's product advantage vis-à-vis its competitors.[5] Led by Prahalad and Hamel, in the late 1980s and early 1990s, strategic management shifted again to look beyond the product/market mix toward the underlying *core competencies,* sets of skills or capabilities that make new product development and process improvements possible.[6] Rather than encouraging companies to build strategy exclusively around products or customers, Prahalad and Hamel urged them to build around a central set of corporate skills. Although their essays focus primarily on technical capabilities underlying a stream of products or services in large manufacturing corporations, other authors have subsequently adopted the core competency theme, identifying an ever-broadening set of underlying capabilities thought to provide competitive advantage. Ulrich and Lake identify four sets of capabilities — financial, marketing, technological, and *organizational learning* — the last referring to an organization's ability to engage employees in problem solving that helps it change.[7] In 1994, Pfeffer identified a trend in strategic orientation away from product and process technology, protected and regulated markets, and access to financial resources toward organizational capabilities — in particular, how the workforce is managed.[8]

As a subdiscipline of sociology, the field of organization theory evolved in a fairly isolated manner from the field of strategic management, with little crossover between the two fields until the late 1980s or early 1990s. To illustrate the subtle shift taking place at the time, consider the changes made to the popular organization-theory text, Daft's *Organization Theory and Design,* between its 1992 and 1995 editions. In the 1992 edition, the chapter on organization effectiveness makes no mention of strategy. In the 1995 edition, Daft combines strategic management and organization effectiveness in a newly titled chapter reflecting this change and includes a new chapter on organizational learning that further expands on strategic management themes.[9] Our book, *Managing the Growing Firm,* originally published in 1992, is also representative of an effort to integrate organization theory and strategic management.

Open-systems theory is one of the most important theories to cross over from organization theory into the general management literature. Though open-systems theory has long been a part of the body of knowledge in organization theory, popular interest in it has only recently reemerged.[10] Apart from our book, several widely read management books published in the early 1990s brought renewed attention to that perspective. Senge's book, *The Fifth Discipline,* based extensively on open-systems-theory principles, highlights the importance to managers of mental models such as open-systems theory to foster more creative problem solving. He points out that by breaking problems into smaller parts, we often lose sight of the whole organization, and he advocates instead a total-system view of the organization.[11] Several books, including *The Boundaryless Organization* and *The Death of Competition,* emphasize the importance of viewing an organization as a social system that, in turn, is part of a larger business ecosystem.[12] Another popular book, *A Simpler Way,* takes a somewhat more anthropomorphic approach to organizations, viewing them as living systems.[13] Explaining system dynamics in more physical terms, Goldstein's *The Unshackled Organization* elaborates on the internal qualities of the organization as a *nonlinear* system: its capacity for *synergy* (the whole being greater than the sum of the parts); its capacity for *self-organization* (spontaneous and radical transformation of the system); the multidirectional and mutual interaction among elements; and the growth potential of the system as a result of a *far-from-equilibrium process* (the tendency of nonlinear systems to change rather than to seek equilibrium).[14]

In sum, our work is influenced by a convergence between strategic management and organization theory. We adopt the view from strategic management that visioning, direction setting, and the identification of core competencies and competitive advantage are useful in building the effective organization. We also benefit from the long-standing body of research on open-systems theory, helping us to identify more clearly what some of those internal core capabilities ought to be. We identify these core capabilities as part of the DSP Model, which is described in the next section.

A SCHEMATIC REPRESENTATION OF THE DYNAMIC SYSTEM PLANNING MODEL

Several readers of our first edition suggested we provide an introductory schematic presentation of the DSP Model, even though we discuss these points later in the text. To this end, we organize this section into four parts. The first three describe the underlying assumptions of the DSP Model:

- The organization is humankind's "ultimate" tool.
- The organization needs to combat entropy to survive.
- The organization is a dynamic social system.

The fourth part outlines the seven DSP issues we derive from these three assumptions, including a full schematic diagram.

The Organization Is Humankind's "Ultimate" Tool

Think of those people who have accomplished great things in history. In many cases, great individuals probably would not have reached such greatness without organizations to back them. Could President Abraham Lincoln have freed American slaves without the enthusiastic support of his government? How many people would John Wesley have reached, then and now, with his new view of Protestantism, if he had not founded the Methodist Church? Consider Bill Gates. He might have designed a few software packages alone, but could he have dominated the global software industry in the 1990s without his software company, Microsoft Corporation? We think not.

The organization is humankind's ultimate tool, because it is the means by which two or more people, working together in cooperation, can accomplish what a single person cannot. Just as a hammer adds physical leverage to the human arm, the organization extends the mental leverage of the human brain and, in many cases, the collective spirit. Do not assume, just because the organization is a powerful tool, that a CEO can or should be a dictator or ruler. However, a truly effective organization will allow dozens, hundreds, or even thousands of individuals to network together to accomplish a vision and shared objectives provided by its leadership. In the entrepreneurial firm, founders have a picture or vision of what they want to accomplish. The organization is their primary tool to help realize that vision. And as with any tool, the more clearly the organization's purpose and its workings are understood, the more likely that purpose or vision will be realized.

The Organization Needs to Combat Entropy to Survive

Open-systems theory leads us to the second key principle of the DSP Model — the concept of *entropy*. Every organization needs to combat entropy, or disorder, to survive. The natural course of the universe is toward further disorder, according to the second law of thermodynamics. But on a local level, order can be restored. You can counter entropy within your own company by understanding how all open systems fight chaos: Inputs are brought into the system, transformed in some manner, and then exit as outputs. These outputs (your products or services) are then exchanged for new inputs. To counter entropy, this input-transformation-output (I-T-O) cycle must continually repeat itself during the life of the enterprise. The more efficient the transformation process, the more resources are left over for future use.

Consider the for-profit enterprise. As illustrated in Figure I–1, inputs of money, people's efforts, information, and materials enter the system and are transformed in a way that adds value to the inputs. When the finished products or services are sold, output is returned to the environment in exchange for more inputs (usually capital). The inputs used in the transformation process might be viewed as costs in operating the system. For the system to operate efficiently, the ratio of outputs to inputs must be greater than or equal to one. The system must operate efficiently over time, or it will eventually run out of resources. To operate effectively, the system must also add value to the inputs as they are being transformed, or no one will desire the product. Adding value may take many forms: The manufacturer takes raw materials and converts them to finished goods; the distributor transports goods to a more central location; the retailer helps to build awareness of various product lines through advertising and by bringing product close to the end user. In the service business, employee skills and information are combined to provide a service. Usually the biggest challenge at start-up is to get this cycle going — to determine a need to fill, to locate the resources to get started, to produce goods or services of adequate quality, and to build up a reliable customer base so that fresh inputs (typically money generated from sales) enter the system on a predictable

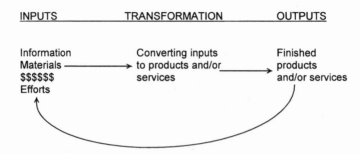

FIGURE I–1   The Basic Input-Transformation-Output Cycle to Combat Entropy

basis. In most start-ups, this simplified model provides a sufficient explanation of the key challenges faced by the new business.

At first glance, the I-T-O cycle may not seem to apply to nonprofit firms. But the recipient of the output does not have to be the same as the provider of new input. Trade associations, a form of nonprofit organization, do indeed provide direct services to their paying members. But many charity organizations follow a less direct path in the I-T-O cycle. Consider for instance the American Red Cross. Though disaster victims sometimes join future ranks of volunteers, many key supporters of the American Red Cross never directly benefit from its activity. Nevertheless they contribute, valuing the services it provides to society — the larger social system. Most philanthropic organizations can be viewed this way. But make no mistake: A nonprofit group not perceived to provide a valuable service eventually ceases operations.

The Organization Is a Dynamic Social System

Once created, your company begins to take on a dynamic of its own. In spite of your best efforts, you eventually discover that you cannot control every action or outcome within your company, much less those actions impinging on it from outside. Why? According to open-systems theory, your company is part of a multitiered set of social systems. At one tier, your company is made up of individuals with freedom to choose and act, creating their own dynamic situation within the organization. In turn, your company interacts with individuals and organizations at higher levels of social systems beyond the organization's own boundaries, further adding to its dynamic qualities. Figure I–2 illustrates this idea.

Some interactions with the larger environment are a result of the I-T-O cycle. For instance, at the input stage, your company interacts with individuals (to recruit them as employees), a bank (to apply for a loan), investors (to pressure them for equity), suppliers (to buy raw materials), or a library (to obtain information). At the output stage, customers buy your products. But not all interactions are intentional or a direct result of the I-T-O cycle. Your

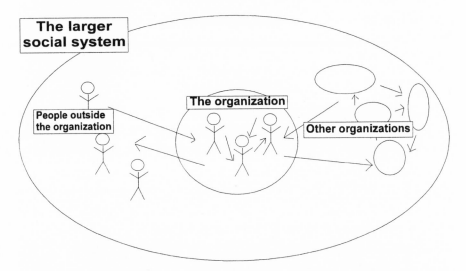

FIGURE I–2 The Organization Is Part of a Multitiered Set of Dynamic Social Systems

company may be buffeted by higher interest rates, new government regulations, or a spate of nasty weather. Your company may benefit from an unexpected new technological discovery or be threatened with extinction by the introduction of a substitute product. Paying attention to these interactions with the larger social system is also essential to your company's survival and growth as a dynamic social system.

In short, even though you create your own firm, once this process of interaction is set in motion, many consequences are beyond your control. Consider the following image created in a training film to demonstrate chain reactions. A room is filled with Ping-Pong balls set on mousetraps. Someone (from off-camera) tosses a ball into the room. First, two other balls are released, then four, then eight. Before long, bouncing Ping-Pong balls fill the room. Fortunately in the real world, chain reactions usually occur less randomly and more slowly. But the multiple interactions among individuals, groups, and organizations in multitiered levels of social systems can result in a scene that appears almost as chaotic. When you create your company, you toss the first ball. After that, don't expect to control all the subsequent dynamics. But do pay close attention to the dynamics that result from your actions and those of others around you, both within and outside the company.

The Seven DSP Issues Are a Direct Result of the Previously Stated Open-Systems-Theory Assumptions

Let us recap our presentation. View your company as a powerful tool used to realize your vision and objectives. But realize that it is also bound by certain natural laws. To overcome entropy, you must develop a reliable and effective input-transformation-output (I-T-O) cycle for your company. Also, you must recognize that your company is part of a dynamic network, affected by multiple layers of people, groups, organizations, societies, and global forces, all interacting dynamically and, at times, unpredictably with one another.

These three assumptions help us to define the core challenges you face as the leader of a dynamic enterprise. First, you must have a vision for your company. Just as every tool has a purpose, you must always keep clearly in mind why your organization exists. You may have personal objectives, such as making money or gaining a sense of accomplishment. But to grow, the organization needs its own reason for being. Sometimes the vision in a new enterprise is inseparable from the products or services offered (e.g., to develop a profitable Web site). But growing companies often benefit from a broader vision. For example, from the start, the mission at Apple Computer was not just to make and sell computers — it was also to produce an affordable, user-friendly computer. Steven Wozniak's personal dream, carried into the fledgling company, was to make personal computer ownership affordable at a time when most computers cost as much as a new car or even a house. Steven Jobs's added inspiration, guided by visits to Xerox Research Park in Palo Alto, California, was to make a computer simple enough for a child to use. In addition to their own contributions, Wozniak and Jobs adopted and modified existing technologies from other Silicon Valley inventors to realize that vision.

The second and third assumptions underlying the DSP Model define the seven issues you must manage effectively to realize your company mission or vision. They include the following:

- resource acquisition,
- resource allocation,
- work flow,
- human relations,
- technical mastery,
- market strategy, and
- public relations.

To survive, grow, and remain profitable, your company must develop an effective strategy and action plan at a specific point in time for each of seven issues, regardless of your company's stage of development (infancy or maturity) or its market niche.

Each of the first six listed issues is necessary to assure smooth functioning of the I-T-O cycle. Ignoring any of these items will thwart your efforts to fight off entropy, although when your company is young and small, some issues, such as work flow and human relations, are apt to be relatively easy to resolve. Ignoring the seventh issue, public relations, may lead to threats to the survival of your firm, not from the damaging effects of entropy but from outside elements potentially opposed to your company's existence. Or stated in a more positive light, the inclusion of public relations as a strategy acknowledges that your eventual success depends not only on your successful struggle with entropy but also on the degree to which your company exists in harmony with its outside physical and social environment.

To be most effective, the approach you take in managing all seven issues should contribute toward, and be consistent with, the overall vision you have for your company. The more compatible these strategies are with one another and with your overall vision, the more powerful the synergy you will be able to achieve among them. They need not be expensive, and they need not change every day. But ignoring any one area may eventually create a breakdown in the I-T-O cycle or even prevent your survival within a sphere of other social systems. Although you are responsible for managing each issue appropriately, others in your company (or outside) may actually carry out the work. Figure I-3 provides a schematic illustration to go along with our description of the model.

Let's now consider each of these issues in a little more detail:

- *Resource acquisition.* You must make sure that your company obtains needed money, people, materials, and external information. Strategies for recruitment, investor relations, purchasing, and research and development are all part of this issue.
- *Resource allocation.* Once inputs are obtained and enter your company, as a first step in the transformation process, you must assign or allocate those resources appropriately throughout the organization, whether by budgeting and corporate planning, attending to the squeaky wheel, or use of intuition. Adequate cash flow and having the right material at the right place in the organization are two indicators of effective resource allocation.
- *Work flow.* As part of the transformation process, you must also decide how to assign or divide and coordinate work to be done. If work slips through cracks, work is delayed, or too many people are saying, "That's not my job," you need to rethink your approach to work flow. Think of your company as a giant jigsaw puzzle with each individual standing on a piece. Overall realization of your vision and objectives requires the smooth and timely fitting of these pieces into the whole picture.
- *Human relations.* As another aspect of the transformation process, you must make sure that employees meet their own needs and wants while simultaneously fulfilling company goals. Loyal, satisfied, motivated employees are more likely to help you meet your company's goals than alienated employees. Low absenteeism and turnover (especially of your better employees) are signs that you are effectively managing the human relations issue.[15]
- *Technical mastery.* At the interface between the transformation process and the output part of the I-T-O cycle, technical mastery requires that you produce your output with adequate quality, speed, and quantity and with the appropriate technical features, all consistent with your company's overall mission and objectives. Hiring and training people with the right technical skills, investing in appropriate tools and materials, and in-house product testing and development are just a few of the strategies you might use to enhance technical mastery.[16]

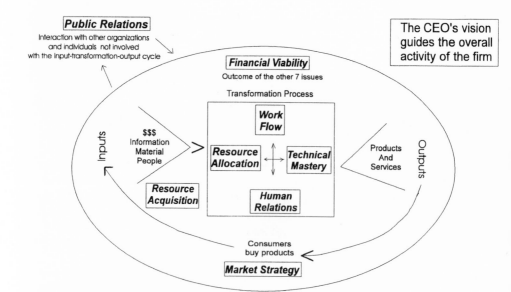

FIGURE I–3   The Eight DSP Issues Essential to Management of a Dynamic Social System

- *Market strategy.* Finally, as products and services exit the company, you must assure that you have adequate customer interest, that is, enough customers willing to pay the right price to cover your costs, in order to generate sufficient revenues to keep your company (and the I-T-O cycle) going. Market strategy involves decisions about which products or services to offer, and with what benefits, and about which customers and markets to target, and at what prices. Effective market strategy is reflected in total sales, rate of sales growth, and steadiness of sales growth.
- *Public relations.* The seventh and final strategy issue requires that you relate effectively with any systems in your company's external environment, *apart* from those external groups — customers, suppliers, investors — directly involved with the I-T-O cycle. Other groups of relevance include various government entities, the communities in physical proximity to each company location, and, in many companies, the family from which ownership may draw. Litigation, fines, tax delinquency, and bad publicity are all signs of inadequate management of this area. Favorable public image, general goodwill, and community acceptance of your company's existence are positive signs.[17]

In our book, we refer to financial viability as an eighth issue, although this might be slightly misleading. In our view, survival and profitability result from effective management of the other seven DSP issues already described but cannot themselves be directly managed.[18]

A system is more than the sum of its parts, and thus the list of seven issues only partially captures the overall intent of the DSP Model. The effective management of each issue changes dynamically over time as the company changes internally and as the world outside changes. Further, the strategies pursued to handle each issue should stem from an overall picture or vision of the company.

THE DSP MODEL CAN PROVIDE A CROSS-FUNCTIONAL PERSPECTIVE

The DSP Model addresses the key functional challenges faced by managers in most companies while providing a more cross-functional perspective. For instance, consider the human resource function. At first blush, you might assume that the human resource function and human relations issue are one and the same. But they are not. Consider the following ways in which a human resource department potentially impacts each of the DSP issues:

- Recruitment is a type of resource-acquisition strategy.
- Administration of compensation and benefits and compensation planning may be viewed as resource-allocation strategies.
- Job description and job design development affect work flow.
- Employee involvement and team building may affect both work flow and human relations.
- Planning company meetings, preparing employee manuals, and writing newsletters help to communicate the company's vision and corporate culture to employees (aspects of human relations).
- Design and execution of managerial, technical, and supervisory training and development programs may affect a variety of DSP issues depending upon the content of the programs. Sales training programs may boost sales (market strategy); technical training may improve product quality (technical mastery); managerial and supervisory training may clarify work role expectations and improve a manager's skill at motivating and leading employees (work flow and employee relations).
- Tracking and enforcing affirmative-action requirements or OSHA requirements are aspects of the public relations issue.

So what? you might ask. First, in a functionally structured company, people from many departments may contribute to (or potentially thwart) your company's ability to operate as an effective open system. To manage each of the DSP issues effectively, you may need to coordinate the efforts of individuals across several departments. The automobile industry recognized this in restructuring the manner in which new products are developed. To improve their technical mastery (the speed, cost, and time involved in developing new products), Toyota and Chrysler Corporation have moved to a cross-functional approach, placing experts from each of the functional areas on one product team, which has reduced development costs and cut down product development time from five years to three or less. Integration of functions may produce economies in management of the other DSP issues.

HOW THE DSP MODEL CAN BE USED
IN MORE FAMILIAR STRATEGIC
PLANNING METHODOLOGIES

In the most simplified approach, which we describe fully in Chapter 3, the DSP Model can stand alone as a strategic management planning tool. Clarify your company's vision. Then consider your current strategy for each of the seven DSP issues. How do you manage each issue now, and how well is that strategy working out? Take market strategy, for instance. First consider the products or services offered, your target market, and how you set market direction. Then consider your current sales. Are they steadily growing, cyclical, or flat? How about your market share? Consider some of the other internal or external factors affecting the strategy. If you are not satisfied with the results obtained from your current strategy, consider the changes you would like to make.

If you run a small company in a slowly changing industry that you understand well, you tend not to introduce new product changes frequently, and you are generally satisfied with your overall firm performance and just want to "tweak" it a bit, our simplified approach may be more than adequate. However, as your firm grows, your approach to strategic management may benefit from a more formal, sophisticated approach, as taught in strategic management courses at most universities. If so, the DSP Model can also be easily incorporated into more familiar strategic planning methodologies. The standard approach described in most modern strategic management texts involves three phases:

Phase 1: Assessment of the current situation
In the first phase, you review your company's current situation: its mission and/or vision, strategies, objectives, strengths, weaknesses, and environmental opportunities and threats. You might also want to identify the company's core competencies (skill sets underlying its ability to make competitive products and services) and competitive advantage (why customers buy from you instead of from your competitors).

Phase 2: Development of a new vision and/or strategy
Once you assess your current situation, you decide what changes are needed, if any, in your overall mission or vision, objectives, and key supporting strategy(ies).

Phase 3: Development of an action plan
Finally, to execute your strategy successfully, you need to develop a detailed action plan.

The DSP Model can be very helpful in all three phases:

- In Phase 1, use the DSP Model to identify your company's current strengths, weaknesses, core competencies, and competitive advantages.
- In Phase 2, use the DSP Model to revise your overall mission and objectives and the key strategies for achieving those objectives.
- In Phase 3, use the DSP Model to develop a comprehensive action plan.

Let's look at each of these three applications briefly, in turn.

DSP as a Tool to Identify Strengths, Weaknesses, Core Competencies, and Competitive Advantage

Most strategic planning guidelines for identifying your company's key strengths and weaknesses are organized along functional lines. They provide a good beginning, but important ideas may also slip between the cracks. The DSP Model quickly helps both novice and professional to pinpoint strengths or weaknesses that might have been overlooked using the functional approach. Because the DSP Model is theory driven and cross-functional, it can provide a working framework for assessing the important aspects of your business, either as a supplement or as a replacement to the functional approach, especially if your company does not fit the functional categories (e.g., marketing, production, accounting, design, etc.) very well. Our students have used the DSP Model for strategic planning case analysis in well over a hundred companies, with generally satisfactory results. Companies with strengths in all seven areas tend to be successful, growing companies.

For an issue to serve as a strength, you must be as good as everyone else. But to have a competitive advantage, you must be *better*. Further, to be a competitive advantage, a strategy needs to make your product or service *more* desirable to your customer than the product or service of your competitors. Again, the DSP Model may provide fresh insights as to your company's real competitive advantage. The core competency approach can also fit into the DSP Model. You may have sets of capabilities relating to one particular DSP issue. Further, the DSP Model may help you to locate those technical skill sets or capabilities that underlie your greatest or most unique strengths.[19] Some of the big corporate successes from the 1980s and 1990s came from companies gaining new markets by developing a core competency around a certain organizational capability.

As an illustration, consider Wal-Mart. From the marketing perspective, it is true that Wal-Mart grew in the 1980s and early 1990s by entering small-town markets ignored by other large discounters. But Wal-Mart could not have implemented this strategy successfully without a parallel organizational strategy. Wal-Mart controlled its inventory costs—a major determinant of profitability in retailing—by designing and implementing a unique regional distribution system tied by computer to each of its stores. This system allowed Wal-Mart to track and inventory its products more rapidly, accurately, and cheaply than any of its competitors, using a point-of-sale information system. Because information was available instantly on what had sold (or what had not), and because backup inventory was kept in warehouses instead of on expensive retail shelves, Wal-Mart was able to create smaller stores, affordably moving into smaller communities that competing discounters such as K-Mart or Sears, Roebuck, and Company had to pass over. In short, Wal-Mart's capabilities or competencies in distribution, an aspect of resource allocation within the DSP framework, are arguably the cornerstone of its competitive advantage.

Note that you use the DSP Model primarily to analyze the situation inside your firm. Before designing an appropriate direction for your firm, you also need to consider environmental trends. Then from these trends, you need to infer what threats or opportunities the environment provides for your company. Most modern strategic management texts outline three categories of trends you should track: the general environment, your industry, and your immediate competition. To begin your analysis, you might use some or all of the commonly used environmental analysis tools:

- STEPE (social-technological-economic-political-ecological) analysis to consider general environmental trends;
- Porter's Five Forces competitive analysis and profile of industry economic characteristics to structure information about the industry;
- Competitor matrix and strategic group mapping to describe the immediate competition.[20]

Note that once these analyses are complete, a lot of intuition and luck are required to identify those trends most important to your company's future and in turn to figure out what their implications might be (positively or negatively) for your own company — especially when changes are in early stages of development. Tom Watson, Jr., spied the right trend when he realized that computers would eventually replace the office machines being made at his father's company, International Business Machines. The Internet provides another good example. In the early to mid-1990s, start-up companies such as Netscape Communications observed the Internet's potential and jumped in to develop the market well before such computer monoliths as Intel or Microsoft Corporation.

To sum up, the DSP Model, together with environmental analysis tools, provides a fairly simple-to-learn analysis of both internal and external factors that can be used to describe the current situation. By reviewing the strengths and weaknesses inside your company, using the DSP Model, and the opportunities and threats external to the company, with the help of some of the previously described analytical tools, you may develop new ideas about the direction you should take. Hamel and Prahalad caution that you should not base your strategic thinking entirely on the current strengths within your company. You might be able to stretch current resources and capabilities rather than fit strategy into your existing repertoire, especially if you identify a really timely opportunity.[21] But whether you decide to stretch resources or fit strategy to your company's current situation, a clear assessment of your strengths and weaknesses is a useful starting point for consideration of your overall strategy or direction.

DSP as a Tool to Recommend New Strategic Directions

In the world of business, nothing ever stays the same. Today's competitive advantage may be copied by competitors and rendered useless tomorrow. Developing new products and entering new markets are two ways to maintain a competitive edge. But in a fast-paced market, imitators can often quickly follow: Even patented items are frequently difficult to defend in a global market. The globalization of commerce has stimulated a shift in thinking about competitive advantage. In many industries, more enduring advantage can come from development of new underlying organizational capabilities, as we have already seen in the Wal-Mart example. Once you have assessed your company's current strengths, the DSP Model may help you to identify areas around which you can develop a new or stronger advantage.

Consider the Japanese automobile manufacturers. In the 1980s, they gained significant global market share for two key reasons: (a) their ability to deliver high-quality goods (with the lowest recall rates in the industry); and (b) their ability to churn out new product in almost half the time of their American counterparts, bringing new platform development time down from five to three years. Key to success in executing these strategies were competencies tied to both technical mastery and work flow. Much has been written about how the Japanese achieved quality improvements. We also now know that it was their use of a cross-functional semiautonomous team design — a work-flow strategy — that provided the key to moving new product to market at breakneck speed, relative to American manufacturers, giving them an edge in responding to customer desires. In the early 1990s, Chrysler Corporation was able to test this theory, bringing its own platform development time down to three years from a previous five-year cycle, introducing its successful LH series to the marketplace in record time.

Wal-Mart and the Japanese automobile makers provide just two examples of how companies are tapping into organizational capabilities to provide a competitive edge. Our key point is this: Depending upon your own industry, immediate competition, and company, any one of the DSP issues could serve as a potential source of competitive advantage. In an era when product, service, and retailing ideas can be quickly mimicked and rolled out to market, building unique organizational capabilities into your company may provide you with a competitive advantage that assures more rapid sales growth or profitability.

The DSP Model Can Be Used to Develop Action Plans

The third and equally important though often neglected phase of strategic planning is the development of an effective implementation plan. Once again, following the traditional path, you can develop action plans along functional lines (marketing, production, etc.) as many strategic planning books suggest. However the DSP Model provides an alternative, cross-functional perspective for considering needed changes in executing a new strategy. To illustrate this point, we share a rather detailed description of an implementation plan carried out by the Canadian McDonald's Corporation and its Soviet joint partner in a Russian joint venture during the late 1980s and early 1990s. In 1976, George Cohan, president of the Canadian McDonald's Corporation, introduced the idea of a joint restaurant venture to Soviet officials at the Montreal Olympics. Negotiations took 12 years, with 2 years more to build the first location, which finally opened on January 31, 1990. McDonald's broke its own world's sales record on opening day, serving over 30,000 customers. That location served over one million customers in the first month. This success did not come about due to luck. Publicly available information about the planning process reveals amazingly detailed attention to each of the seven DSP issues.[22] For each point, we include in parentheses the aspects of the DSP Model supported by this part of the action plan. Consider the following:

- A clear vision guided the overall project. The locations to be opened in Moscow were to serve the Soviet people, not just the tourists and the elite. (Overall vision)
- In keeping with this mission, the restaurants accepted only rubles. The first location was located in a major downtown location. To retain its ethnic attraction, a strictly American menu was served. (Market strategy)
- To assure a local food supply (and to support local farmers, again consistent with the overall vision), McDonald's Corporation invested in a joint partnership with the Kashira farming collective to boost farming yields and improve the quality of their potatoes. McDonald's also arranged for milk, beef, and other supplies from local producers. (Resource-acquisition strategy — materials)
- Key management personnel were all drawn from the Soviet citizenry. Further, the top 4 candidates spent nine months in Toronto and at Hamburger University in Oakbrook, Illinois. These trainees received extensive technical and supervisory training to assure quality control and an understanding of McDonald's approach to work division and coordination and also to develop an understanding of McDonald's corporate culture and how it was enforced. McDonald's also sent an additional 27 assistant managers to Toronto for training, again revealing its strong commitment to employee training. (Technical mastery, work flow, and human relations)
- McDonald's avoided excess in developing its recruitment program, again revealing a thorough understanding of its environment. It placed a one line advertisement in the Moscow paper for employees and received over 27,000 applications as a result. But in the follow-up effort, managers carefully screened and interviewed applicants. (Resource-acquisition strategy — recruitment)
- The Moscow McDonald's restaurants, though modeled on the American menu and technology, are far larger than most of McDonald's other restaurants. The joint venture's first location alone seats 700 inside and an additional 200 outside the restaurant. Therefore, though many aspects of the Soviet operations were copied from their American model, to assure smoother work flow, the joint venture created a separate food-processing plant to better service the large-scale restaurants it had in mind. The plant takes care of much of the food preparation, such as baking, patty preparation, and cutting potatoes into pieces ready for frying. (Work-flow strategy)

- By probing deeply into the Soviet system and patiently making many trips to Moscow over a 12-year period, George Cohan and his management team at the Canadian McDonald's Corporation succeeded in making the Soviet government a part of the McDonald's team rather than a potential adversary. This was a truly amazing accomplishment, especially when one realizes that negotiations began well before the cold war had even ended between the Soviet Union and west bloc countries. This thoroughness, and the related efforts to build trust, may explain why McDonald's Corporation's presence in Moscow survived the collapse of the Soviet regime and remains a success. (Public relations)
- Some of this same evidence also supports the view that McDonald's had a thoughtful approach to resource allocation: It spent large sums on certain areas (e.g., for the food-processing plant, training in the United States and Canada, potato farming venture) and acted frugally in others (using local contacts for other foodstuffs, placing a short ad in the newspaper). (Resource-allocation strategy)

Whatever planning system McDonald's Corporation intentionally used, as we review these facts and others publicly available about this joint venture, we find evidence that McDonald's developed implementation strategies supporting all seven DSP issues, helping to explain its success. We find McDonald's thorough approach to implementation of the joint venture remarkable, perhaps as remarkable as its resulting sales success.

At this point you may well ask: Don't all major corporations pay attention to such details? Perhaps. The question is hard to answer, other than by inferring from company actions, since implementation plans are not generally made available to the public. But based on press reports, there is evidence to suggest that companies do not always succeed so well in anticipating appropriate details. Consider for instance the launching of EuroDisney by Disney Corporation. We won't go into a full case analysis here, but consider just one DSP issue — resource acquisition, and recruitment in particular. At start-up, Disney Corporation so miscalculated the availability of local citizens interested in employment at EuroDisney that it was forced to build dormitories on site, temporarily housing many out-of-town employees in high-rent Parisian apartments many miles away. Disney could have done a better job of anticipating this recruitment problem. At the time EuroDisney was scheduled to open, Western Europe historically had faced entry-level labor shortages, due to a combination of relatively low unemployment and generally attractive unemployment entitlement programs. In fact, the Dutch and German vocabulary includes the term *guest worker,* which refers to immigrants brought into those countries to fill entry-level, lower-skilled positions. Did Disney Corporation misjudge the attractiveness of its jobs to the local population or simply overlook consideration of the recruitment issue altogether? We may never find out the real story, but we can't help wondering whether a more thorough implementation plan could have provided Disney with a smoother, more profitable launch of its EuroDisney project.

In devising your own action plans, how do you avoid overlooking obvious details? We recommend a fairly simple approach. First, consider each of the seven DSP issues carefully, relative to your overall direction or vision. Then for each issue, complete the following information as specifically and thoroughly as possible:

- Describe the *specific* strategy you plan to follow. Be sure to consider how this might support the overall strategy and/or vision for your company.
- Define the anticipated *outcomes* you expect as a result of following this strategy (e.g., improved work flow, boost in market share, profitability, etc.). Be as specific as possible, although not all goals have to be numerically defined.
- Define your *time schedule*: When will the project begin? What are the key milestones? When must the project be completed?
- Describe the *resources* required to carry out the plan (staffing, capital, information, raw materials, equipment) and who will provide these resources.
- Outline the specific *steps* to be followed to execute the strategy or any other details defining the actual tasks to be carried out.
- Assign the *person* responsible for overseeing the action plan.
- Finally, develop a *feedback* system so that the assigned person can report to you on a timely basis (perhaps at certain milestones and/or time intervals) and be made accountable for the success of the plan. The report should cover steps taken, resources spent, and any surprises encountered along the way, which might suggest a change in direction.

Summary of How the DSP Model Is Used in Strategic Planning

If you want to use the DSP Model as part of a formal strategic planning process, you can use it in all three phases: (1) to assess current strengths and weaknesses, including core competencies or capabilities and competitive advantage; (2) to trigger ideas for a unique overall strategy or new competitive advantage; and (3) to organize more detailed action plans. The same seven issues are considered at each step, making the overall system relatively easy to learn. A successful overall strategy requires a clear vision, considerable creativity in devising new strategy, and an ability to sift through a lot of extraneous information confronting you on a daily basis to identify the important trends about your immediate competition, your industry, and general social, political, technical, economic, and ecological trends. And equally important, the strategy needs a carefully thought-out implementation plan. We cannot give you a pat formula for producing a powerful strategy. But as a mental model, the DSP Model may trigger your awareness of aspects of your company you otherwise might have overlooked.

UPDATE ON CURRENT STRATEGY AND SALES GROWTH LITERATURE

In this final section of the introduction, we update the reader on relevant research published after (or overlooked by) the first edition of our book. Some readers may prefer to come back to this material after reading the remainder of the book. This section is organized as follows: First, we compare the DSP Model to other classification schemes. In the remainder of this section we report upon and discuss research results linking various management strategies or actions with sales growth. Note that when we mention our own research, we are referring to the results of the project "Managing the Growing Firm," reported in this book and related publications.

Other Classification Schemes of Growth Problems

One of the considerations in developing any typology is the degree to which it should be driven by theory or by an empirically supported, factor analytic base. One of the questions we faced in developing our original model was whether the DSP Model should be theory driven or data driven. Our DSP Model is a blend of the two. For instance, we fully expected certain issues, such as resource acquisition, to be multifaceted, covering a range of strategies used to attract personnel, capital, materials, and information. On the other hand, factor analytic results partly influenced our final determination of the aspects to be included in resource allocation and work flow.

Though many studies have created their own lists of issues, only a handful actually test categorization schemes. Studies avoiding an a priori determination of categories *and* empirically testing at least some of these categories with factor analysis are rarer still. Thus, we must piece together ideas from different studies meeting at least one of these criteria.

Hambrick and Crozier's classic article on strategy and growth provides an interesting starting point. In examining a sample of INC. 100 companies from the early 1980s, they identify several internal transformation issues as key to success, including resource acquisition (hiring experienced managers and being able to recruit effective middle managers); work flow (formal systems and decentralized teams); human relations (develop and reinforce the culture); and resource allocation (paying attention to frugality and variable cost compensation).[23] Although this listing is not meant as a comprehensive classification scheme, its focus on internal issues is noteworthy, especially given the relative lack of attention to many of these issues in empirical research on strategy and sales growth.

In a different study, Terpstra and Olson develop a listing of issues, avoiding an a priori classification scheme, with a technique very similar to the one we used to identify key growth problems in our own research (see appendix A).[24] Using an open-ended interview format with CEOs of 121 INC. 500 companies, they identify key problems at start-up and at later stages of growth.[25] Since they do not factor analyze their results, their clustering (based on functional categories) is relatively arbitrary. More interesting, we think, are the actual problems they identify at start-up and later stages of growth, which are very similar to the list we developed in our own research. There are two exceptions, including the problem "managing growth," which is probably a rather general problem that can apply to the whole process, and lack of management experience, which can be linked with either the recruitment component of the resource-acquisition strategy or any of several other issues, depending upon whether the CEO is referring to skills at time of hire or inadequate training within the company.

Kazanjian's research is noteworthy for a different reason. He does not derive his set of 18 issues from open-ended interviews but rather from a review of the literature. Not surprisingly, this produced considerable gaps. For instance, he omits coverage of any problems we would classify within human relations, public relations, or the quality component of technical mastery. However, his factor analysis provides further insight into some of the other dimensions of the model — for instance, it confirms our own conceptualization of the work-flow issue. In particular, he identifies an *organizational systems* factor including the following variables: develop management information systems; control costs; define organizational roles, responsibilities, and policies; develop financial systems and internal controls; and cut administrative burden and red tape.[26] Readers looking over our approach to work flow in Chapters 7 and 8 will find a strong similarity to our work-flow construct. Indeed, this was one area for which we also used factor analysis to develop the final construct. Kazanjian's second factor, *sales/marketing,* also provides interesting comparisons with our concept of market strategy. Dominant problems loading on this factor include the following: meet sales targets; attain profit and market-share goals; penetrate new geographic territories; and (weaker) provide product support and customer service (also loading on production). Kazanjian's third factor, *people,* really involves two recruitment-related issues: attract capable personnel; and achieve management depth and find talent. Table I–1 indicates how the 18 problems are grouped according to his analysis into the following six factors: organizational systems; sales/marketing; people; production; strategic positioning; and external relations. Table I–1 also presents a clustering of Kazanjian's individual variables according to the DSP Model.

D'Souza and McDougall also report results of a factor analysis of strategies.[27] They empirically identify four clusters of strategies, including resource allocation, operational efficiency, market/product, and value emphasis. Their research most clearly validates the resource-allocation concept, with such diverse variables as investment in advertising and investment in research and development loading on the same factor. However, their factor analysis suggests that technical mastery may really be two dimensions: one focused on productivity and costs (operational efficiency); the other focused on quality and value added (value emphasis).

It would appear that most of the issues described by other researchers can fit within the overall framework of the DSP Model, although more extensive work on the empirical verification of these different dimensions will be helpful.

TABLE I-1 Comparison of the Dynamic System Planning Model with Other Classification Schemes of Problems in Growing Firms

DSP MODEL	KAZANJIAN	TERPSTRA AND OLSON
Resource Acquisition	Secure financial resources and backing (external relations) Acquire key outside advisors, board members (external relations) Develop network of reliable vendors and suppliers (production) Attract capable personnel (people)	Obtaining financing for growth Inadequate working capital Suppliers/supplies/raw materials Recruitment/selection
Resource Allocation	Control costs (organizational systems) Develop financial systems and internal controls (organizational systems)	Cash flow problems Collection of accounts receivable Controlling margins/profits/expenses Other or general financial management problems Production capacity problems Becoming computerized
Work Flow	Develop management information systems (organizational systems) Cut administrative burden and red tape (organizational systems) Define organizational roles, responsibilities, policies (organizational systems) Develop financial systems and internal controls (organizational systems)	New division Changing from custom programming to product Training/development (depends on topic) Other or general organization structure/design problems Other or general production/operations management problems
Human Relations	NOT COVERED	Training/development (depends on topic) Satisfaction/morale Turnover/retention Other or general human resource management problems

(continued)

TABLE I–1 (*Continued*)

DSP MODEL	KAZANJIAN	TERPSTRA AND OLSON
Technical Mastery	Produce in volumes that meet demand (production) Develop new product or technology application (strategic positioning) QUALITY ISSUES NOT COVERED	Product development Becoming computerized (also listed in resource allocation) Training/development (depends on topic) Quality control (product or service)
Public Relations	NOT COVERED	Insurance Licensing/bonding
Market Strategy	Meet sales target (sales/marketing) Attain profit and market-share goals (sales/marketing) Penetrate new geographic territories (sales/marketing) Provide product support and customer service (sales/marketing) Establish position in new product market segments (strategic positioning)	Low sales Dependence on one or few clients/customers Marketing or distribution channels Promotion/public relations/advertising Other or general marketing problems
Other		Lack of management expertise CEO overworked/overwhelmed Managing growth Planning/leading/other general management problems

NOTE: Environmental problems (e.g., increased competition, poor economy, etc.) deleted from this table.

The Focus of the Review: Management Actions and Sales Growth

In the remainder of this chapter, we focus specifically on research predicting sales growth in small to medium-sized companies. Using a rather broad definition of strategy, we include research measuring some type of management activity or strategy subsequent to a company's formation.[28] We group our conclusions by DSP issue and, in turn, by specific independent variables.

We choose sales growth as the dependent variable rather than profitability primarily for pragmatic reasons. Much of the recent research in entrepreneurship focuses on sales growth, making it easier to compare findings across studies.[29] Both profitability and sales growth are important, however, and on the basis of research to date, evidence suggests that they should both be included but as separately measured dependent variables. Although they correlate to some extent, the correlation is fairly weak. Furthermore, independent variables that predict sales growth do not always predict profitability and vice versa. For instance, the choice of a broad strategy at start-up may stimulate greater sales growth but will not necessarily optimize the level of profitability, at least in the short run.[30] Ideally, future research would include both as dependent variables, so that we can better understand what these trade-offs might be and where they occur.[31]

We focus on empirically and statistically based published research, omitting the vast majority of case-based articles without statistically analyzed data. We eliminate most studies using employment growth because of research showing weak correlation with sales growth.[32] We also omit studies with profitability as a dependent variable unless it is combined with sales growth into a measure of financial performance, although we caution you to view studies with such hybrid measures as exploratory. We are by no means certain that we have covered all the relevant research, but we hope to provide a fairly representative introduction to current research on strategy and sales growth.[33]

Although the quality of research is improving steadily, the field of entrepreneurship is very young, with most empirically and statistically based research dating back only to the early 1980s. Samples are generally small (a few hundred companies or less) and not always randomly drawn. (The most frequent nonrandom studies are done on INC. 500 companies.) Few results are confirmed by more than a handful of studies, and often only one or two studies provide confirmation. We have some distance to go before we can start conducting metanalyses on groups of studies. In the meantime, conclusions need to be interpreted cautiously.

Proper research interpretation is also hampered by the tendency of some researchers to mix measures of different constructs into one heterogeneous variable. These measures are often not highly correlated, and they are conceptually distinct. Though scale development can improve reliability, this must always assume that items logically measure the same concept. The approach to financial performance provides a case in point. In an otherwise promising stream of research, a number of published entrepreneurship studies measure financial performance using a measure that combines ratings of sales growth, profitability, cash flow, and other financial indicators. Yet research to date demonstrates relatively limited variation among these variables (typically with less than 25 percent shared variation explained). Such low correlations might warrant creation of a scale when attitudinal measures are used that clearly capture the same idea. But sales growth and profitability are clearly measurable and distinguishable from one another. Companies can grow and not be profitable, or they can be profitable and not grow. Combining the two measures into one scale may lead to misleading conclusions about the real influences on sales growth and profitability.[34] Given the limited amount of research on sales growth, we include some of these studies in our review, but the reader should interpret results of studies using such hybrid measures of financial performance quite cautiously. Research on entrepreneurial strategic profile or orientation provides a second example of this construct problem. Using factor analysis, recent research by Lumpkin and Dess verifies that measures of the variable, entrepreneurial strategic orientation, may be made up of as many as four independent factors, not one factor, as other research has inferred, and thus should not be combined into one scale. And whereas *proactiveness,* one of these four factors, predicts sales growth, another, *competitive aggressiveness,* does not.[35] Lumping both together may lead to improper conclusions about the impact of competitive behavior on financial performance.

In sum, given the limited number of studies done on most topics and the methodological limitations of some of those same studies, you should interpret our conclusions in the remainder of this section tentatively. As research in the field grows and our methodology improves, we will eventually build a more accurate picture of how and why firms can grow and succeed.

Market Strategy and Sales Growth

In this section, we cover a wide variety of variables that may be viewed as aspects of market strategy, including the planning process itself and the types of strategies chosen. In particular, we cover the following variables: formal strategic planning, market positioning and market research, product innovation, breadth of strategy, and customer relations and sales tactics, as well as a few related industry characteristics, including industry growth and market demand. We include industry variables along with other market strategy variables because in our view, the industry selection process is not random. CEOs consider the type and characteristics of industry both at start-up and at later points as a company diversifies or reorients its strategy.

Formal strategic planning. Strategic management authors urge use of the business plan. In fact, the business plan forms the cornerstone of most introductory entrepreneurship courses. And yet very few companies in randomly drawn samples of small businesses actually do formal planning. Indeed, only 5 percent of CEOs in our own study claim to plan formally. One informal indicator of the business plan's value is the much higher incidence of its use among INC. 500 companies, with about 50 percent reportedly having prepared a business plan at start-up.[36]

Research evidence suggests that formal business planning may be valuable but only if it is approached with sufficient understanding and motivation. Keats and Montanari suggest that successfully integrating strategic planning into normal operations is a function of cognitive development.[37]

The planners' backgrounds, the intensity of planning, and the type of strategy may all change the relationship between formal strategic planning and sales growth. Admittedly on the basis of fairly limited research, we may tentatively conclude that

- Companies using professionals to develop a formal business plan grow faster than those who do not.[38]
- Formal planning may also require a certain type of CEO, one either with more formal management training and experience or with more openness to new information. For instance, one study finds that formal planning spurs sales growth but only in companies led by CEOs fitting the "opportunistic" profile — well educated, flexible, confident, and with an awareness of and orientation toward the future. For those with the opposite profile ("craftsman"), researchers find no relationship between formal planning and sales growth.[39]
- The quality of business planning matters: The more intense the formal planning — that is, the more time and effort spent and the more functions considered — the faster a company appears to grow.[40]
- The usefulness of formal planning may depend upon the type of strategy — innovative vs. duplicative or "copycat." The findings of a study by Olson and Bokor indicate that though neither formal planning nor type of strategy (i.e., product innovation vs. a copycat strategy) alone predicts sales growth, interaction effects are statistically significant. In particular, these researchers find that the fastest growing companies use both an innovative strategy and formal planning. These companies grow faster than innovative companies that use an informal approach and also faster than copycat companies regardless of planning approach. Yet the study raises an interesting caveat: Among copycat companies, those using informal planning grow faster than those using a formal approach.[41]
- The importance of strategic planning may depend on size: In a sample of post–start-up mid-sized firms, systematic strategic planning was found to be a factor in continued growth, although conclusions were drawn from case analysis only.[42]

Market positioning and market research. Market positioning is an important part of strategy. Seeking new markets for products is important to maintain growth over time:

- One major study of more mature small companies finds that developing new markets for existing products in existing industries boosts sales more than does the design of new products.[43]

- Another article reports that larger private firms that continue to grow must find ways to extend the market, adding adjacent market niches.[44]
- To develop a more effective marketing plan, it is important to learn more about the customer and marketplace. In one study, businesses were found to grow faster when the company views marketing as an important strategy, and conducts market research and when someone in management has particular expertise in marketing at start-up.[45] In particular, from a rather comprehensive list of company, owner-founder, and strategy characteristics, "conducting market research" is the single strongest predictor of sales growth, explaining 14 percent of the variance in a large sample of small manufacturing firms in Great Britain.[46]
- Geographic positioning, especially when exporting, has also been linked with faster growth for certain subsamples, including larger, more established firms and firms in particular regions whose local markets are seriously constrained, as in Northern Ireland.[47]

Product innovation. Product innovation is a topic that can cut across at least two DSP issues: market strategy and technical mastery. In particular, the decision to offer new and different products vs. duplication of products can be viewed as market strategy. But how *well* a company is able to innovate (e.g., number of patents) might be viewed as an aspect of technical mastery. We try to include only the former orientation in this section. Comparison of results is especially difficult in this area because terminology varies widely from study to study. For some, innovation relates to product development truly new to the world. For others, it may include product or even process improvements. Also, as with formal planning, we cannot look at innovation in isolation. The type of planning as well as external environmental characteristics may interact with the innovation variable in predicting sales growth. We draw the following tentative conclusions from existing research:

- The impact of innovation on sales growth may depend on formal planning as well as level of management experience. Olson and Bokor's study, previously mentioned in the formal planning discussion, is also of relevance here. Their study finds no significant main effect between product innovation and sales growth. But for companies carrying out formal business planning, innovation and sales growth are significantly linked although the sample size is very small. Further, the nature of management experience also appears to play an important role in determining the impact of innovation on sales growth — innovation boosts sales growth in companies led by experienced managers but not necessarily in companies led by inexperienced managers.[48]
- In a much larger sample of companies, a different pair of researchers, Acs and Audretsch, do indeed find a linkage between innovation and sales growth but only at a different level of analysis and taking a time delay into account. Grouping small to medium-sized manufacturing companies (those with less than 500 employees) by industry, they find that small companies in innovative industries grow faster than those in less innovative industries, but this effect is delayed by four years. Furthermore, sales growth is also greater for small companies in industries where smaller companies disproportionately contribute innovations.[49]

A growing stream of entrepreneurship research uses a subjective rating for financial performance, combining profitability, market share, and sales growth into one measure. Though this rating is not directly comparable to the findings of research on sales growth alone, we include it here because it partially represents the dependent variable, sales growth, and is becoming a generally accepted measure for overall firm performance.[50] An example of use of this approach follows:

- Covin, Slevin, and Schultz find that a high orientation toward product innovation and risk-taking (referred to as strategic posture) is associated with better firm performance for companies aiming to increase sales and market share (a "build" mission) but is unrelated in companies aiming to maximize profitability and cash flow in the short term (referred to as a "harvest mission").[51]

Breadth of strategy. At start-up, entrepreneurs are often urged to focus on a narrow niche. But on the basis of research to date, a narrow strategy is not always advisable. In our own research, we find no link between breadth and sales growth. However, with respect to profitability, we do find that smaller companies (fewer than 80 employees) suffer from a more diversified approach, whereas companies with more than 80 employees benefit from such an approach. Other researchers confirm the importance of company size in altering the relationship between strategic breadth and firm performance:

- In two separate studies of fairly small firms (one with less than 50 employees; the size of the other not stated) firms focusing on a single product or narrow product line were found to grow more quickly than more diversified companies.[52]
- But for older and/or larger firms, just the opposite occurs. Those who diversify or plan to diversify grow faster.[53]

Industry growth rate is another factor that may alter the relationship between diversification and sales growth:

- Focus appears to boost sales growth in a highly competitive, low-growth, mature industry. But for companies in higher growth industries, a broader strategy appears to bolster sales growth — even for start-ups. It is not clear however whether such a strategy is as beneficial for profits. In the same study, start-up firms in the high-growth industry following a broader strategy achieved only moderate return on sales, at least for the short term.[54]

Industry growth. Industry growth has also been looked at as an independent variable. The limited work in this area provides mixed results:

- One applied economics study, aggregating firms by similar industry, finds no relationship between industry growth and the rate of growth for all small firms under 500 employees.[55]

- In another study, smaller, start-up companies do not grow any faster in rapidly growing industries. But in a different sample examined by the same research team, larger, older companies in more rapidly growing industries do grow faster.[56] Given these results, we need to consider the possible moderating effects of company size or age.
- And data from a different study suggests that being a pioneer, that is, being in a rapid-growth industry, may not pay off in retaining higher market share or in a lingering cost advantage.[57]

Market demand. Market demand is another variable linked to sales growth.

- In a study of small manufacturing firms (fewer than 50 employees), CEOs were asked about a number of constraints on company growth. The perceived lack of demand for the main products and/or a declining market were the single most important constraints, predicting 10 percent of the variation in sales growth.[58]

Customer relations and sales tactics. Finally, some studies look at the quality of customer contacts and the sales staffing used to achieve sales. Sales growth is greater where

- Close customer contact is made.[59]
- External sales agents (e.g., manufacturers' representatives) are not relied upon to market goods.[60]

Conclusions related to market strategy and sales growth. Research in this section confirms the importance of market strategy as a predictor of sales growth. Results also suggest that rather than one streamlined answer, the appropriate market strategy is likely to change as a company grows, especially if that growth begins to saturate market demand. Successful companies are keenly tuned into market research, positioning themselves in new markets as needed over time. Although product innovation can be useful, other approaches can substitute as long as the company maintains sufficient demand for its product (either by seeking out new markets or by making improvements to existing products). Market demand, though crudely measured in Barkham's research in Great Britain, may provide the key to understanding the interactive effects of company size and industry growth. While a narrowly focused strategy may help a start-up, it may hamper long-term growth unless the company is able to adapt to new markets or products as it grows out of its niche. Yet there may be less of a need to diversify for companies in growing markets, as long as demand within the existing market niche continues to outpace the company's ability to meet that demand.

Resource Acquisition and Sales Growth

In contrast with research into market strategy, only a handful of studies empirically test the contributions of capital, information, and human resource–

acquisition strategies to sales growth in small to medium-sized firms. Those studies support our conclusions that sales growth is associated with the ability to obtain capital and personnel. One study also sheds light on types of external information associated with growth. Companies are likely to grow faster where

- They have good relations with banks or other established funding relationships;[61] and they have outside investors and/or are willing to share equity among two more individuals.[62]
- They have stronger personnel recruitment procedures and are able to recruit non-owning managers.[63]
- They are able to obtain needed external information, especially in the areas of business strategy, personnel and recruitment, public relations and advertising.[64]

Resource Allocation and Sales Growth

Few resource-allocation variables in our own study directly affect sales growth, though several impact profits. In our study, among a variety of financial indicators tracked, only the CEO's reported tendency to track sales progress over time predicts more rapid sales growth. In addition, we find a strong linkage between sales growth and the adequacy of cash flow, though the latter lags in time, suggesting that sales growth provides better cash flow rather than the reverse. Other research identifies the following two predictors of sales growth:

- Using investment in machines to improve the production process is linked with faster growth.[65]
- Also, among start-up firms (but not among larger, older firms), those operating on a leaner basis (fewer managers, fewer physical assets, lower compensation per employee) grow more quickly.[66]

Work Flow and Sales Growth

Our own research shows that sales growth is related to several aspects of work flow, including effective work-division strategies, effective role assignments, effective coordination strategies and more widely shared information.[67] Only a few studies in the fields of entrepreneurship and strategy include aspects of work flow and organization design as factors predicting sales growth. Researchers have found that faster sales growth is associated with

- delegation of authority or other organizational changes that give senior management more time;[68]
- the presence of a functionally balanced management; and[69]
- the presence of work standards and also the presence of monitoring systems.[70]

In the discussion of research on market strategy and sales growth, we mentioned the use of a subjective measure of financial performance.[71] Although this measure only partially reflects sales growth, we include research predicting this measure, because, to date, other than our own work, it represents the bulk of research on work flow and entrepreneurial financial performance. Specifically, work by Covin, Slevin, and colleagues draws the following conclusions:

- An organic organization structure is associated with higher firm performance in firms with a build mission but not in those with a harvest mission, as defined previously.[72]
- In a separate study, Covin and Slevin find that organically structured/ entrepreneurially managed firms and mechanistically structured/conservatively managed firms had higher performance than firms otherwise matched on organization design and management style. *Entrepreneurial management style* is a term for a rather broad class of measures, basically emphasizing product innovation, breadth of strategy, active search for big new opportunities, and a charismatic leadership; the conservative style is just the opposite.[73]

Although we find the broadly defined, multidimensional approach to definition of variables in this research stream to be somewhat confusing, it presents an exciting research direction.

Changes in work flow are a common theme in life cycle models.[74] Such studies support the dynamic changes of work-flow strategies over time — toward more formal control and feedback systems, coupled with greater delegation of authority. Unfortunately, these studies fail to correlate such changes with sales growth, examining instead at which stages such changes might take place. Nevertheless, such evidence clearly points to the important organizational changes companies experience as they grow. Those results, the findings from our study, and the promising work of Covin and Slevin, and their colleagues suggest that far more research is warranted in the area of work flow and sales growth than has been done to date. Furthermore, contingency theories may be extremely important to aid in understanding of ideal structures.

Human Relations and Sales Growth

In our study, effective communication of values and employee goal integration are predictors of faster growth. Other researchers emphasize the importance of human relations and effective human resource management in rapidly growing firms.[75] Yet in spite of the overall wealth of research in organization behavior, most of the research predicts satisfaction, absenteeism, turnover, and other organizational variables. In short, the body of literature statistically testing relationships between human relations concepts and sales growth is extremely limited. Clearly more work is needed in this area.

Public Relations and Sales Growth

Our research data covered public relations in a fairly limited manner for the project reported in this book, although we did identify a strong linkage between community image and sales growth. There also appears to have been little empirical examination of this important variable on the part of other researchers. However, Dyer provides an excellent discussion of the public relations concept and how it differs from marketing.[76] Dyer supports our view that public relations may provide yet another source of competitive advantage, although he presents no empirical data.

An emerging research area, environmental entrepreneurship, may spur more research in one aspect of public relations: ecological interests inside and outside the government. One aspect of public relations is a company's impact on the physical environment, which may stimulate support or contempt from the public and may generate fines or tax benefits from government, depending upon its actions. One study finds a link between voluntary emission reduction and firm performance.[77] A company's environmental stance may influence other aspects of strategy as well. For instance, Ferrone suggests that environmentally conscious product design strategy may serve as a competitive advantage.[78] But few studies to date have actually tested links between environmental policy and sales growth. Part of the problem in testing this hypothesis is that although companies face considerable environmental pressure, only a small minority have responded by changing their business strategy focus.[79] A recent article provides a more detailed discussion of the application of the DSP Model to environmental entrepreneurship, with illustrative cases.[80]

Technical Mastery and Sales Growth

In our study, faster sales growth is linked with better technical skills and quality of output. In addition, better technical skills, quality of output, and productivity are all linked with steadier growth. A few other studies examine related aspects of technical mastery. Although we do not touch on new product development in our original project, it is an essential component of the technical-mastery strategy and is included in our treatment of technical mastery in subsequent writings.[81] Studies we reviewed suggest that technology and product improvements may boost sales, depending on the circumstances:

- Age and/or size may influence the impact of technology on sales growth. In one study, young, start-up companies grow faster with new, more advanced technology. However, the same effect was not found for older, larger firms.[82]
- Studies on innovation need to separate truly new product invention from improvements to existing products. In a different study of small firms (less than 50 employees), companies installing new machinery in a quest for improved process also tend to grow more quickly.[83] In the same sample of small manufacturing firms (all

with less than 50 employees) improvement of *existing* products boosts sales more effectively than the creation of truly novel products.[84]

- Innovation may be a stronger requirement in high-technology than in low-technology industries. In one study of companies in the biotechnology industry, pioneering use of applied R and D and internal sources of innovation are associated with greater sales growth.[85]

- And once again, we include results from Covin and Slevin's group even though they predict a hybrid dependent variable, only partially reflecting sales growth. In particular, these researchers find an interactive effect of the environment: Refinement of existing products and services is likely to boost financial performance, including sales growth, in low-risk (benign) environments but not in high-risk (hostile) environments.[86]

- In another study by their research team, Covin, Slevin, and Schultz find that companies with a harvest-oriented strategic mission perform better when they emphasize research and development activity geared toward the development and refinement of existing products, but their work indicates that such emphasis has no effect on performance for build-oriented firms.[87] Furthermore, neither new product development nor product refinement is correlated with firm performance in that study.

Whereas our original research project limits itself to potential outcomes of a well-executed technical-mastery strategy, Zahra has developed an extensive research program to identify potential technical-mastery strategies, including pioneering (a company's commitment to developing and introducing radical technologies), product portfolio breadth, process portfolio breadth (the commitment to applied research in developing manufacturing process technologies), commitment to internal R and D, use of external technology, and forecasting.[88] These strategies are correlated with return on assets. Zahra then develops a contingent set of recommended technology strategies based on the degree to which environments are dynamic, hostile, or heterogeneous. Although Zahra predicts return on sales, rather than sales growth, the depth of development of the conceptual approach to technology strategy should spur more research in this area.

Summary of Research on Sales Growth

The growing number of research studies and improved quality of research are quite encouraging. No field of knowledge can build effectively without the concerted efforts of many researchers examining the same issues. Published research to date has been dominated by the marketing field. However, several researchers have broadened their perspective to look at other organizational strategies and sales growth, in the process identifying additional variables that may serve to provide better prediction of sales growth in the future.

Contingency or interactive effects, long hypothesized to be of importance in organization effectiveness and design, are beginning to be examined in a systematic way in the entrepreneurship and strategic management literature.

Some internal issues within the firm interplay with one another — firms pioneering new technologies and products may need to approach planning and organization design differently than less innovative companies. Size and age may also create potentially important interactions, as do the skill level and experience of top management. And companies set up the same way may succeed or fail, depending on the nature of the environment. Size is a very important determinant, but past research has often failed to distinguish clearly enough between the effects of size or age and the direction of causality. Since companies growing rapidly are also getting bigger in size, we need studies that more carefully control for these two effects. For instance, does formal business planning really stimulate growth, or is it a correlate that emerges as a company increases in size? The predictors are far from simple, yet certain clarifying patterns are appearing. One thing is clear: More research is needed, especially quantitative, multivariate research that examines the interrelationships of these different factors.

CONCLUDING REMARKS

In this introduction, we have attempted to provide a firm basis of understanding for the material we present in the rest of this book. In particular, we emphasize the following points:

- Certain strategic actions determine continued growth and profitability in the small to medium-sized firm.
- The fields of strategic management and organization theory have each begun to take advantage of ideas from the other discipline.
- We schematically present the Dynamic System Planning (DSP) Model, derived from three key assumptions: that organizations are humankind's ultimate tool; that surviving and growing companies must combat entropy with an effective input-transformation-output cycle; and that organizations must be viewed as dynamic entities in the context of a network of larger social systems. These three assumptions define the key management strategy issues of the DSP Model: resource acquisition, resource allocation, work flow, human relations, technical mastery, market strategy, and public relations. The first six help to combat entropy. The seventh assures that the organization relates appropriately to a large network of other social systems outside the organization. These seven issues are guided by the founder's or current leader's company vision.
- The DSP Model can be helpful in viewing organizations more cross-functionally.
- The DSP Model can be used for quick feedback in strategy development. It can also be used in all three phases of more conventional strategic planning: to identify current and potential strengths, weaknesses, core competencies, strategies, and competitive advantage; to develop alternative strategies; and to develop an implementation plan.
- Finally, we update interested readers on research in strategy and sales growth of small to medium-sized firms. Although we are already able to draw practical

implications, research on strategy and sales growth is in its infancy. However, we share what we view to be the most validated and promising findings.

We attempt to superimpose the DSP Model as an organizing theory to review findings on strategy and growth, many findings otherwise being scattered and appearing unrelated. We find a recurring theme in our literature review: Predictors of sales growth may change as a company grows and/or its environment alters. Some findings, taken collectively, suggest that perhaps the determination of their founders can help new, small companies squeeze into a market niche. But as a company grows, it becomes more essential that the CEO be able to understand the many complex requirements imposed by a company's environment and to alter the way the firm is managed in response to these requirements. Our understanding of these dynamics is still in its infancy, frequently hampered by the primitive statistical and data techniques we have available to us for understanding complex, multidimensional, and dynamic processes. Hopefully what we learn over the next few decades will guide us toward more effective, dynamic management of the growing firm.

NOTES

[1] Zoltan J. Acs and David B. Audretsch, "The Determinants of Small-Firm Growth in US Manufacturing," *Applied Economics,* 22 (1990), 143–53. This article provides a good example of testing for industry effects on companies, although companies are aggregated by industry type.

[2] Murray B. Low and Ian C. MacMillan, "Entrepreneurship: Past Research and Future Challenges," *Journal of Management,* 14, no. 2 (1988), 139–61. Low and MacMillan identify these four directions.

[3] Richard Barkham, Graham Gudgin, Mark Hart, and Eric Hanvey, *The Determinants of Small Firm Growth: An Inter-Regional Study in the United Kingdom 1986–90,* Regional Policy and Development Series 12 (London: Jessica Kingsley Publishers and Regional Studies Association, 1996), p. 47. In Barkham's study, strategy aims and methods explain 28 percent of sales growth variation, compared with 14 percent explained by company characteristics and only 5 percent explained by entrepreneur characteristics. As a group, variables together explain 46 percent of the variation in sales growth. In William R. Sandberg and Charles W. Hofer, "Improving New Venture Performance: The Role of Strategy, Industry Structure, and the Entrepreneur," *Journal of Business Venturing,* 2 (1987), 5–28, Sandberg and Hofer predict profitability, rather than sales growth. They find several statistically significant interactions among these three sets of variables, concluding that interactive effects have a far greater effect than any of these variables alone.

[4] Robert M. Grant, *Contemporary Strategic Analysis: Concepts, Techniques, Applications* (Cambridge, MA: Blackwell Publishers, 1995). For a history of the field of strategic management, refer to Chapter 1.

[5] For his classic presentation of generic competitive strategies, refer to Michael Porter, *Competitive Strategies* (New York: The Free Press, 1980), pp. 34–46.

[6] C. K. Prahalad and Gary Hamel, "The Core Competence of the Corporation," *Harvard Business Review,* 68, no. 3 (1990), 79–91. See also Gary Hamel and C. K. Prahalad, *Competing for the Future* (Boston, MA: Harvard Business School Press, 1994).

[7] Dave Ulrich and Dale Lake, "Organizational Capability: Creating Competitive Advantage," *Academy of Management Executive,* 5, no. 1 (1991), 77–92.

[8] Jeffrey Pfeffer, *Competitive Advantage Through People: Unleashing the Power of the Work Force* (Boston, MA: Harvard Business School Press, 1994), pp. 6–26.

⁹See Richard L. Daft, *Organization Theory and Design,* 5th ed. (Minneapolis/St. Paul: West Publishing Co., 1995), Chapters 2 and 14. For comparison, see Richard L. Daft, *Organization Theory and Design,* 4th ed. (Minneapolis/St. Paul: West Publishing Co., 1992).

¹⁰Open-systems-theory applications to organizations can be traced to two streams of applications in the early 1960s — a "subsystems" approach defined by Daniel Katz and Robert L. Kahn, *The Social Psychology of Organizations,* 1st ed. (New York: John Wiley & Sons, 1966) and an organization problem-solving model developed by Basil Georgopoulos and colleagues. See Basil Georgopoulos and F. C. Mann, *The Community General Hospital* (New York: Macmillan, 1962); and for more recent discussion and research application, see Basil S. Georgopoulos, *Organization Structure, Problem Solving and Effectiveness: A Comparative Study of Hospital Services* (San Francisco: Jossey-Bass, 1986). For a more detailed presentation of our perspective, see Chapter 4 and also Lorraine U. Hendrickson, "Bridging the Gap Between Organization Theory and the Practice of Managing Growth: The Dynamic System Planning Model," *Journal of Organizational Change Management,* 5, no. 3 (1992), 18–37.

¹¹Peter Senge, *The Fifth Discipline: The Art and Practice of the Learning Organization* (New York: Doubleday/Currency, 1990).

¹²Ron Ashkenas, David Ulrich, Todd Jick, and Steven Kerr, *The Boundaryless Organization: Breaking the Chains of Organizational Structure* (San Francisco: Jossey-Bass Publishers, 1995); James F. Moore, *The Death of Competition: Leadership and Strategy in the Age of Business Ecosystems* (New York: HarperCollins Publishers, 1996).

¹³Margaret J. Wheatley and Myron Kellner-Rogers, *A Simpler Way* (San Francisco: Berrett-Koehler Publishers, 1996).

¹⁴Jeffrey Goldstein, *The Unshackled Organization: Facing the Challenge of Unpredictability Through Spontaneous Reorganization* (Portland, OR: Productivity Press, 1994).

¹⁵In naming this issue, we were seeking a shorter phrase and more familiar words to replace the rather technical-sounding term *social-psychological integration* used by Basil Georgopoulos and his colleagues. (See Georgopoulos, *Organization Structure.*) We drew upon the familiarity of the human relations movement of the 1950s, stressing the importance of employee commitment, satisfaction, and motivation. But for many of our readers, the term *human relations* was mistakenly thought to include relationships with all constituents, within or outside the company, overlapping with aspects of other issues (e.g., resource acquisition, market strategy, and public relations). An alternative label, "employee relations," was thus used in some of our more recent publications: Lorraine Uhlaner Hendrickson and Nesa L'abbe Wu, "Technical Mastery: Basis for Strategic Manufacturing Management," *Productivity,* 34, no. 2 (1993), 199–207; and Lorraine Uhlaner Hendrickson and Dale B. Tuttle, "Dynamic Management of the Environmental Enterprise: A Qualitative Analysis," *Journal of Organizational Change Management,* 10, no. 4 (1997), 363–82.

¹⁶The technical-mastery issue is more fully described in Hendrickson and L'abbe Wu, "Technical Mastery." In our original research project, we inadvertently overlooked the importance of new product development strategy, admittedly a major oversight that is corrected in subsequent publications and in the introduction to the second edition.

¹⁷As with the term *human relations,* we have had second thoughts about the term *public relations.* The same term has been used in marketing to refer to strategies and tactics to create awareness among potential customers or more broadly to refer to relationships with any internal or external constituencies, neither of which captures our intended meaning. (See Samuel Dyer, "Public Relations Strategies for Small Business Growth," *Public Relations Quarterly,* 41, no. 3 [1996], 43–47.) In more recent publications, we have chosen to refer to this DSP issue as "community/government relations." (See Hendrickson and L'abbe Wu, "Technical Mastery," and Hendrickson and Tuttle, "Dynamic Management of the Environmental Enterprise.") But based on recent discussion with colleagues, it is apparent that this label may be too narrow in focus, since another important external constituency outside the I-T-O cycle in many organizations is the owner's family — not really a part of the company but potentially having tremendous impact on its effective functioning.

¹⁸In our research, we include adequate cash flow, or liquidity, as a dimension of financial viability. However, unlike with profitability, management can take several actions to dramatically modify cash flow, including the following: appropriately allocating funds; instituting good collection policies; and negotiating favorable payment terms, just to name a few examples. Although in this book, liquidity is treated, along with profitability, as part of the eighth issue of financial viability,

Hendrickson and Tuttle, "Dynamic Management," 376, suggest that the topic of cash flow management be included within the resource-allocation issue. Future work is likely to incorporate adequate cash flow into the resource-allocation issue.

[19]For the classic presentation of the core competency concept, refer to Prahalad and Hamel, "The Core Competence of the Corporation," 79–91. See also James Brian Quinn and Frederick G. Hilmer, "Reading 3.3 Core Competencies and Strategic Outsourcing," in Henry Mintzberg and James Brian Quinn, *The Strategy Process: Concepts, Contexts, Cases,* 3rd ed. (Upper Saddle River, NJ: Prentice Hall, 1996), pp. 63–73.

[20]See for instance, Fred R. David, *Strategic Management,* 5th ed. (Englewood Cliffs, NJ: Prentice Hall, 1995), Chapter 4, pp. 113–47, for a more detailed description of environmental tools to analyze the general environment, industry, and immediate competitors. Also see John A. Pearce and Richard B. Robinson, Jr., *Strategic Management: Formulation, Implementation, and Control,* 5th ed. (Burr Ridge, IL: Irwin, 1994), pp. 183–88, for an excellent description of the value chain approach. They also provide a detailed description of environmental analysis tools and an overall introduction to strategic management.

[21]Gary Hamel and C. K. Prahalad, "Strategy as Stretch and Leverage," *Harvard Business Review,* 71, no. 2 (1993), 75–84.

[22]We derive our facts from the video *McDonald's in Moscow* originally prepared by the Canadian McDonald's Corporation and later distributed through Dryden Press to accompany the marketing text, Louis E. Boone and David L. Kortz, *Contemporary Marketing,* 7th ed. (Orlando, FL: Dryden Press, 1993).

[23]Donald C. Hambrick and Lynn M. Crozier, "Stumblers and Stars in the Management of Rapid Growth," *Journal of Business Venturing,* 1 (1985), 31–45.

[24]For more detailed discussion of the technique we used to develop the model and the specific problems we categorized into the different DSP issues, refer to Hendrickson, "Bridging the Gap Between Organization Theory and the Practice of Managing Growth."

[25]David E. Terpstra and Philip D. Olson, "Entrepreneurial Start-up and Growth: A Classification of Problems," *Entrepreneurship Theory and Practice,* 17, no. 3 (1993), 5–20.

[26]Robert K. Kazanjian, "Relation of Dominant Problems to Stages of Growth in Technology-Based New Ventures," *Academy of Management Journal,* 31, no. 2 (1988), 257–79.

[27]Derrick E. D'Souza and Patricia McDougall, "Exploring the Competitive Strategies of High-Growth Manufacturing Firms," presentation, 1995 Southern Management Association Conference.

[28]This broader definition of strategy is consistent with the approach taken by British researchers Storey and Barkham. See D. J. Storey, *Understanding the Small Business Sector* (London: Routledge, 1994). See also Barkham et al., *The Determinants of Small Firm Growth.*

[29]Storey, *Understanding the Small Business Sector,* provides a major literature review on strategy and growth, although the reader should be cautioned that some articles on employment growth are intermingled with those on sales growth. Barkham's study represents another major study done recently on sales growth (Barkham et al., *The Determinants of Small Firm Growth*). Brush and VanderWerf find that from a sample of 34 studies, "changes in sales" was overwhelmingly the most popular operationalization, with 16 of 34 studies reviewed utilizing this measure. (See C. G. Brush and P. A. VanderWerf, "Measuring Performance of New Ventures," in *Frontiers of Entrepreneurship Research,* ed. Neil C. Churchill, William D. Bygrave, John A. Hornaday, Daniel Muzyka, Karl H. Vesper, and William E. Wetzel, Jr. [Wellesley, MA: Babson College, 1990].).

[30]See Patricia Phillips McDougall, Jeffrey G. Covin, Richard B. Robinson, Jr., and Lanny Herron, "The Effects of Industry Growth and Strategic Breadth on New Venture Performance and Strategy Content," *Strategic Management Journal,* 15 (1994), 537–54. They find that although broad breadth strategy ventures in high-growth industries exhibit significantly highest sales growth rates, they showed only modest return on sales (see p. 550).

[31]Tsai et al. warn of possible trade-offs between sales growth and profitability. See W. M. H. Tsai, Ian MacMillan, and Murray B. Low, "Effects of Strategy and Environment on Corporate Venture Success in Industrial Markets," *Journal of Business Venturing,* 6 (1991), 9–28.

[32]Several studies present empirical evidence questioning the strength of relationship between sales and employment growth, including Sue Birley, "New Ventures and Employment Growth," *Journal*

of Business Venturing, 2 (1987), 155–65; William C. Dunkelberg, Arnold C. Cooper, Carolyn Woo, and William Dennis, "New Firm Growth and Performance," in *Frontiers of Entrepreneurship Research*, ed. Neil C. Churchill, John A. Hornaday, Bruce A. Kirchoff, J. Krasner, Karl H. Vesper (Wellesley, MA: Babson College, 1987), pp. 301–21. See also Carolyn Y. Woo, Arnold C. Cooper, William C. Dunkelburg, Urs Daellenbach, and William J. Dennis, "Determinants of Growth for Small and Large Entrepreneurial Startups," in *Frontiers of Entrepreneurship Research*, ed. Robert A. Brockhaus, Sr., Neil C. Churchill, Jerome A. Katz, Bruce A. Kirchoff, Karl H. Vesper, William E. Wetzel, Jr. (Wellesley, MA: Babson College, 1989), pp. 134–47.

[33]We would appreciate being alerted to empirically based research we have overlooked.

[34]Depending upon the study, the correlation between sales growth and profitability ranges between about .3 and .5 (explaining between 0 percent and 25 percent of the variation between them, hardly warranting, in our opinion, treating them interchangeably). See, for instance, Scott Shane and Lars Kolvereid, "National Environment, Strategy, and New Venture Performance — A Three Country Study," *Journal of Small Business Management*, 33, no. 1 (April 1995), 37–50, who find a correlation of .28 between sales growth and a subjective profitability rating. See also Gregory G. Dess, G. T. Lumpkin, and J. G. Covin, "Entrepreneurial Strategy Making and Firm Performance: Tests of Contingency and Configurational Models," *Strategic Management Journal*, 18, no. 9 (1997), 677–95, who find a correlation of .4 ($p < .05$) between sales growth and profitability.

[35]Lumpkin and Dess find that two aspects of entrepreneurial orientation — proactiveness and competitive aggressiveness — are conceptually and empirically distinct, loading on two separate factors and correlating in different ways with sales growth and profitability (proactiveness being positively related, whereas competitive aggressiveness is unrelated to the two dependent variables). (See G. T. Lumpkin and Gregory G. Dess, "Proactiveness and Competitive Aggressiveness: Separate Dimensions of a Firm's Entrepreneurial Orientation," in *Frontiers of Entrepreneurship Research*, ed. Paul D. Reynolds, William D. Bygrave, Nancy M. Carter, Per Davidsson, William B. Gartner, Coln M. Mason, and Patricia P. McDougall [Wellesley, MA: Babson College, 1997]. See also G. T. Lumpkin and Gregory G. Dess, "Clarifying the Entrepreneurial Orientation Construct and Linking it to Performance," *Academy of Management Review*, 21, no. 1 [1996], 135–72.) For two research examples incorporating both proactiveness and competitive aggressiveness in the entrepreneurial orientation construct, see Jeffrey G. Covin and Dennis P. Slevin, "Strategic Management of Small Firms in Hostile and Benign Environments," *Strategic Management Journal*, 10 (1989), 75–87; and Jeffrey G. Covin and Dennis P. Slevin, "Competitive Aggressiveness, Environmental Context, and Small Firm Performance," *Entrepreneurship: Theory and Practice*, 14, no. 4 (1990), 35–50.

[36]Jeffrey C. Shuman, John J. Shaw, and Gerald Sussman, "Strategic Planning in Smaller, Rapid Growth Companies," *Long Range Planning*, 18 (1985), 48–53. Also see Jeffrey C. Shuman and John A. Seeger, "The Theory and Practice of Strategic Management in Smaller Rapid Growth Firms," *American Journal of Small Business*, 10 (1986), 7–18.

[37]B. W. Keats and J. R. Montanari, "Stages of Strategic Sophistication: A Developmental Model," paper presented at Decision Sciences Institute National Meetings, Honolulu, 1986, and cited in Jeffrey S. Bracker, Barbara W. Keats, and John N. Pearson, "Planning and Financial Performance Among Small Firms in a Growth Industry," *Strategic Management Journal*, 9 (1988), 591–603.

[38]See Richard B. Robinson, "The Importance of 'Outsiders' in Small Firm Strategic Planning," *Academy of Management Journal*, 25 (1982), 80–93. Also see Richard B. Robinson, Jon A. Pearce, George S. Vozikis, and Timothy S. Mescon, "The Relationship Between Stage of Development and Small Firm Planning and Performance," *Journal of Small Business Management*, 22 (1984), 45–52.

[39]For research on moderator effects of opportunistic vs. craftsman profiles, see Bracker et al., "Planning and Financial Performance." Though not statistically tested, Olson and Bokor's work suggests a trend that formal business planning appears to spur sales growth to a greater extent for more experienced managers. See Philip Olson and Donald W. Bokor, "Strategy Process-Content Interaction: Effects on Growth Performance in Small, Start-up Firms," *Journal of Small Business Management*, 33 (1995), 35–44. Finally, while not specifically measuring management characteristics, Robinson suggests that there may be a possibility that those business owners choosing to work with the Small Business Development Center may have a greater openness to new ideas or greater

commitment to economic success, consistent with certain elements of the opportunistic profile. See Robinson, "The Importance of 'Outsiders,' " 91.

[40]Robinson et al., "The Relationship Between Stage of Development and Small Firm Planning and Performance," 45–52. Duchesneau and Gartner also find a link between independent variables, time in planning, using professional advice, and planning breadth, and the dependent variable, profitability. (See Donald A. Duchesneau and William B. Gartner, "A Profile of a New Venture Success and Failure in an Emerging Industry," in *Frontiers of Entrepreneurship Research,* ed. Bruce A. Kirchhoff, Wayne A. Long, W. Ed McMullan, Karl H. Vesper, and William E. Wetzel, Jr. [Wellesley, MA: Babson College, 1988], 372–86.

[41]Olson and Bokor, "Strategy Process-Content Interaction," 39–40.

[42]See Richard L. Osborne, "Second Phase Entrepreneurship: Breaking Through the Growth Wall," *Business Horizons,* 73 (1994), 80–86.

[43]This was an unpublished study by David Smallbone, David North, and Roger Leigh, "Managing Change for Growth and Survival: The Study of Mature Manufacturing Firms in London During the 1980s," Working Paper No. 3 (Cambridge Planning Research Centre, Middelsex Polytechnic, 1992), conclusions of which are described in Storey, *Understanding the Small Business Sector,* p. 157.

[44]Osborne, "Second Phase Entrepreneurship," 81. Once again, note that this study is nonempirical, based on case study.

[45]Barkham, et al., *The Determinants of Small Firm Growth,* p. 37.

[46]Ibid.

[47]See Smallbone et al. in Storey, *Understanding the Small Business Sector,* p. 157. Storey also refers to another study by Kinsella. See R. P. Kinsella, W. Clarke, D. Coyne, D. Mulvenna, and D. J. Storey, *Fast Growth Firms and Selectivity* (Dublin: Irish Management Institute, 1993).

[48]Olson and Bokor, "Strategy Process-Content Interaction," 42. We drew this conclusion by combining raw data presented in Tables 5 and 6, but a statistical test was not performed.

[49]Acs and Audretsch, "The Determinants of Small Firm Growth."

[50]See A. K. Gupta and V. Govindarajan, "Business Unit Strategy, Managerial Characteristics, and Business Unit Effectiveness at Strategy Implementation," *Academy of Management Journal,* 27 (1984), 25–41.

[51]Jeffrey G. Covin, Dennis P. Slevin, and Randall L. Schultz, "Implementing Strategic Missions: Effective Strategic, Structural and Tactical Choices," *Journal of Management Studies,* 31, no. 4 (1994), 481–505.

[52]Barkham et al., *The Determinants of Small Firm Growth,* p. 38. Also see Robin Siegel, Eric Siegel, and Ian C. MacMillan, "Characteristics Distinguishing High-Growth Ventures," *Journal of Business Venturing,* 8 (1993), 169–80, esp. 173.

[53]Siegel, Siegel, and MacMillan, "Characteristics Distinguishing High-Growth Ventures," 175. See also Smallbone et al. in Storey, *Understanding the Small Business Sector,* p. 157.

[54]McDougall et al., "The Effects of Industry Growth and Strategic Breadth," 537–54.

[55]Acs and Audretsch, "The Determinants of Small Firm Growth," 150.

[56]Siegel, Siegel, and MacMillan, "Characteristics Distinguishing High-Growth Ventures," 174.

[57]D. A. Aaker and G. S. Day, "The Perils of High Growth Markets," *Strategic Management Journal,* 7 (1986), 409–21.

[58]Barkham et al., *The Determinants of Small Firm Growth,* p. 40.

[59]Siegel, Siegel, and MacMillan, "Characteristics Distinguishing High-Growth Ventures," 175.

[60]Barkham et al., *The Determinants of Small Firm Growth,* pp. 82–83.

[61]Siegel, Siegel, and MacMillan, "Characteristics Distinguishing High-Growth Ventures," 175–76.

[62]Four studies support the relationship between external equity and sales growth. These studies are reviewed by Storey, *Understanding the Small Business Sector,* p. 146.

[63]P. Wynarczyk, R. Watson, D. J. Storey, H. Short, and K. Keasey, *The Managerial Labor Market in Small and Medium Sized Enterprises* (London: Routledge, 1993), cited in Storey, *Understanding the Small Business Sector,* pp. 150, 311.

[64]See Smallbone et al., in Storey, *Understanding the Small Business Sector,* p. 157.

[65]Barkham et al., *The Determinants of Small Firm Growth,* p. 140.

[66]Siegel, Siegel, and MacMillan, "Characteristics Distinguishing High-Growth Ventures," 174.

[67]Lorraine Uhlaner Hendrickson, "Size, Growth or Uncertainty: What Matters in Design of the Firm?" *Proceedings of 1990 International Council for Small Business Conference,* Washington, DC, June 7–10, 1990.

[68]See Smallbone et al., in Storey, *Understanding the Small Business Sector,* p. 157.

[69]Siegel, Siegel, and MacMillan, "Characteristics Distinguishing High-Growth Ventures," 175.

[70]Hendrickson, "Size, Growth or Uncertainty."

[71]Covin, Slevin, and Schultz, "Implementing Strategic Missions," 481–505.

[72]Ibid.

[73]Jeffrey G. Covin and Dennis P. Slevin, "The Influence of Organization Structure on the Utility of an Entrepreneurial Top Management Style," *Journal of Management Studies,* 25, no. 3 (1988), 217–34.

[74]For the classic article, see L. E. Greiner, "Evolution and Revolution as Organizations Grow," *Harvard Business Review,* 50 (1972), 37–46. For just a few of the other articles discussing this topic, see Charles W. Hofer and Ram Charan, "The Transition to Professional Management: Mission Impossible?" *American Journal of Small Business,* 9, no. 1 (summer 1984), 1–11; Eric Flamholtz and Yvonne Randle, "How to Avoid Choking on Growth," *Management Review* (May 1987), 25–29; Steven H. Hanks and Gaylen N. Chandler, "Patterns of Functional Specialization in Emerging High Tech," *Journal of Small Business Management,* 32, no. 2 (1994), 23; R. K. Kazanjian and R. Drazin, "A Stage-Contingent Model of Design and Growth for Technology Based Ventures," *Journal of Business Venturing,* 5 (1990), 137–50.

[75]John Kotter and Vijay Sathe, "Problems of Human Resource Management in Rapidly Growing Companies," *California Management Review,* 21 (1978), 29–36.

[76]Samuel Dyer, "Public Relations Strategies."

[77]S. L. Hart and G. Ahuja, "Does It Pay to Be Green? An Empirical Examination of the Relationship Between Emission Reduction and Firm Performance," *Business Strategy and the Environment,* 5, no. 1 (1996), 30.

[78]R. Ferrone, "Environmental Business Management Practices for a New Age," *Total Quality Environmental Management,* 5, no. 4 (1996), 41–46.

[79]B. Garrod and P. Chadwick, "Environmental Management and Business Strategy: Towards a New Strategic Paradigm," *Futures,* 28, no. 1 (1996), 37.

[80]Hendrickson and Tuttle, "Dynamic Management of the Environmental Enterprise."

[81]Hendrickson and L'abbe Wu, "Technical Mastery: Basis for Strategic Manufacturing Management," 205.

[82]Siegel, Siegel, and MacMillan, "Characteristics Distinguishing High-Growth Ventures," 178.

[83]Barkham et al., *The Determinants of Small Firm Growth,* p. 88.

[84]Ibid., p. 84.

[85]Shaker A. Zahra, "Technology Strategy and New Venture Performance: A Study of Corporate-Sponsored and Independent Biotechnology Ventures," *Journal of Business Venturing,* 11 (1996), 289–321.

[86]Covin and Slevin, "Strategic Management of Small Firms in Hostile and Benign Environments."

[87]Covin, Slevin, and Schultz, "Implementing Strategic Missions," 481.

[88]Shaker A. Zahra, "Technology Strategy and Financial Performance: Examining the Moderating Role of the Firm's Competitive Environment," *Journal of Business Venturing,* 11 (1996), 189–219.

CHAPTER 1

Preparing Yourself for Managing Growth

How do you manage a growing company? What can you learn from other CEOs facing the dual challenges of maintaining growth and profitability? What issues are you likely to face and how can you best resolve them? We address these questions and more.

We believe our book is unique. We combine extensive interviews and data from nearly two hundred companies along with first hand experience in building J. P. Industries (JPI), a FORTUNE 500 company.[1] Our diverse research and management experience confirms that companies are dynamic and must be managed that way. We sum up our guidelines in the Dynamic System Planning Model that, we will show, is practical yet based on well-tested theory. We especially address challenges faced by small, growing firms. But the model applies whether or not your company is growing right now. It applies whether you have five employees or five thousand, whether you face a maelstrom of growth and change or stagnation and decline. The model provides a means to develop a more successful company strategy for higher profits and growth.

THE DECISION: TO GROW OR NOT

Consider this unusual concept: You don't have to grow to be self-employed and financially secure.

Ron started several businesses during his life. But once each venture was underway, he eventually reached a point at which the business managed him rather than the other way around.[2] Although adept at identifying new markets and making

1

sales, when it came to working with other employees, assigning tasks, and coordinating their efforts, he never seemed quite able to make the transitions needed to assure business success. After several such failures, Ron hit upon a suitable niche for his talents—as a promoter of trade shows. He has no employees to contend with; each show is of relatively short duration; and he can move on to the next project before he gets bored or runs into complex management challenges.

Ron opted for *zero* growth—no employees, no hassles, and a good income.

Jeff is CEO of a tool-and-die shop.[3] At one time he was committed to growth of his firm but when the firm approached about twenty employees, Jeff had to make a decision. If he continued to grow, he would have to add middle managers. As things stand, he is making an extremely good income and is able to house all his employees in one large unpartitioned quonset-style building. With this physical layout, and an organization of project teams, he can oversee his whole operation alone. His wife does the bookkeeping and he is able to handle all administrative and sales work in one small room in the front of the shop floor. He has made his decision: simplicity. This is not to diminish his staff's technical accomplishments. Even the Japanese have toured this little plant, which produces some of the most innovative work in his industry.

WARNING FROM AN ENTREPRENEUR OF THE YEAR

If you are reading this book, you may not identify too closely with Ron or Jeff. Self-employment and financial independence are not your only goals. You probably also relish the challenge of seeing how far and how fast you can grow. Growth can be an exhilarating experience and public recognition of growth accomplishments abound. Most honor rolls of business, such as the FORTUNE 500 and INC. 500, base selection on sales or sales growth.

But beware. So much hoopla accompanies rapid sales growth that the question of profitability may go unexamined until major problems set in. Our data confirms the critical point that growth alone does not guarantee profitability or long-term survival—and can actually spell disaster if improperly managed.

The case of a large retail computer entrepreneur highlights this point. At one point in his firm's meteoric growth, he received many local, state, and national awards honoring his accomplishments, including Entrepreneur of the Year. But he had not put basic control systems in place. Lack of control took its toll on profits and the firm struggled for survival. Fortunately, the CEO did some reading on other fast-growth firms, including a case written about L. L. Bean in Maine, and identified his unmet needs. He hired several full-time experts to install the necessary systems. For several years following, his firm remained an industry profit leader and eventually merged with another successful computer retailer. But he still remembers the irony of receiving so many awards when his business was in such serious financial trouble and cautions the aspiring entrepreneur to beware the hubris that comes with that first honor-roll award.

OUR BASIC PHILOSOPHY: IDENTIFY
THE PROBLEM FIRST

Our strategy for managing the growing firm is called the Dynamic System Planning Model. But first, we would like to present our basic philosophy of running a successful business that underlies the model's application.

It can be stated simply: If you know what kinds of issues or problems to look for, it is much easier to find the right solution. The challenge is in learning what kinds of problems or issues to anticipate. Your technical training can be very helpful, but learning *how* to learn is even more important. Once you can identify the problem, whether it is technical, human relations, or marketing in nature, you can look and find the relevant solution.[4]

Once you master the Dynamic System Planning Model, you will be much better prepared to anticipate the problems that lie ahead and to set up an ongoing strategy to cope with them.

THE DYNAMIC SYSTEM PLANNING MODEL

The Dynamic System Planning Model is a model of organization effectiveness based on both the classical goal approach and open-systems theory ideas pioneered by researchers at the University of Michigan's Institute for Social Research, including Daniel Katz, Robert Kahn, and Basil Georgopoulos.[5] Borrowing from the classical goal approach, for-profit firms depend upon *financial viability to survive*. A financially viable company can pay its bills when they are due and operates at a profit.[6]

Simple enough. But achieving financial viability is much more complicated than merely determining objectives for profit and production of goods and then setting out to achieve those goals. The DSP Model defines the issues you must manage to assure financial viability, including market strategy, work flow, resource acquisition, human relations, resource allocation, public relations, and technical mastery. Successful corporate strategy must tackle each of these issues.

Each issue raises key questions about how you run your company:

1. Market strategy: What is your market niche—who are you selling to and why are your customers buying?

2. Work flow: How do you assure the best flow of work? First, how should you divide work among everyone in your firm—and, once divided—how can you assure that everyone's activities fit smoothly together?

3. Resource acquisition: How do you acquire the resources you need—money, people, supplies, information—to begin and/or continue to operate your business?

4. Human relations: How can you maintain adequate human relations—esprit de corps, employee motivation—so employees can really contribute? What values do you share with employees?

5. *Resource allocation:*   As you acquire the resources you need, how can you best make use of them? How should you spend your money, assign your staff, or otherwise allocate raw materials, information, equipment, and supplies?

6. *Public relations:*   Who else outside your firm can shut you down—or help you out? What groups or individuals should you be paying attention to other than your customers and suppliers?

7. *Technical mastery:*   How do you maintain the highest productivity and quality? Do you have the needed technical know-how?

8. *Financial viability:*   Can you pay your bills when they come due? Are your assets growing, and do you operate at a profit?

Though critical to the firm's survival, financial viability is fundamentally different from the other seven issues in one respect: It cannot be managed directly. How well you manage the first seven issues determines how much cash you have, how profitable you become, how quickly your assets grow, and how long your company survives.

THE ORGANIZATION IS A DYNAMIC SYSTEM

Each word in the term *Dynamic System Planning Model* has a special meaning. We use the term *dynamic* to signify the ever-changing conditions that organizations face outside the firm—and changing management strategies required to keep up with these changes on the inside. Global competition, court rulings, and the changing caliber of job applicants are all examples of these external dynamics. Because of these dynamics, effective strategy requires frequent review and assessment.

When we speak of a *dynamic system,* we are alluding to qualities of organizations defined by open-systems theory.[7] According to that view, frequent response and adaptation to environmental changes is critical to survival. Although the eight issues remain the same, to grow profitably, the approach you must take to manage each issue changes over time.[8] The open-systems view also sees the organization as a collection of interdependent parts. Change one, and it affects the others. You cannot treat any one aspect—be it accounting, marketing, or technical mastery—in isolation.

The words *planning model* are also important. The Dynamic System Planning Model offers a new way of thinking about planning that guides your daily thinking. Planning should not be looked at as an annual report you file in a drawer or shelve on the bookcase until next year but as a program you can use on an ongoing basis to guide your decisions and action. Strategy for dealing with the eight DSP issues forms the backbone of the plan, guided by your vision for your company. As events change over the course of the year, you need to revisit your strategy frequently to make sure it still adequately addresses each issue.

One common problem faced by CEOs of rapidly changing firms is being blindsided in one area while concentrating too hard in another. For example, perhaps you put all your energy into improving sales but ignore medical-insurance concerns your employees have. Sales are dependent on positive customer relations. Can you really improve customer relations while your employees feel miserable about their benefits? You may not be able to resolve all the challenges at once but you are less likely to confront an unexpected crisis if you track all eight issues on a regular basis.

HOW TO READ THIS BOOK

In this book, we intentionally avoid a style that makes strong prescriptive statements about how you should run your own business. Companies are complex and unique. The problems are the same but the solutions are different: What works for someone else may not work for you. Rather than give pat answers, we try to help guide you toward the right questions. We include self-assessment tools (like those we used in our research) to help you identify your own strengths and weaknesses. Whether or not you run a company right now, skimming the questions will also give you a quick idea of how we define each issue and the kinds of strategies that can be used for resolving each issue. Though the questions we provide are very straightforward, accurate answers may be more difficult to come by. For a true assessment you may want to obtain confidential responses to many of these questions from your managers, employees, or even your customers. In Part III, we provide some tips about how to do this appropriately.

Based on your self-assessment, wherever you think improvement is in order, you'll want to consider approaches other CEOs have taken that are described throughout the book. Though we don't advise that you copy another strategy verbatim, their experiences may help trigger an idea of your own and expand your repertoire of solutions to consider.

Part II also presents findings from our research that you may want to know about—*linkages* between management practices and strategies that lead to profitability and cash flow. Linkage is the term we use to refer to a statistically supported relationship between two or more variables in our two-hundred-firm sample. Predictably, linkages don't correlate 100 percent to success measures. What works for one firm may not work for another. But the linkages are supported strongly enough, statistically speaking, to warrant special mention. In this way, we show how our data dispels some commonly held beliefs and sustains others.

EXAMPLES OF SOME LINKAGES

Let's look at a few examples of linkages.

LINKAGE 1-1: NET PROFITS ARE HIGHER IN FIRMS that emphasize quality as a part of the mission.
Perhaps you have wondered whether to emphasize quality more in your own firm. However you define it, we find quality to be a significant success factor for

many companies we studied. Our findings agree with those from another large study by Buzzell and Gale.[9] The topic of quality is explored further in several chapters, including Chapters 6 and 13.

LINKAGE 1-2:   NET PROFITS ARE HIGHER WHERE CEOs have a clear vision.

A lot is said about the importance of having a strategic plan or vision. Does this really matter, or is it just business school mumbo-jumbo? Our study confirms the importance of a clear focus. Vision does not necessarily pertain solely to products or services. It may relate to emphasis on quality, low cost, focus, or diversification. JPI was founded on a clear vision—to create a high-quality, low-cost producer of durable goods by acquiring underperforming firms in which the founder could use his expertise in manufacturing and management. Underperformers in automotive and plumbing supplies were targeted, in particular. Of course more than vision alone was required. Detailed strategies were designed to turn around each firm, including the narrowing of product lines, selling off excess inventory, consolidating marketing and administrative staff, training personnel at all levels, and replacing managers when needed. This clear vision catapulted JPI into the FORTUNE 500 just ten years after start up, with strong profits throughout the period.

LINKAGE 1-3:   NET PROFITS ARE HIGHER WHERE work flows smoothly, especially in manufacturing and business service firms and in larger firms.

Some linkages apply in all firms. Others appear to be especially critical in certain industries or size ranges. Work flow is an example of the latter.

Smooth work flow means making sure efforts of different individuals and groups in the firm converge properly in the right time and place. Achieving smooth flow of work sounds simple. In very small firms, the owner sees everything that goes on and corrects mistakes. But as a firm exceeds 20 employees, difficulties crop up. Sometimes owners figure if they keep putting in more hours they can continue to iron things out. But sooner or later direct oversight simply stops working. At that point, only more sophisticated techniques will assure smooth work flow, such as a clear chain of command and control systems. Chapters 7 and 8 explore how work flow can be improved and its effect on other aspects of the organization.

LINKAGE 1-4:   NET PROFITS ARE HIGHER WHERE CEOs communicate specific values to their employees.

Our data—and our personal experiences—support the importance of clearly stated values. This is explored more fully in Chapter 10, including the types of values emphasized by JPI and how they were communicated to employees.

The four linkages summarized in this section are only a sampling of those noted throughout the rest of the book. Each chapter of Part II is based in large part on additional linkages we found in data collected from interviews with CEOs and managers in nearly two hundred small and medium-sized companies. In Appendix C, we list the linkages specifically supported by our research. We also illustrate points throughout the book with specific comments from CEOs.

SUMMARY OF THE EIGHT KEY ISSUES

The Dynamic Systems Planning Model is centered around eight basic issues, including:

1. Resource acquisition: obtaining key capital, personnel, information, and material inputs

2. Market strategy: establishing and maintaining a market niche

3. Public relations: maintaining or enhancing adequate relationships with significant outside groups other than customers and suppliers

4. Resource allocation: optimally assigning all types of resources—capital, supplies, personnel—appropriately inside the firm

5. Work flow: assigning and dividing work, and in turn, coordinating these efforts in a manner that assures task accomplishment

6. Human relations: maintaining adequate motivation and morale among employees, so that personal needs of employees are met coincident with the meeting of organizational goals

7. Technical mastery: assuring the firm knows how to make and improve on what it sells

8. Financial viability: Having adequate capital and cash left over to operate the business and make it grow

If you can keep these eight issues in mind, you will be less likely to waste time on crisis management. Crisis management comes from a lack of ability to anticipate problems. Knowing what those problems are reduces the risk of overlooking them. If a firm is able to resolve each of these eight issues adequately over time, it is more likely to remain profitable, with better cash flow and less tension.

OUTLINE OF THE REMAINDER OF THE BOOK

The remainder of Part I (Chapters 2–4) elaborates the framework and theoretical underpinnings of the Dynamic System Planning Model. Chapter 2 presents a case that illustrates the model and how each issue evolves over time. It also describes briefly how each issue tends to change over time. Chapter 3 presents a practical step-by-step CEO's guide for using the DSP Model in planning. Chapter 4 delves more deeply into the practical implications of viewing your company as a dynamic system, with some additional pointers to consider if you plan to use the DSP Model.

Chapters 5–13 make up Part II of the book. At least one chapter is devoted to each issue. We start with financial viability in Chapter 5—the key issue of profit and cash flow. In Chapter 5 we also summarize key linkages between financial viability and the other seven issues. Chapters 6–13 elaborate each of the other seven issues in turn. We review more thoroughly the importance and meaning of each issue, and how each relates to the others. We describe the strategies CEOs use to manage each issue, how these strategies change with circumstances, and which appear to be more effective under particular conditions. At the beginning of each chapter is a self-assessment guide to help acquaint you with the issue, and to pinpoint your company's own strengths and weaknesses. Each chapter concludes with specific recommendations for coping with that issue. Because work flow is one of the most complex issues, we have divided that discussion into two segments: Chapter 7 addresses work division; Chapter 8 deals with coordination of effort.

Chapters 14 and 15 make up Part III. Chapter 14 addresses the problem of organization change. How can you involve your employees? Suppose you have identified areas of weakness or programs you would like to introduce. How can you introduce change in a way that maximizes your chances of success? Chapter 15 summarizes major conclusions made throughout the book.

Appendix A provides more detail about research methodology and research results. Appendix B includes some additional questions to supplement the self-assessments throughout, which were used in the original study for *Managing the Growing Firm*. Appendix C provides a list of linkages supported by our data discussed throughout the book.

NOTES

[1] Details of the research study are presented in Appendix A.

[2] This story is based on an account shared in a telephone conversation with Ron's daughter, who is also a show promoter.

[3] This example is drawn from information gathered in the research project. Names and identifying information are deleted throughout the book to protect confidentiality of the participants in the project.

[4] These ideas were also discussed by John Psarouthakis in an interview, *Wall Street Transcript*, January 18, 1988, p. 88,081.

[5] Daniel Katz and Robert L. Kahn, *The Social Psychology of Organizations*, 2nd ed. (New York: John Wiley & Sons, 1978). Basil S. Georgopoulos, "The Hospital as an Organization and Problem-Solving System," in *Organization Research on Health Institutions*, ed. Basil S. Georgopoulos (Ann Arbor: Institute for Social Research, 1972). Basil S. Georgopoulos, *Organization Structure, Problem Solving, and Effectiveness: A Comparative Study of Hospital Services* (San Francisco: Jossey-Bass, 1986).

Ours is not the first application of open-systems theory to entrepreneurship. Also interesting reading by another Michigan graduate is Eric G. Flamholtz, *Growing Pains: How to Make the Transition from an Entrepreneurship to a Professionally Managed Firm*, rev. ed. (San Francisco: Jossey-Bass, 1990).

[6] James L. Price and Charles W. Mueller, *Handbook of Organizational Measurement* (Marshfield, MA: Pitman Publishing, 1986), pp. 128–30.

[7] Our approach is an adaptation of Georgopoulos's complex problem-solving model, which defines "enduring" problems faced by the system. See Georgopoulos, *Organization Structure*.

[8] Kenneth Boulding, "General Systems Theory—the Skeleton of Science," in *Modern Systems Research for the Behavioral Scientist*, ed. W. Buckley (Chicago: Aldine, 1968). Also refer to footnote 5 in this chapter.

[9] Robert D. Buzzell and Bradley T. Gale, *The PIMS Principles: Linking Strategy to Performance* (New York: The Free Press, 1987).

CHAPTER 2

How Your Management Challenge Changes with Growth

In the first part of this chapter, we illustrate the eight issues of the Dynamic System Planning Model with the case of Lou and Jane's photographic firm—first when they are just starting out, and again ten years later when the company has grown substantially.

In the second part of the chapter, we describe typical changes CEOs experience in managing each of the issues, especially as the company grows in size.

AN ILLUSTRATION: LOU AND JANE'S PHOTOGRAPHIC FIRM

When companies first form, the entrepreneur's primary attention is usually centered on the product or service itself—what products or services should be offered, how they are made, who will buy them and how they can best be sold.

When Lou and Jane decided to go into business for themselves,[1] neither thought about building a large organization, or making much money. They were 1960s-style activists who wanted to avoid traditional jobs and whose primary goal was self-employment. They loved photography, so they decided to start a photo lab.

One of their first challenges was finding enough capital to purchase needed start-up equipment *(resource acquisition)*. They had excellent credit references from prior employment and a solid business plan, so they went to the bank. The bank wanted their house as collateral; and because Lou and Jane were confident about the quality of their work and the demand for affordable, fast, customized work in their area, they agreed.

They struggled in the early months to keep up with the loan. They concentrated on selling quality services to customers interested in custom work, since they knew they could have difficulty competing for standard film-development business *(market strategy)*. Few permits or regulations were involved, other than filing for a state tax code number permitting them to operate a retail business *(public relations)*.

They informally checked with each other about the day's orders and about who would solicit which customers and complete the orders for the next day. Thus, the work flow issue, though it existed, was very easily resolved through informal means. And since both Jane and Lou were partners in both marriage and in a business they loved, their personal needs were directly met through their work *(human relations)*.

Because some of Lou's customers wanted finishes he had little experience with, he enrolled in a special photography course *(technical mastery)*. After awhile, Lou and Jane found they needed to work out a usage schedule for their more expensive camera so that orders could be filled on a timely basis. A simple schedule board worked quite nicely after some trial and error.

They also began to budget for additional equipment *(resource allocation)*, monitoring cash and profits with the help of a local bookkeeper, who provided them with quarterly reports. After a profitable first year *(financial viability)*, they were able to meet their bank-loan repayments, pay themselves a living wage, and purchase another piece of more sophisticated finishing equipment *(resource allocation)*.

Of all eight issues noted during the early stages of the business, market strategy and resource acquisition received the most attention.

LOU AND JANE'S FIRM: TEN YEARS LATER

Ten years later, Lou and Jane's photographic firm has grown to 40 people. They still face the same eight issues. But they approach them differently.

They have a strong reputation for timely, high-quality, customized photography work at a reasonable price. The quantity of sales is less an issue now than is the pace of demand. Peaks and valleys in sales put a strain on employees and make it difficult to complete all jobs quickly. The firm is experimenting with leveling demand peaks by charging more for rush jobs and less to customers willing to wait a few extra days *(market strategy)*.

With an excellent credit history and retained earnings from several years of slow, steady growth, Lou and Jane are able to equip and supply the firm with whatever is needed *(resource acquisition)*. Their biggest challenge now in the resource-acquisition area is recruitment—where to find capable personnel trained in the more sophisticated photography techniques used by their firm. Lou has developed some close ties with area instructors in photography. One professor at the local community college sent him three decent recruits last year.

As for *public relations,* few major challenges have yet presented themselves. However, Lou and Jane have found it doesn't hurt yearbook business to donate some free services regularly to some of the area school fund-raising campaigns. Jane is also fairly active in the town's chamber of commerce.

Production is beginning to pose a major challenge. Maintaining smooth *work flow* involves much more sophisticated approaches than before. Lou and Jane now have three mid-management people—one to supervise inside sales, one to oversee production, and a third to handle field sales. This way, Lou and Jane delegate many routine decisions. They still make the major decisions, such as equipment purchases, diversification of photography services, and compensation *(resource allocation)*.

However, they hired a full-time bookkeeper who makes budgeting recommendations to them. This has become fairly routine and is not a major challenge.

Human relations probably poses the greatest challenge at the moment. Lou and Jane lament that the firm no longer feels like a family. Back when the firm had about 15 or 20 employees, there seemed to be a homey quality to the place. Some had even been college friends. Now many recently hired employees, though competent, show little commitment to the firm.

Technical mastery offers an ongoing challenge. Sometimes sales growth outpaces the ability to recruit and train new people. Lou and Jane no longer have the time to supervise directly all the work that is produced. From time to time, as quality begins to slip, they get an increase in customer complaints and have to work closely with production people to get things back on track.

Overall, Lou and Jane have been very fortunate. Their development of successful strategies for the issues described thus far is reflected in a healthy financial picture. They maintain good cash flow, and the firm grows slowly but steadily. Their profit picture continues to be strong as well *(financial viability)*.

In summary, Lou and Jane face the same eight issues that they did ten years ago. Some of these issues require more attention now, others less. But few are handled in the exact manner that they were back then. None of the areas are being ignored and this is reflected in financial health—sales growth, profitability, and cash flow.

ATTENTION SHIFTS TO DIFFERENT ISSUES OVER TIME

At this point, you may feel that the task of managing all eight DSP issues may appear overwhelming. But keep in mind, in a well-run company, you are not likely to face a major challenge in all eight areas at once. The ease with which particular issues are resolved shifts with size and age of the firm. Early on, the most commonly mentioned problems involve aspects of market strategy (finding your customers) and resource acquisition (finding capital and people to work for you).[2] As orders surge, your next major challenge typically is improving work flow.[3] Human relations, an almost trivial issue in the early stages when the company feels almost like family, can become your greatest challenge as you near the 100-employee mark.[4]

THE GRADUAL NATURE OF CHANGE

Once a CEO establishes a strategy for each of the DSP issues, that approach may continue in use for a long time. A shift in approach may be phased in very gradually, one issue at a time over a several-year period. To illustrate, we share some

TABLE 2–1   **The Percentage of Firms That Report Change in the Type of Strategy Used to Manage Different Issues**

	NOW DONE DIFFERENTLY FROM THE PAST
Type of Strategy for:	
Coordinating efforts	46%
Setting direction	43
Assigning roles	33
Finding key managers	29
Allocating equipment and dollars	22
Sharing values	21
Sample Size = 168	

information we gathered in our interviews. For five of the issues, we asked CEOs whether they had changed the type of strategy used or whether they used the same strategy they always had. Table 2–1 summarizes these results.

As Table 2–1 shows, for any one issue, a minority of CEOs remember shifting their strategy for addressing that issue over time. Strategy for coordinating efforts is most frequently mentioned as having changed since the firm's founding but even here, fewer than half report major changes. Setting direction, a component of market strategy, is the next most frequently mentioned issue involving change. At the other end of the spectrum, only about one in five CEOs have changed their approach to allocating equipment and dollars (most still using the squeaky-wheel approach) and a similarly small proportion (21 percent) have changed their approach to sharing values, an important component of the human relations issue, since their firm's founding. In between, about a third had changed strategies for assigning roles (33 percent) and finding key managers (29 percent).

Of course these data are based on the recollections of the CEOs being interviewed and should not be taken as perfectly accurate or even representative of all small to mid-sized firms. We share our data, however, to make the following practical point that these numbers suggest: The growing firm is not likely to confront the need for change in strategy for all eight DSP issues at the same time. On the contrary, change is phased in over a period of years. Perhaps it is the gradual nature of these shifts that makes them harder to identify. But if you are alert to them, be comforted that you will have plenty of time to plan for them. Ignore them, however, and let major problems slide, and run the risk of being overwhelmed by the accumulated challenges later on.

WITH GROWTH, TYPICAL SHIFTS IN THE NATURE OF EACH ISSUE

For each of the eight issues, let's take an introductory look at some typical changes in both problems and solutions with company growth.

Resource Acquisition: A Shift from Money to People

For most new firms, one of the first problems is start-up capital. Most firms capitalize using the owner's personal savings, credit lines and/or money from relatives and friends. Only a very small percentage obtain money from venture-capital firms.

With growth, the biggest resource challenge often shifts from money to people. Lack of available managerial and technical talent is a frequent complaint among CEOs of more successful growing firms.

Market Strategy: Outgrowing Your Niche

Identifying products or services that sell is at the core of any business. Market strategy continues to challenge most CEOs. A frequent problem faced by growing firms is that they outgrow their niche—typically broadening or diversifying the range of products or services to fuel growth.

In devising new market strategy, CEOs of growing firms retain an informal, intuitive approach, more rarely shifting to a formal strategic planning approach. However, even without formal planning, CEOs of successful firms integrate a vast array of information about their own firms, their industry, and the marketplace.

Public Relations: A Broadening Constituency

Until the middle part of the twentieth century, businesses typically paid attention to two outside groups: customers and suppliers. Alas, the environment is becoming increasingly complicated. Today's CEO needs to address a much broader grouping, including various levels of government and public-interest groups. Government agencies have become enmeshed in a growing array of issues—environmental quality, product liability, hiring and promotion practices, safety and health conditions for employees, and zoning, just to name a few. Many agencies ignore the smallest firms. Many laws even exclude firms below a certain size. Though helpful at first, this can catch the growing firm off guard later. As a firm grows, it can become a target for regulation, litigation, and tax audit.

Resource Allocation: Work Volume Leads to Budgeting

Resource-allocation strategy is a direct function of work volume. In small firms, the CEO may not need a formal budget. Very little excess money may be available and needs are basic, anyway. The firm may be able to get by with a simple bookkeeping system and with what several in our study refer to as the "squeaky-wheel" budgetary approach.

As the firm expands, the volume of transactions becomes too great to rely on mental arithmetic and checkbook balancing alone. Budgeting becomes more formal. Resource allocation appears to be one issue for which you can plan well ahead. Many entrepreneurs with prior business experience find it easier to set up a computerized accounting system right from the start. This reduces the disruption faced in converting over to such a system once the operation is in full swing.

Work Flow: More Information Leads to Specialization

In young businesses, roles are usually fluid. The owner is right there directing everything and on different days, people may rotate and perform overlapping tasks. Later on, however, specialization emerges. The partner who is a better salesperson handles sales. The more technically oriented partner may cover installations, engineering, or production. As the firm expands, roles become even more specialized. The more specialized they become, the more challenging the coordination of efforts. Specialization implies a greater interdependence. If everyone were to sell, install equipment, and service their own customers, less communication and interaction would be required than when one group sells, another installs, and a third group services the same units. Work volume and information complexity, the same forces that tend toward specialization, push the firm into an ever more complicated spiral of interdependence. At a certain point, overload of information becomes a driving force for change.[5]

Growth in the raw number of employees also complicates coordination and triggers the need for change. Using simple formulas for permutations and combinations, one sees that the number of possible pairs of relationships jumps from 45 for a group of 10 employees to 190 for a group of 20 employees, and then to 1,225 pairs for 50 employees—the typical size at which a crisis arises in work flow. Checking with your neighbor to see what she or he is doing—the self-regulation of activity so effective and common to small firms—quickly becomes an impossibility. And for many types of work, the CEO becomes overwhelmed with information, as well. CEOs manage information overload by delegating decisions about many aspects of the firm's operations as it grows.

Human Relations: Founder Loses Touch

Rather than diminish, the human relations issue tends to grow in complexity and challenge with sheer growth in size and the passage of time. The human relations issue is frequently ignored until it has reached a crisis stage. At start up, the CEO's charisma, the excitement of a newly formed team and informal conversations are usually enough to hold a small firm together. Even subordinates in a young firm usually share in the excitement. Rapport is simple to build because the founder is right there, frequently sharing his or her values and beliefs, or reflecting them directly into actions for all to observe and learn. With a little planning, such values and beliefs can form the foundation for a company culture that will maintain a positive atmosphere as the company grows.[6] More typically, the CEO is too busy attending to other aspects of the business until it's too late. Then a cavernous gulf separates the CEO from third- and fourth-generation employees, whom the CEO fails to impress and whom the employees don't understand.

One founder of a successful office-supply firm was surprised and hurt when he first faced this fact at a sales meeting. His sales people were quite upset about a change in the sales-commission structure. By their words, it was clear that many reps did not know him or trust his motives. They didn't understand what his company stood for, what his values were, and why he had built the firm. At the time of the interview, he and his managers were considering major corrective steps to improve communication of his values and restore a positive atmosphere to the firm.

Technical Mastery: More Expertise Is Needed

All firms must master their particular industry. In the small and young firm, a founding partner is often the company's technical expert.[7] Alternatively, the CEO may hire outside expertise, although very small firms run the risk that this person will start his or her own firm, leaving them stranded. Or worse, the expert may sink the ship with large fixed-pay requirements.

As firms grow, at some point, it is usually necessary to hire and/or train technical people. Also, firms are more likely to expand research and development to move beyond the know-how of the founder and to capitalize on unique information.

Quality assurance is another aspect of technical mastery. Many firms rely only on visual inspection and simple scrapping of efforts. However, as quality demands and cost constraints escalate worldwide, more sophisticated strategies are being implemented to improve quality of output. During the 1970s and 1980s, many observers of the United States noticed a decline in attention to the issue of technical mastery—taking for granted the once superior know-how and skill level of American workers. Magaziner and Patinkin show how Samsung Corporation of Korea succeeded in dominating the microwave-oven industry in less than ten years by focusing on technical mastery.[8]

Financial Viability: No Firm Immune

Profits and cash go up and down depending on how well the other seven issues are managed. Financial viability is not in itself directly managed. Although young firms often struggle with cash flow and profit, older firms are hardly immune to these same problems.

NOTES

[1]This fictionalized account is closely based on one of the companies participating in our research. To provide a complete introduction to each of the eight issues and how they change over time, we added a few minor details. Unless otherwise noted, cases presented in the book are based on our research study.

[2]Guvenc G. Alpander, Kent D. Carter, and Roderick A. Forsgren, "Managerial Issues and Problem Solving in the Formative Years," *Journal of Small Business Management,* 28 (1990), pp. 9–19.

[3]D. Miller, "The Structural and Environmental Correlates of Business Strategy," *Strategic Management Journal,* 8, pp. 55–76.

[4]This conclusion was drawn from analysis of data in our own research.

[5]The seminal work on the information-processing model was done by Jay Galbraith. See for example, Jay Galbraith, *Organization Design* (Reading, MA: Addison-Wesley, 1979).

[6]Edgar Schein, *Organizational Culture and Leadership: A Dynamic View* (San Francisco: Jossey-Bass, 1985). For other discussions on culture, see W. Gibb Dyer, Jr. *Cultural Change in Family Firms: Anticipating and Managing Business and Family Transitions* (San Francisco: Jossey-Bass, 1986).

[7]Michael Gerber, *The E-Myth: Why Most Businesses Don't Work and What to Do About It* (Cambridge, MA: Ballinger, 1986).

[8]Ira C. Magaziner and Mark Patinkin, ''Fast Heat: How Korea Won the Microwave War,'' *Harvard Business Review,* 67 (1989), pp. 83–93.

CHAPTER 3

Using the DSP Model to Plan Your Business

Studies repeatedly show the same results: Few business owners follow the text when it comes to strategic planning. In a rapidly growing company and, for that matter, in most companies today, it is often very difficult to predict what will happen next week, let alone five years from now. Yet, planning is essential for company success.

This chapter is our how-to guide to strategic planning for turbulent times. Although similar to conventional planning in some respects, it differs in other significant ways.[1] In the first part of the chapter we describe our approach. In the second part, we summarize distinctions between our approach and more traditional planning approaches.

STRATEGIC PLANNING ACCORDING TO THE *DSP* MODEL

Strategic planning according to the DSP Model can be summarized in the following seven steps:

1. Clarify your company vision.
2. Track each of the seven organizational DSP issues, using the DSP Grid.
3. Watch your financials closely—especially cash flow. It is your firm's pulse.
4. Constantly reassess your strategy in each area and take action, as needed, to modify strategy to fit new conditions.
5. In making changes, plan for the people side, not just the technical side. Anticipate resistance to change and take steps to prevent it.
6. Create feedback loops so that you can evaluate progress for every issue.
7. Repeat steps 1 through 6 as often as needed to stay on course.

Now let's look at each step in more detail.

Step 1: Clarify Your Vision

The basic premise of conventional strategic planning is a sound one: Company planning must be guided by a corporate vision. What are you really trying to accomplish with your company? What sets your firm apart? Some visions are too narrow, addressing only the specific products or services offered. The word *vision* also reflects insight into the future. Steven Jobs was not just producing microcomputers when he founded Apple Computers. He had uncanny insight into the way microcomputers could revolutionize business in America, a way that bypassed data-processing departments and brought information right to the point at which it was needed. Ray Krok had a vision for McDonald's Corporation that went beyond hamburgers to fill a need for consistent, fast, and good-tasting food. The founding partners of Holiday Inn had a hunch that the Interstate Highway Act would spur an enormous increase in family-vacation road travel (which it did). And Henry Ford of Ford Motor Company wasn't just making cars. He envisioned the marriage of the assembly-line process with automobile technology to produce low-cost cars the middle class could afford. The great visionaries in industry, in short, see something beyond the mere product or service being made.

A strong vision is probably the most important step in the planning process. Come back to this step as often as you like, until you really feel secure in knowing where your firm is now headed and where you would like it to end up. In almost all successful firms, large or small, planning is top-down, driven by the CEO's vision of the firm.

Step 2: Complete the DSP Grid

Second, track each of the seven organizational DSP issues, using the DSP Grid. The term *DSP Grid* refers to a matrix that you can easily set up to track your company's progress. Figure 3–1 presents a sample worksheet you may consider in planning according to the DSP Model. It provides a relatively simple format you can keep in mind in analyzing the seven organizational DSP issues (all but financial viability). Over time, you may need more space to complete your grid than the squares provide. But conceptually you can use the grid to keep in mind the way to proceed.

Note that the DSP Grid addresses only the first seven organizational DSP issues. Financial viability requires a different treatment that we explain in Step 3 of the strategic-planning process we have outlined. Note that column 1 simply lists each of these seven issues to be considered.

Figure 3–2 provides a little more detail to help you complete your grid. In column 2, note how effectively that particular issue is now being handled in your firm. We present a few examples here and again in the chapters referred to for each issue on the chart. In column 3, list the strategies or approaches you are using currently to handle that issue. Keep in mind that each strategy should be consistent with your overall company vision. In column 4, consider the context of each issue. The context includes both external factors and factors internal to the firm that may affect the way in which this issue is resolved. Consider here not only current conditions but also a forecast of changes that may be particularly relevant for each issue. In column 5, reflect on any changes you may want to make now or consider for the future in

COMPANY VISION: _____

1: DSP ISSUE	2: EFFECTIVENESS OF CURRENT STRATEGY (criteria)	3: CURRENT STRATEGY TAKEN (think in terms of vision)	4: CONTEXT (INTERNAL/ EXTERNAL) NOW OR IN THE NEAR FUTURE	5: YOUR NOTES ON CHANGES YOU WANT TO MAKE (in light of col. 2–4 and company vision)
Market strategy				
Work flow				
Resource acquisition				
Human relations				
Resource allocation				
Public relations				
Technical mastery				

FIGURE 3–1   Worksheet for Your Company DSP Grid for the Seven Organization Issues

COMPANY VISION: _____

1: DSP ISSUE	2: EFFECTIVENESS OF CURRENT STRATEGY (sample criteria)	3: CURRENT STRATEGY TAKEN (think in terms of vision: sample areas to consider)	4: CONTEXT (INTERNAL/ EXTERNAL) NOW OR IN THE NEAR FUTURE (sample factors to consider)	5: YOUR NOTES ON CHANGES YOU WANT TO MAKE (in light of col. 2–4 and company vision)
Market strategy	Sales level? Market share?	Products/services offered; who sets direction and how	Industry analysis; competitor analysis; general economy	See Chapter 6
Work flow	Does work slip through the cracks? Do efforts fit together?	Degree of specialization; coordination methods used	Company size; growth rate	See Chapters 7, 8
Resource acquisition	Access to capital? Able to recruit good managers? Access to supplies?	Methods to recruit; capital/ supply sources	Interest-rate levels; labor market—general and job-specific	See Chapter 9
Human relations	Are employees committed to the company? Are absenteeism/ turnover low?	How values are shared; how corporate culture is defined; formal incentives used	Company size; effectiveness of other strategies; general economy	See Chapter 10
Resource allocation	Funds/staff/ equipment assigned to proper areas?	Method of allocating cash: method to allocate equipment/ supplies/ personnel	Company size; volume of purchases, transactions	See Chapter 11
Public relations	Facing litigation? Public image and reputation?	Method to track laws, new regulations; policies on environment	New regulations on affirmative action, environ- ment, antitrust; new government funding	See Chapter 12
Technical mastery	Are products/ services delivered on time/expected quality/quantity needed? Is technology improving?	Techniques to train personnel; production methods used; type of equip- ment used	Supplier expectations; technological developments; competitors' plans	See Chapter 13

FIGURE 3–2   Guidelines for Developing the DSP Grid for the Seven Organization Issues

light of your responses in columns 2–4. Consider how well your current strategy is working out, whether the current strategy effectively supports the overall mission and vision for the firm, and whether you expect changes in the near future that will make your current strategy obsolete. Let's look at columns 2–5 in a little more detail.

Column 2: How adequately is each issue currently being managed?
When you first start working with the DSP Grid, your responses may be rather rudimentary. As you progress, you may want to evaluate each issue according to specific, measurable criteria—consistent, hopefully, with your overall vision for the firm.

To get you started, here are some sample questions that you may want to consider for each issue. Additional assessment questions are provided throughout Part II and Appendix B:

- For market strategy, are you selling your goods or services at the expected levels?
- For resource acquisition, are you able to get the supplies/capital/people you need to do the work?
- For public relations, are you on good terms with others in the larger community within which you operate? Are you facing any litigation as a result of an oversight of one or more outside constituencies (environmental group, government, citizens' rights group, etc.)?
- For resource allocation, are you able to allocate your resources to projects, departments, or activities where they are needed?
- For work flow, is work well coordinated and appropriately assigned?
- For human relations, is morale good, and are employees committed to the company and to high performance?
- For technical mastery, can you produce the goods or services for customers as promised with respect to quantity, timing, quality, and technical improvements?

Your dissatisfaction in answering any of these questions may signal a need to probe deeper into self-assessment of your company and may also provide an opportunity to develop a more effective strategy for managing your firm.

Column 3: How are you approaching each issue right now?
What is the nature of the strategy you are currently using to resolve each issue? Consider in particular the strategies that best support your overall mission and vision for the firm. If product quality is a critical factor, consider the approach you take to recruiting personnel. Are your methods sufficient to find suitable talent? If being a low-cost producer is a critical competitive factor in your business, have you paid enough attention to the way in which work is set up (the work flow)? If your vision of the firm is that customer service is number one, have you instilled these values in your employees and do you use specific techniques to do so (human relations)?

In sum, the way you approach every issue gives you an opportunity to support the corporate mission and your future vision of your firm.

Column 4: What is the relevant context—external and internal— for each issue?   Has the internal or external situation that might affect this issue changed recently? Is this context relatively stable or will anticipated changes alter the way you handle this issue in the near future? For market strategy are new competitors opening their doors nearby? In public relations, is a new government regulation going to affect your business? Is sheer size going to affect your strategy for managing the flow of work? By paying close attention to the changing context, you may get early warning of a need to change your strategy for a particular issue, or even to rethink the vision for your firm.

The most common internal trigger for change is sheer growth. Having more people creates a need for qualitative changes in the way most of the DSP issues are managed. External dynamics are myriad—new competitors, a change in the caliber of the labor market, change in suppliers. Effective CEOs constantly scan the environment for changes that may affect their business. Marketing and strategy texts often provide excellent techniques for analyzing your market, your industry, and your competition. These techniques are especially relevant for your market strategy but are useful as a starting point for other issues, too.[2]

You also need to consider how change in each of the eight issues may affect the other seven. For instance, declining morale may hurt quality or slow down work flow. To make significant changes in one issue, you may need to consider changes in two or more areas at the same time. The interrelationships among the eight DSP issues are carefully considered throughout Part II.

Column 5: What changes do you want to make?   In column 5, reflect on any changes you may want to make now or consider for the future in light of your responses in columns 2–4. If you are less than completely satisfied with the results you are getting from your current strategy, it may be time to rethink your approach and try something new. Consider not only how well your current strategy is working out by itself, but also whether your current strategy effectively supports the overall mission and vision for the firm, and whether you expect changes in the near future that will make your current strategy obsolete. Column 5 on the grid is also a placeholder for any additional observations or remarks—either specific changes you have thought of, or just a general reminder that you need to investigate alternatives in this area.

On the chart in Figure 3–2, we have indicated the chapters in Part II that treat each of the issues in much more detail. Although the chapter references are located in column 5, these chapters will also be useful in developing the rest of your grid.

Step 3: Watch Your Financials Closely

Financial viability cannot be managed directly as noted on the DSP Grid. It is a yardstick of how well you are managing the other issues. It certainly can be measured, however, and should be tracked on an on-going basis.

At JPI, the most important financial information concerned cash flow, not profits. The controller tracked cash daily and then prepared a Statement of Cash Flow—a summary of sources and uses of cash for operating, financial and investment purposes—that the president reviewed every Monday morning. The balance sheet and income statement, though prepared monthly, were not considered useful from a planning perspective. They merely provide a picture of *where you have been, not where you are headed.* If you don't already do so now, you should have your accountant prepare a cash-flow statement for you or set up an internal system that can track this information for you.[3]

Step 4: Take Action

Constantly reassess your strategy in each area and take action as needed to modify strategy to fit new conditions. Once your DSP Grid is complete, don't just stick it in a drawer and forget about it. Keep it on hand as a daily guide for running your business. Think of the eight issues as parameters that you must always watch in order to stay on course in realizing your vision. Review your assumptions as often as necessary and revise your strategy as needed, but always in the context of the total picture that you have developed. This is your preventive-maintenance program. It is far superior to the alternative of crisis management.

At JPI, we used an annual, formal business-planning cycle to review our progress in different areas. The difference with many companies, however, was in following step 4. We continually made adjustments in strategy throughout the year, keeping the original plan in mind, but not using it as a straightjacket when different opportunities arose and changes occurred.

Step 5: Plan Changes Carefully, Especially as They Apply to People

In making changes, plan for "the people side," not just the technical side. Entrepreneurs seem particularly surprised to learn that many other people do not embrace change the way the typical entrepreneur does. In fact, most people naturally resist change, whether that change is technical (such as adding a computer system) or managerial (such as introducing a new team-building technique) in nature. Don't expect employees to be as excited as you are, even about improvements they will directly benefit from. At JPI, careful planning, team building, employee training, participation in operational decision making, and other modern supervision techniques went a long way toward minimizing resistance to change.

Step 6: Create Feedback Loops

Create feedback loops so that you can evaluate progress for every issue. Plans rarely lead to entirely predictable results, especially in rapidly growing companies or those in turbulent environments (which includes almost all companies today). Don't rely on financial data alone to track progress of your plans.

If you set up specific criteria to evaluate the adequacy of each issue in Step 2 (column 2), then this step is fairly easy. Simply track your evaluation over time to see how you do in each area. If you haven't done this, you need to go back to Step 2 and think this through.

Measures do not all have to be highly quantifiable. For public relations, for instance, it may be more significant that you have been involved in major litigation in the last year for pollution at the plant, than exactly how many lawsuits have been filed. However, seize the opportunity for gathering more information when you get sporadic complaints about some problem or even positive feedback about what you do.

Finally, note that although knowing the discrepancies between actual and expected results is helpful, taking full advantage of a feedback system may mean you need to pursue the matter in greater depth to learn what created the discrepancy in the first place. Try to gain a complete understanding of why the discrepancy occurred. Rather than counting defects, solve the problem that caused the defects in the first place.

Step 7: Repeat Steps 1–6

Planning, including strategic planning, should not be viewed as simply an annual activity. It is a frame of reference for guiding your daily activity. If you have a good memory, you may be able to get by without writing anything down. The goal of the DSP planning approach is not to create a large report. On the other hand, notes to yourself, however informal, may help remind you of ideas as you go through the process. Another advantage of writing down your thoughts, if they are written legibly, is that you can pass your ideas around and get input from others in your company—board members, advisors, managers, or employees themselves.

At JPI, we went through the process of developing an annual business plan but also recognize that most CEOs of small to medium-sized companies don't. The importance of the exercise is not what you are writing but what you are thinking about. As your company grows, you may want to shift to a more formal approach, but that isn't the essence of the process. It can be done either way.

CONVENTIONAL STRATEGIC PLANNING VS. OUR APPROACH

Our approach to planning has several similarities with conventional strategic-planning approaches. It also has some specific differences. For instance, both approaches recommend you begin with a clear vision of your firm, sometimes referred to as the mission statement. And with either approach, consider current and future general strategies for achieving that vision. Finally, with either approach, your end goal is to generate specific action plans to implement your general strategies, which support the overall vision.

In spite of these similarities, our approach differs in several important aspects. Let's sum up by reviewing what these are.

Analysis of company strengths and weaknesses is based on issues, not functions.   In the conventional approach, implementation plans are developed functionally—through marketing, engineering, sales, production, and so forth. Some large corporations actually shortcut the planning process, having functional managers develop plans for their areas that are later fused at the top. Obviously, in the latter case, the activities in one area may have little relevance for forwarding the goals in a different area or even the overall aims of the firm. The shift from functional areas to issues may seem subtle, but it represents a fundamental shift in thinking toward a problem-solving perspective, driven by the corporate vision.

Market strategy is only one of several key issues.   Secondly, our approach differs because it elevates the other six organizational DSP issues to the same level of importance as market strategy (as important as it is). Of course, market strategy is often central to the vision; there is no denying this. But our framework allows you to consider other important factors, along with specific products and services, that you may not have previously considered on a strategic level—factors defined by the other issues.

The CEO is central to development of the overall plan.   Strategic planning, and planning in general, is often viewed as so time-consuming that it is delegated to some staff person—a vice-president of planning, or even an outside consultant. Be cautious! Often, delegated plans reflect too little of the CEO's unique vision, knowledge, and instincts to be of any use. For most companies, success is largely due to the CEO's inspiration. As JPI approached $500 million in sales, most of the CEO's duties were delegated to others, but not the strategic-planning function. In our view, that must always remain with the CEO, although others may provide input.

Consider the following example, related to us by an insider at a mid-sized high-technology firm specializing in defense contracts. The company hired a vice-president of strategic planning to develop a formal business plan. The insider listed several weaknesses of the resulting plan:

1. Too little attention had been paid to new markets, as opposed to existing ones.

2. The determination of investment costs in a newly proposed product was unrealistic and didn't take into account the investment other companies had already made.

3. Estimates for the marketing and advertising dollars required to launch the new product were far too low.

In this particular case, the whole staff supposedly had worked with the vice-president; but his plan clearly reflected a lack of input from the top of the organization, where the discrepancies in it would have been noted. The result? No significant actions were taken linked to the plan during the subsequent three years.

Strategic planning is a daily exercise, not an annual event.
Fourth, and finally, unlike many conventional planning approaches, our approach requires frequent, steady monitoring by the CEO. A formal strategic plan is not something you do once a year and stick in a drawer. It must guide your daily actions and be modified frequently to respond to a turbulent world. Developing a big book

report should not be the goal of strategic planning. Having a clear orientation in your mind, you can organize new information coming to you in a much more effective manner.

NOTES

[1]By conventional planning, we mean the approach presented in most contemporary strategic-management college texts. See for instance, John A. Pearce II, and Richard B. Robinson, Jr., *Strategic Management: Formulation, Implementation, and Control,* 5th ed. (Homewood, IL: Irwin, 1994), p. 3.

[2]See Michael E. Porter, *Competitive Advantage* (New York: Free Press, 1985). This book provides an excellent basis for more in-depth analysis of the environment and market-strategy development. See also Arthur A. Thompson, Jr. and A. J. Strickland III, *Strategic Management: Concepts and Cases,* 6th ed. (Homewood, IL: BPI/Irwin, 1992), Chapter 3 for excellent guidelines to carry out your own market, industry, and competition analysis.

[3]For a good review of how to prepare a cash-flow statement, see Charles T. Horngren and Gary L. Sundem, *Introduction to Financial Accounting,* 4th ed. (Englewood Cliffs, NJ: Prentice Hall, 1990), Chapter 11.

CHAPTER 4

Viewing Your Company as a Dynamic System: Practical Implications

Why are the eight DSP issues such important parameters for planning your business? What are some other practical implications of viewing companies as dynamic systems? We address answers to these questions in this chapter. In the second part of the chapter, we also present an expanded version of the DSP model.[1] The expanded version further clarifies your role as CEO—as visionary and as creator of a multibrained system that fulfills that vision.

PRACTICAL IMPLICATIONS OF VIEWING COMPANIES AS DYNAMIC SYSTEMS

To be successful in managing your own dynamic, changing organization, the DSP Model requires that you:

- Develop a successful strategy for all eight DSP issues. Each is vital to company survival and growth.

- Expect that a change—planned or otherwise—in how one DSP issue is managed affects the other seven.

- Effective management requires constant monitoring of all eight DSP issues. Realize that your job is never done.

- Identify specific solutions suited to your own firm. Avoid copying without careful analysis.

- Be alert to changes that require a shift in your attention to different issues over time.

Let's explore these implications in more detail.

All Eight Issues Are Vital to Survival and Growth

The eight issues of the DSP Model are not arbitrarily selected. They arise naturally when one views firms as open systems.[2] In the absence of any energy or force to counteract it, all systems gravitate toward *entropy*, a state of disorganization and chaos. A company fights entropy by "sucking orderliness out of its environment."[3] *Syntropy* (negative entropy) is the process by which all systems combat entropy, building something up.

Syntropy is achieved via the simple cycle of *input, transformation,* and *output*. According to this cycle, a system brings resources (inputs) inside its boundaries, converts or transforms those resources (adding value), and then exports those improved resources (output) back into the environment. To keep going, the system needs a steady supply of inputs. To complete the cycle, outputs must be traded for new inputs on an ongoing basis. In a for-profit company, simply, the product has to sell.

Each of the eight DSP issues relates in a unique way to successful completion of the input–transformation–output cycle—your company's weapon against chaos and disorder.[4]

Resource acquisition—needed at the input stage.   All companies need to import resources on a daily basis. In addition to equipment, supplies, and capital, we also consider employee efforts and new information brought in from outside the firm as "fuel" to keep the system going. In previous chapters, we have identified the firm's ability to obtain needed resources as the *resource acquisition* issue.

Issues pertaining to transformation of inputs.   Four issues relate to the transformation stage of the cycle: resource allocation, work flow, human relations, and technical mastery. *Resource allocation* begins the transformation process. Once resources are brought within the boundaries of the organization, they need to be assigned to certain uses. Allocating cash to different uses is the core resource allocation problem, whether done on an ad hoc or formal budgeting basis.

Another transformation issue, *work flow,* is two-pronged. Organizations form because two or more individuals are needed to get the work done. How do you divide work among employees? This is the first work-flow challenge, often referred to as *structuring*. The direct result of work division is the need to combine individual efforts so that the work of the company is still accomplished. In management, we refer to this as the *coordination* of efforts. Coordination refers to the need to fit employee efforts back together properly to accomplish the company's objectives.

The third transformation issue, *human relations,* addresses the willingness of workers to commit their efforts toward the realization of company goals.

At some point, product comes off the line. *Technical mastery,* the fourth transformation issue, addresses your company's ability to complete the cycle by actually making what it is supposed to make. This is a nontrivial task. Are the products and services produced in the quantity and with the quality you expected and needed? Are you capable of making needed technical changes?

Converting outputs back into inputs—completing the cycle.   Successful resolution of the first five DSP issues assures your company is able to produce the goods and services you set out to make. But now that your product is off the line, will it sell? Will somebody buy the services you are set up to provide? These answers are at the root of the *market-strategy* issue—your ability to convert your outputs back into new inputs—cash, credit, bartered goods, or services.

Managing the interface between the organization and its environment.   So far, the issues we have looked at derive directly from the input–transformation–output cycle itself. The seventh DSP issue, *public relations,* has more to do with your company's relationship to the general environment than to specific customers or suppliers. In this general environment, many other groups, including government agencies, environmental activists, and hungry lawyers can destroy your company or promote it. Family is another external group to consider.

This general environment can also be viewed as a *suprasystem* within which your company is embedded. Although in theory, the suprasystem has always existed, social, political, economic, and technological forces continue to push your company closer to other individuals, groups, organizations, and national governments in an increasingly complex, interconnected web called the global village. Understanding of this fact can save you costly litigation and other unforeseen problems.

Your fight with entropy.   Though the process that counters entropy is long and complicated, your measures of success are straightforward. Your accumulated assets, especially liquid assets and other fixed assets that can be converted to cash, are your ultimate weapons to combat entropy. Without cash from some source—saved, invested, or borrowed—a company quickly ceases to be.

Profits are useful to the extent that they help you to build up your assets. They reflect a measure of the efficiency of the input–transformation–output cycle—in short, how well you manage all the other issues. Without a series of profitable quarters, it is usually difficult to maintain enough cash to operate your business and to obtain needed credit during periods of slow cash flow. Even though slightly different in the role they play in the system, profits and cash flow are thus closely intertwined and we lump them together as the eighth issue, *financial viability.*

The functional versus the DSP approach.   All the issues we discuss derive from easily identified management activities. Yet viewing companies from these eight parameters is fundamentally different from the functional view. Each parameter contributes to the flow of work through the system as a whole. Functional areas are specific divisions within the firm given certain work assignments, some of which overlap two or more of the issues we have discussed. Consider, for instance, the *human-resource* function in the organization versus the human-relations issue. The human-resource function often requires strategy development for at least two or three issues: recruiting the necessary talent (resource acquisition), creating a motivating environment (human relations), and training individuals with the proper technical skills (technical mastery). Thinking in terms of issues rather than functions allows you to put management into a problem-solving perspective regardless of the structure of your company.

Change—Planned or Otherwise—Is One Issue That Alters All the Others

In a dynamic system, variation in one part of the system can create a big variation in the total system. One way to visualize the system is as a giant balloon. If you give it a push in one place, the balloon feels pressure everywhere and needs to compensate somewhere else. Sloppy accounting eventually affects cost controls, which has impact on the ability to purchase needed supplies and equipment or to offer competitive salaries. A personality clash between the sales manager and production manager may affect not only morale in their two departments but eventually the ability of the production department to meet its schedule.

For those of you who think mathematically, we can view overall performance of the system as a multiplicative function:

$$P_{system} = F\,[(a_1I_1)\,(a_2I_2)\,(a_3I_3)\,.\,.\,.\,(a_8I_8)] \qquad \text{(Eq. 4-1)}$$

In Equation 4-1, F refers to function, P_{system} is the symbol for performance of the whole company. I refers to the level of effectiveness, either for the eight DSP issues or for the system as a whole (I_s). The letter a simply refers to the importance or proportional weight of each issue. That is, at any point in time, overall performance may depend more on one issue than on another. In words, what Equation 4-1 is saying is that the performance of the system is a function of the weighted products of effectiveness for each of the eight DSP issues. Notice what happens when any one factor (I_i) equals zero. The performance of the entire system drops to zero. $(x \times 0 = 0)$.

Similarly, we can summarize the effectiveness (I_i) for any one of the eight DSP issues as follows:

$$I_i = F(a_iI_i) = F[(a_1I_1)\,(a_2I_2)\,.\,.\,.\,(a_{n-1}I_{n-1})] \qquad \text{(Eq. 4-2)}$$

In this equation, I_i refers to the effectiveness with which any one issue is managed. In words, we are saying that how well each issue is managed depends in a multiplicative way, again, on the other seven issues.

Of course, the fact that we can state our case mathematically is not meant as a proof. And indeed, we will see less-than-perfect support for the model in Part II. Some issues seem to have much more bearing on each other, at least in the short run, than do others. But they do provide an efficient way to summarize the key assumptions we have been making thus far: If any one issue is poorly managed, it can have negative impact throughout your company. And in the long haul, because of the indirect effects that each issue has on the others, you still probably can't afford to ignore any one issue for very long.

Constantly Monitor to Make Needed Adjustments

Effective management requires constant monitoring of the eight issues for adjustments in strategy. View the eight issues as parameters you always need to watch, not as eight projects that can be designed and completed. As we have already seen, viewing your company as a dynamic system means that it is closely intertwined with an ever-changing environment. As the environment continues to change, so must your firm. But by closely watching the environment as well as parameters defined by the eight issues, you can often spot deviations from desired targets and increase the odds of making needed adjustments well before a crisis occurs. The more turbulent the environment, the more adjustments are needed. Survival demands change. In open-systems theory this is referred to as *dynamic homeostasis*.

Design Solutions Specific to *Your* Needs

Another implication of viewing your company as a dynamic system is to realize that just as what worked for you yesterday may no longer work today, the solution that worked for someone else may not have the desired effect on your own company. Beware of adages and quick-fix solutions before analyzing your own situation.

Consider the adage "Don't bet the store," together with what John Johnson did when he launched *Ebony* magazine.[5] He indeed "bet the store" at one point, but in retrospect it was the right thing to do given his unique set of company strengths and environmental constraints. At the time, Johnson had limited access to sources of start-up capital other than the profits of another venture he owned, a very profitable magazine called the *Negro Digest*. So Johnson subsidized *Ebony* out of those profits for quite some time while building readership and advertisers. He felt he had to do this because although fairly conservative in spending decisions (he notes he kept a close eye on the cash, too), he felt strongly that the format of his mainstay magazine would eventually become obsolete, replaced by new formats with more color and graphics. If he had failed, he would have risked his fledgling empire. But he carefully assessed his own unique situation and figured that this course of action was the correct one for him to follow. And, of course, history proved him right.

Shift Focus Among Issues as Needed

Successful management of dynamic firms also requires shifting your attention to different issues at different times. Market strategy and resource acquisition are often a dual focus for start-ups. But when a company grows so quickly it can't keep up with the sales orders coming in the door, the key decisions shift to matters affecting work flow and resource allocation.[6] And at the bottom of the business cycle, when survival is your main objective, conservation of cash and careful allocation of your other resources become more central; market strategy concerns then take second place.

The focus during a growth period is even different from those periods when a company is trying to expand. The latter look more like the start-up period. Market strategy becomes the renewed focus; although this time resource allocation, rather than resource acquisition, is also key. Your company will have its own pattern of changes. The point is, don't get locked into viewing only the issues that helped you through your last crisis. This time, it may not be the same issue that determines your survival.

AN EXPANDED VERSION OF *DSP*

Figure 4–1 portrays an expanded view of the Dynamic System Planning Model that takes your employees more fully into account.

In particular, it suggests which factors might influence how each of the eight DSP issues are resolved.

What happens with each issue depends on all employees, from you down to the mailroom employee. Your careful planning is helpful, but it is only one influence on the system. The sum total of your employees' performances affects the outcome, too. Employee performance in turn depends on a host of factors: their attitudes and motives, their perceptions about what they are expected to do, and their skills and abilities. Employee performance also depends upon what else is going on in the system. Has your company provided the needed tools, information, and assistance to get the job done? And what factors from outside the company might expedite or constrain each person's work? These are basic issues but are often overlooked when company plans are not realized. Too often, CEOs simply blame employees for lack of motivation when the factors are far more complicated.

Figure 4–1 also suggests some outside variables are especially critical, such as competitive intensity, the rate of technical change, and general economic uncertainty. Let's not overstate the case of the environment, though. It was fashionable in the 1980s in certain academic circles to ignore the role of the individual in influencing the firm's survival and to see the company's fate as more closely tied to the swirl of these largely uncontrollable environmental factors.[7] We acknowledge those factors: It would be foolish to think anyone could control the exact outcomes of all actions undertaken. On the other hand, we feel the ecologists have gone to the other extreme, underrating the impact that people have on their companies, in particular, and on the world as a whole. Our model is based on the simple underlying premise that people *do* make a difference—not just the CEO but each and every person in the company. This leads us to the final point in our chapter—your role as the CEO.

Your Role as CEO

Defining your key role as company CEO is a real challenge. The possibilities are limitless. Some CEOs isolate themselves from day-to-day production. Others produce all the services or goods for the business. Some hire a marketing manager. Others do all the selling. But according to the DSP Model, what is *fundamental* to the CEO's role? What *must* you do that no one else can?

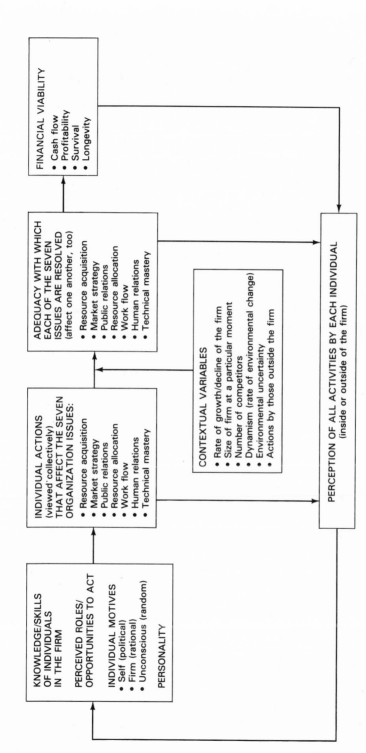

FIGURE 4–1 An Expanded Version of the Dynamic System Planning Model

Be your company's visionary.   We have already discussed the importance of serving as your company's visionary. Clarifying the company vision is the first step in strategic planning. Each of the functional areas can be delegated, but only you can provide the overall battle plan. Otherwise, groups of employees and even entire divisions split off into different, even competing directions. You must understand what your company is aiming for—what it is trying to create. No planning department or outside consultant can do that for you.

As JPI approached $500 million in sales, most of the functional responsibilities were delegated by the founder and chairman—but not overall strategic planning.

Create a multibrained system to realize your vision.   Tools are extensions of the human hand: Organizations are extensions of the human mind. In the twentieth century, private corporations truly rose to the fore, often supplanting governments in accomplishing certain objectives. In 1990, the Communist regime of the former U.S.S.R. struggled to feed its people, yet McDonald's Corporation of Moscow served one million customers in its first month of operation—using locally grown potatoes and beef and Russian employees!

Though vision is essential, it is not alone sufficient to accomplish these feats. Many entrepreneurs operate their companies at far below their true potential because they fail to take advantage of the gifts and talents of those around them. For your company to operate at its highest level and to serve as the most sophisticated tool, you must take full advantage not only of your own brain and its creativity, but of the brains of the employees around you.

We use the term *multibrained* to signify the company that maximizes the use of employee brains to confront and resolve issues facing the company.[8] You can choose to develop the potential lurking in your firm or let it idle. This often requires a commitment to extensive technical training and supervisory-skill development, in addition to restructuring.

The failure of many early experiments in participative decision making and employee involvement was because of a lack of attention to preparing employees for this shift in responsibilities. Not so at JPI. One of the less written-about reasons for JPI's success was its close attention to training and development, coupled with employee involvement and team-building programs that unleashed the human creativity and potential untapped by the previous CEO. Surprisingly few employees at the middle and lower levels were laid off when JPI took over its acquisitions.

SUMMARY: MANAGING THE DYNAMIC SYSTEM

Viewing companies as dynamic systems has several implications. As we have already noted in previous chapters, it means first of all that eight particular issues—the DSP issues we have been talking about—are vital to survival and growth.

Viewing companies as dynamic systems has other implications. It means that you must consider the effects of changing your strategy, not only for one issue but for all eight DSP issues.

Third, viewing companies as dynamic systems means your work is never done. Continual changes in the internal and external environments of the company require constant vigilance regarding the eight issues.

Fourth, in dynamic systems, although the eight DSP issues themselves apply to all firms, the complexity of this interactive system in its ever-changing environment results in a unique combination of specific solutions for each firm. You are asking for trouble if you simply try to mimic a portion of another firm's plan, because the entire context of your firm is different.

Fifth, in dynamic systems, the focus shifts over time from issue to issue. Although each is always present, the issue that requires special attention and modification of plans depends upon changes both internal and external to the company.

Finally, the complexity of the dynamic system—the unpredictable, almost infinitely possible ways in which different parts within the company interact with each other and with the outside environment—can rarely be analyzed by one human brain alone. Successful companies are multibrained, ideally using the human potential of all employees to their fullest.

Your job as CEO is to develop a vision, first and foremost, of what you want your firm to accomplish. Think of the firm as a tool to extend the creativity and talents of all the people working for it, but most important, a tool by which you can realize your dream. Using your own brain alone, however, is like driving a car with one cylinder working. Highly successful organizations develop and use the full talents of all their people. Only these companies warrant the label "multibrained."

NOTES

[1]Many of the ideas of this chapter are discussed further in Lorraine U. Hendrickson, "Bridging the Gap Between Organization Theory and the Practice of Managing Growth: The Dynamic System Planning Model," *Journal of Organizational Change Management* 5 (1992), 18–37.

[2]Basil S. Georgopoulos, *Organization Structure, Problem Solving, and Effectiveness: A Comparative Study of Hospital Services* (San Francisco: Jossey-Bass, 1986). See footnote 5 in Chapter 1 for additional references.

[3]Erwin Schrodinger, "Order, Disorder, and Entropy," in Walter Buckley, *Modern Systems Research for the Behavioral Scientist* (Chicago: Aldine, 1968), pp.143–46.

[4]Georgopoulos, *Organization Structure*.

[5]J. Johnson, *Succeeding Against the Odds* (New York: Warner Books, 1989), p. 154.

[6]In Phase I of our research, described in Appendix A, we asked 30 CEOs of medium-sized established companies in construction, manufacturing, and wholesale to describe critical decisions that they made under these three different conditions. Further discussion of the critical incident technique is also covered in L. U. Hendrickson, P. Weber, and T. F. Grainey, "The Critical Incident Technique Revisited: Application to a Research Problem in Organization Theory," in *Proceedings, Midwest Academy of Management, Thirty-First Annual Meeting*, eds. T. L. Keon and A. C. Bluedorn (Toledo, OH, 1988).

[7]G. R. Carroll, *Ecological Models of Organizations* (Cambridge, MA: Ballinger Publishing Company, 1988), p. 2.

[8]Multibrained systems are the eighth level of Boulding's Hierarchy of System Complexity, which he refers to as multicephalous. See Kenneth Boulding, "General Systems Theory—the Skeleton of Science," in *Modern Systems Research for the Behavioral Scientist*, ed. W. Buckley (Chicago: Aldine, 1968). We are indebted to Louis R. Pondy, also, for inspiration from many of his unpublished papers on this topic, especially "Beyond Open-System Models of Organization," presented at the Annual Meeting of the Academy of Management, Kansas City, MI, August 12, 1976, which describes Boulding's eight levels as "multibrained."

CHAPTER 5

Financial Viability:
Your Yardstick
for Organization Achievement

Most employees, the media, and even entrepreneurs measure success by sales and sales growth. Most "lists," such as INC. 500 and FORTUNE 500, rank companies this way. In Chapter 1 we discussed pitfalls of this approach. But if banners and plaques are not a good measure of success, what is? Seasoned business owners realize that profits and asset growth provide better assurance of a firm's long-term survival and ability to thrive. Liquidity, or the availability of cash, is also a hallmark of the well-run business.[1]

ASSESSING YOUR FINANCIAL VIABILITY

What does financial viability mean? How well does your company stack up? By taking a few minutes to answer the following questions, you can get a quick feel for this issue. Or if you prefer, you may just want to skim through these questions for now, returning to them after completing the chapter.

I. Liquidity and Cash Flow

Question 5-1: Liquidity. How would you describe your current cash position (cash in the bank, whether obtained by a bank loan, retained earnings, or from start-up capital):

[1] Significant liquidity, available for major investment—e.g., a new plant, building, large piece of equipment
[2] Some liquidity, available for minor investment—a new truck, smaller piece of equipment, office equipment

[3] Little liquidity, available only for high-priority items to keep current operations going
[4] Very little liquidity—difficult to cover even essential items to keep current operations going

The median firm in our study reported "some" liquidity ([2] above). Yet 45 percent report having "significant" liquidity.

Question 5-2.   Has your level of liquidity hampered business operations any time during your firm's growth? If yes, in what way?

Question 5-3.   Was there any particular reason that your cash position has been unusually good or poor in the past few years—purchase of a building or a large drop in sales or profitability, for instance?

II. Profitability

Question 5-4: Subjective rating of profits.   What has your profit picture been like for each of the past five years? Rate your firm for each year separately.

[1] Very profitable
[2] Fairly profitable
[3] Somewhat profitable
[4] Break even
[5] Somewhat unprofitable
[6] Fairly unprofitable
[7] Very unprofitable

At the time of the study, the median firm reported being "somewhat" profitable ([3] above). About one in five CEOs reported being "very" profitable ([1]).

Question 5-5: Tracking net profit.   Do you track your net profit, that is, your rate of return on gross revenues, on a regular basis?
Only about 70 percent of the CEOs we interviewed track their net profit closely. When we asked the following question, some CEOs had memorized their numbers but others needed to dig through the files to determine whether or not they were even profitable.

Question 5-6: Percentage estimate of return on sales (ROS).
What would you estimate your net profit (pretax) as being, in percentage terms (that is, dollars of net income divided by total annual revenues), for each of the past five years?

In the fiscal year during which the study took place, the median net profit of firms under study was about 2 percent, the average net profit being about 4 percent. Profits ranged between an 18 percent loss and a 35 percent gain.

WHAT WE MEAN BY FINANCIAL VIABILITY

An organization that is financially viable can pay its bills when due and operates at a profit.[2]

Short-Term Profit: Why We Use It to Measure Financial Viability

When companies such as General Motors lose billions of dollars a year and yet you still see plenty of Oldsmobiles and Buicks cranking off the assembly line, it gives many people the impression that short-term profit and loss are not all that important. But large companies are usually very different from most small to medium-sized firms in a fundamental way—they have accumulated huge assets from previous years of profitability—assets that include investor confidence in their ability to survive to another upturn. Some small companies are asset-rich enough that they can also survive severe periods of unprofitability. These are usually older firms that have socked assets away in a manner that is reasonably liquid. Among rapidly growing firms it is less common, since much capital is absorbed in fueling growth. Although short-term profits may have their pitfalls, they still provide a reasonable snapshot of a small firm's financial health—good enough for our purposes.

We do caution against putting exclusive emphasis on short-term profits. Capital investments that may be required in long-term growth will suppress a firm's profit and cash position even though the long-run effects may be positive. On the other hand, they need to be done judiciously or else long-term profitability will also suffer.[3]

Cash Flow: Another Important Aspect of Financial Viability

One overlooked financial measure is the flow of cash, as distinct from paper profits. Many books and seminars have been dedicated to the problems and solutions for managing cash flow effectively.[4] Though related to profitability, cash flow is not guaranteed just because a firm is profitable. For instance, a firm may be cash poor but profitable when it has tied up too much of its capital in inventory, buildings, and expensive equipment. Rapidly growing firms are almost by definition in cash-poor situations, because more money is needed to produce the products or services than was realized by previous sales. Absolute limits on internally financed growth can be calculated this way. Taking out short-term loans, including renegotiating better creditor terms, stretches these limits. However, prolonged use of such techniques often increases risks. The riskiest technique of all is to refinance growth via deferral of withholding taxes. Yet many owners have to admit they've done it, unwise as it is.

Because of the critical importance of being able to pay one's bills, the cash-flow indicator is examined in parallel with profitability as an indicator of financial viability throughout our book.

DIFFERENT WAYS TO MEASURE PROFIT

There are three commonly accepted ways to measure profit: as return on assets (ROA), return on investments (ROI), and return on sales (ROS). Which is best to use in evaluating your firm?

ROI (your net income divided by total equity) is an important number for managers because it is a good indication of whether you are wasting your time in the business you are in. If ROS (your net income divided by total sales) is fairly low but your need for capital is also quite limited, it will still be a very worthwhile endeavor. On the other hand, if running the business requires a heavy investment, you should weigh your use of money invested in your business against simply putting it into the bank. It is easy to become so preoccupied with sales growth that you forget to evaluate the cash you put into your business the way you would choose your passive investments. But tracking your ROI is important. It allows you to compare investments in different instruments and types of firms. Even small passive investors evaluate their investments on this basis, comparing rates of return and risk factors for treasury bills, certificates of deposit, mutual funds, and so forth. Business owners emphatically need to do exactly the same for their active investments.

Assume you are sole owner and have set aside a rainy-day fund for your company. Does it really make sense to reinvest the fund in the firm or would you be better off closing this business and starting over? ROA and ROI more realistically help you to answer this question than return on sales. Many entrepreneurs get trapped psychologically, pouring more and more money into a dying business—taking equity out of homes, borrowing against life insurance policies—just to keep a doomed or marginal business afloat. Any calculation should also factor in the time you spend, compared with your likely earnings in a salaried position, working for someone else.

Why, then, did we use ROS as the primary yardstick for profitability? Our choice is a compromise between theory and pragmatism. Most firms we studied were privately held. Most of the CEOs were hesitant to share even return on sales figures, much less balance-sheet figures. And many were confused by the terminology of ROS and ROI. To offset the instability of one year's profit performance, two years of data were collected from most firms.

Although ROS is not perfect, it still provides a sound basis for comparing firms. In a study of several thousand business units in 450 companies, Buzzell and Gale find not only that ROS and ROI are linked with each other, but linked in very similar ways to most of the company practices and characteristics they studied.[5] The relationships differ principally in variables associated with capital intensity of the business—the investment per dollar of sales. Greater capital intensity itself is linked to lower ROI; the relationship with ROS is negligible. With this caveat, we feel comfortable that ROS provides useful insights into effective management of small, growing firms.

CASH FLOW AND NET PROFITS

We all read about highly leveraged companies taking big risks with other people's capital. You might think such cases are rare among small firms. But think again. Many entrepreneurs take huge risks with inheritances, college savings, bank loans, and even money for withholding taxes. Although it seems a more conservative approach, those with better cash flow are also those with higher profits and longer survival. There is something to be said for the adage: "Don't spend what you don't have."

Many top performers in our study make a religion out of flexibility. They anticipate lean periods during the peak of the business cycle. Though they will expand somewhat, they accumulate cash during good years to operate comfortably in lean years. Ready cash also helps them respond to unanticipated opportunities.

One of the hardest decisions facing smaller firms is when to make a major capital improvement—purchase of a new building or a new technology. Successful capital improvements have "many fathers." But several CEOs we interviewed regret untimely or excessive expansion decisions, especially those made in anticipation of sales that never materialize. In one typical case, a CEO built a large plant addition to handle increased orders from a key customer, a large automobile manufacturer, who pulled out just after the plant completion date. The CEO had now lost his flexibility to downsize during the next recession and struggled to find alternate business to justify the expense of the new plant.

On the other hand, consistent careful incremental expansion of just one or two trucks a year by a trenching firm is proving sufficiently competitive. He enjoys profit levels well above industry norms. The large fleet he has gradually amassed has helped him to attract and maintain utility company clients, which provide the firm with steady profitable work.

Managing one's cash flow thus does not mean a zero-growth strategy, but does require careful attention to available cash, not just paper profits.

FINANCIAL VIABILITY AND THE DYNAMIC SYSTEM PLANNING MODEL

Profit is a yardstick of how well the entire system functions. When the system runs efficiently, money, time, and other resources are left over; the firm makes a profit. Some firms watch the short-term costs so closely that long-term opportunities are overlooked. On the other hand, several consecutive quarters of the operating loss caused by recent heavy investment will test survivability. Profit is what the firm has available to it to combat entropy and the general uncertainty of the environment.

Further, profitability is one powerfully important way to judge the efficiency of different solutions chosen to resolve the seven organization issues of the DSP model. If coordination can be handled through direct observation by the owner, why waste money on elaborate controls and time-consuming meetings with managers? If design of the machine can be done in someone's basement, why build a laboratory? The CEO's challenge is to find the solution suitable to the needs of the firm at a given size and complexity.

As with profitability, cash flow is heavily influenced by the way in which each of the seven organization issues are managed. Take resource allocation: If too much working capital is tied up in inventory, precious funds may not be available for critical opportunities and emergencies. Poor response to other issues can also hurt cash flow. If sales suffer from poor marketing or product selection (a market-strategy issue), cash flow suffers. If sales are strong, but overstaffing is required because of inefficient coordination, cash will be unnecessarily depleted. Poor motivation will have similar results. Just as with profits, efficient responses to every issue will augment overall cash flow. Poor response will diminish it.

Let's summarize key linkages between financial viability and the other organizational issues to reinforce their importance. The results are based on two or more years of profits, unless otherwise noted. In this section we also say a little about how effectiveness of the other seven DSP issues is measured.

Market Strategy and Financial Viability

We measured five components of market-strategy effectiveness: (1) The CEO's rating of direction-setting effectiveness; (2) relative size compared to competition; (3) steadiness of sales growth; (4) rate of sales growth; and (5) total revenues. Notice that size is examined both in absolute dollar terms and terms relative to the industry.

Market share—not absolute size in dollars—is linked to profitability. Firms that are larger, relative to others in the same industry, tend to be more profitable. This is true despite the fact that absolute size of the firm as measured in total revenues is not positively linked to profitability at all. This suggests that it is *market share,* not size per se, that predicts profits.

Steady growth is linked to profitability. Firms that generate steady growth have a higher two-year ROS average than those with peaks and valleys. Steady growth also contributes in the longer term to a better cash position in the firm.

Faster-growing firms are generally more profitable. The rate of sales growth, though sometimes a profit handicap, generally predicts ROS.

CEOs of profitable firms tend to like the way they set company direction. Finally, CEOs who rate their direction-setting strategy as effective are more likely to report higher ROS and a better cash position.

Chapter 6 explores some of the strategies CEOs use to achieve a higher *and steadier* rate of growth.

Work Flow and Financial Viability

Work flow is made up of two components: (1) division of tasks and authority; and (2) coordination—assuring that everyone's efforts and overall information fit together in a timely way and efficiently.

CEOs who are satisfied with their work-flow strategies are also likely to make a profit. CEOs who rate the strategy for assigning work as more effective are likely to have higher profits. Ratings of coordination effectiveness are also connected to profitability and better cash flow. Effective work flow is one of the most important predictors of ROS for small and medium-sized firms.

Resource Acquisition and Financial Viability

Within the resource acquisition issue, we look at all types of resources: capital, information, equipment and supplies, subcontractors, managers, and nonmanagement employees.

Only ability to acquire capital is linked to profits. The ability to obtain resources is surprisingly weakly linked to profitability. Only the ability to obtain *capital* is linked to profitability, and only during the same year. Not surprisingly, ability to obtain capital is linked to the firm's cash position in the same and succeeding years. Resource acquisition is strongly linked with other aspects of organization effectiveness, however, besides profits.

Human Relations and Financial Viability

Though they overlap somewhat, we look at five components of human relations effectiveness: (1) morale: overall job satisfaction and commitment of employees; (2) goal integration: consistency of organization and individual goals; (3) a consistent view of the mission by CEO and managers; (4) a consistent view of values; and (5) how effectively values are shared.

Morale and profits are linked. Consistent with a decades-old but controversial hypothesis, we find a clear link between morale and profits.[6] The firm's cash position is also reported to be better in the same year but does not seem to be influenced in following years by the level of morale, whereas profitability is also higher in subsequent years.

Companies with strong corporate cultures are more profitable. CEOs and managers were queried about values emphasized within the firm. In strong corporate cultures, where CEO *and* managers report the same values, the firm is more profitable. Similarly, where CEOs and managers share a similar understanding about the firm's mission and direction, ROS is higher—though here we find a "lagged" effect, an influence delayed by six months or a year.

CEOs who can communicate their values head more profitable firms.   Finally, CEOs who rate the way in which they communicate their values as effective also tend to run more profitable firms.

Resource Allocation and Financial Viability

We look at resource allocation from a few different angles: how well people and material are allocated across departments; the quality of budget information (how quickly and accurately you get it); and the effectiveness of the allocation strategy (how well it is working).

Certain aspects of resource allocation are strongly linked to profits, though less so with our measure of cash flow.

Effective resource-allocation strategy is linked to profit.   CEOs who rate their resource-allocation strategy as effective also report higher ROS. The better able the firm is to assign people to the right departments in the right numbers, according to its managers, the more profitable the firm is likely to be.

Managers (other than the CEO) were also asked to rate the firm's ability to assign equipment, dollars, and material so that all work groups have sufficient resources to operate. Though not related to profits, these were positively linked to cash flow.

Public Relations and Financial Viability

Effective public relations and profits are linked.   Our focus on public relations was fairly limited in the research study: We asked CEOs and managers to rate their company's reputation and image in the community. This rating is linked to both ROS and cash flow.

Technical Mastery and Financial Viability

Technical mastery and profits are linked.   We identify four components of technical mastery: technical performance of employees; technical skills of employees; productivity—the firm's ability to meet schedules and fill customer orders on time; and quality of the services and/or products the firm provides. All four aspects link to ROS and cash flow.

IN SUMMARY

Financial viability is the key to company success. Few firms survive long without sufficient profits and cash flow. This chapter reviews different ways to measure profits. It also provides a quick overview of the linkages between financial viability and the other seven issues of the Dynamic System Planning Model. In the remaining chapters of Part II, we pay individual attention to each of those seven issues, in turn.

NOTES

[1]Cecil J. Bond, *Hands-on Financial Controls for Your Small Business* (Blue Ridge Summit, PA: Liberty Hall Press, 1991).

[2]James L. Price and Charles W. Mueller, *Handbook of Organizational Measurement* (Marshfield, MA: Pitman Publishing, 1986), pp. 128–30.

[3]Robert D. Buzzell and Bradley T. Gale, *The PIMS Principles: Linking Strategy to Performance* (New York: The Free Press, 1987), pp. 135–62.

[4]Bryan E. Milling, *Cash Flow Problem Solver: Procedures and Rationale for the Independent Business-man* (Radnor, PA: Chilton Book Company, 1981) and Bond, *Hands-on Financial Controls for Your Small Business,* are two excellent sources that are written in plain language.

[5]Buzzell and Gale, *The PIMS Principles,* discuss pros and cons of ROS and ROI at length, preferring ROI since it "relates results to the resources used in achieving them" (p. 25).

[6]Rensis Likert, *New Patterns of Management* (New York: McGraw-Hill, 1961).

CHAPTER 6

Market Strategy: Finding Your Niche

Market strategy is the first of the seven organizational DSP issues you must directly and continually confront to assure your company's success. This chapter explains more about what we mean by market strategy and how to plan for it. Ask yourself the same kinds of questions we asked CEOs in our research, so that you begin to visualize market strategy more clearly in your own setting.

ASSESSING YOUR MARKET STRATEGY

Question 6-1: Direction-setting strategy. Do you have a particular way of setting the overall company *direction*—in other words, a way to decide on the types of products or services you offer, the customers you serve, distribution channels to use, etc.? If so, what do you do?

Question 6-2: Strategy analysis. If you answered yes to question 6-1, then for each of the items (a) through (d) listed below, choose one of the following four answers:

[1] Not done at all
[2] Done on an informal, ad hoc, basis
[3] Done systematically, on a scheduled basis
[4] Written down as part of a formal business plan

WHICH OF THE FOLLOWING, IF ANY, DO YOU REVIEW
TO SET COMPANY DIRECTION?

——*a.* Analysis of the competition

——*b.* Analysis of general economic, social, and technical trends that affect your industry.

——*c*. Market analysis—assessing present and future market demand.

——*d*. Organization assessment—your organization's strengths and/or weaknesses.

Question 6-3: Change in direction-setting strategy. Considering your answers to questions 6-1 and 6-2, have you set your firm's direction in this way

[1] Always

[2] For quite a while, but *not* since the start of the firm

[3] Only *now* changing this approach? (If you have made changes, what triggered this change?)

Question 6-4: CEO's rating of direction-setting strategy effectiveness. Considering your responses to questions 6-1 through 6-3, how well do you feel your strategy for setting direction is working out?

[1] Extremely well

[2] Very well

[3] Fairly well

[4] Not so well

[5] Not well at all

Question 6-5: Relative size. How would you rate the *size* of your firm relative to your industry?

[1] Very High: Top 2% of the industry

[2] High: Within the top 10%

[3] Well Above Average: Top 25%

[4] Above Average: Within top one-third

[5] Average: About the middle of the industry

[6] Slightly Below Average: Two-thirds are bigger

[7] Well Below Average: Bottom 20% of the industry

Question 6-6: Steadiness of growth. How would you characterize your growth in the last 5–10 years (or if your firm is not that old, then since the birth of your firm)?

[1] Lower than the previous period

[2] Flat, or with cycles that end up with about the same peak sales each time

[3] Growth and then leveling

[4] Cyclical but each time end up with a higher peak in sales

[5] Growth/plateau/growth; or flat for awhile and then growth for a few years

[6] Steady growth without any annual drop in sales

Question 6-7: Rate of growth. How rapidly has your firm grown in the past five years? Calculate total percent increase in annual revenues for a five-year period.

Question 6-8: Total revenues. What are your total annual revenues in dollars?

Question 6-9: Specific industry. What specific products do you carry or services do you offer?

Question 6-10: Competitive niche. What do you see as your unique competitive advantage or niche?

Question 6-11: Your firm's mission. What is the firm's primary mission—its main direction and purpose (other than the specific products or services offered)?

Question 6-12: Your vision. Where would you like to see your company go in the next few years?

▶

Questions 6-4 through 6-8 help you to figure how successful your market strategy is. The other questions define your market strategy in more detail: who is involved in defining the firm's direction, what that direction is, and how you go about defining your firm's direction.

The typical CEO in our study rated the direction-setting strategy as working out "very well" ([2], on question 6-4). Almost one in three CEOs rate their strategy as working out extremely well. If you gave yourself a [3] or less, you may want to consider some ideas from this chapter.

The median firm in our study made only about $3.3 million in sales but put their firm in the top 25 percent in relative size within their industry (question 6-5). Almost one-fourth (22 percent) put themselves in the top 2 percent. This suggests that although the firms are small in an absolute sense, many have defined selectively narrow niches—by product, service, customer, or region—where they can dominate.

WHAT IS MARKET STRATEGY?

Where do you fit in the marketplace? What kinds of products or services do you offer? Do you offer a product or service in a way that especially makes customers want to select you rather than your competitors? Market strategy comprises your answers to these sorts of questions.

We measured five components of market-strategy effectiveness: (1) the CEO's rating of direction-setting effectiveness—question 6-4, above; (2) relative size compared with competition—question 6-5; (3) steadiness of growth—question 6-6; (4) rate of growth—question 6-7; and (5) total revenues—question 6-8. Notice that size is examined both in absolute dollar terms and in terms relative to the industry.

How do the above five components of market-strategy effectiveness relate or link to one another? According to our research, these components interlink strongly, with only three exceptions. Total annual revenues are not linked to either steadiness of growth or to the CEO's rating of direction-setting effectiveness. And relative size of the firm is not linked with rate of growth.

IMPORTANCE OF THE MARKET-STRATEGY ISSUE

Our research supports the view that market strategy is central to company success. Market strategy is linked to all other DSP issues except resource allocation.

Debunking Myths About Growth

Many of our findings debunk popular myths. One might think, for instance, that rapid growth would harm profits. Yet growth and financial viability go hand in hand. Our data even hints at the possibility that growth fuels profitability, rather than the reverse.

Another myth about rapid growth is that it necessarily undermines smooth work flow. Though growth certainly poses a challenge, we find no evidence for this claim. In fact, firms that grow more rapidly (and more steadily) are likely to have *more* effective division of work and *better* coordination of efforts.

Steadiness of growth is as important as its rate.   We find a lagged effect between steadiness of growth and cash flow and lack of connection between growth *rate* and cash flow. This is consistent with textbook treatments that recommend steadiness of growth over volatile growth.[1]

Another finding debunking a myth about growing firms relates to recruitment. Although CEOs of growing firms complain a lot, based on our data, they have an easier time filling management positions than do CEOs of stagnant firms. We find steadier and more profitable growth where CEOs more clearly communicate their values and the company mission. Growth can be stressful but we find the growing pains are outweighed by positive aspects of growth, including more positive attitudes among employees.

Debunking Some Myths About Company Size

Several myths also abound about the impact of size. One myth is that larger firms have more problems with coordinating efforts than do smaller ones. Our data shows, instead, that neither relative size nor total revenues link with any component of work flow.

Neither relative size nor total revenues are linked with any components of human-relations effectiveness. This dispels another myth that increased firm size necessarily contributes to poor morale.

Larger firms have some advantages when it comes to acquiring resources. They are better able to obtain managers and capital. But smaller firms have advantages obtaining supplies—perhaps it is easier with the smaller volumes required.

In sum, size per se does not help or hinder effective resolution of many issues. Although firms often must change their issue-resolving approaches as they grow, this does not automatically lead to poorer outcomes. Conversely, firms more effective at resolving each issue are also apt to grow more steadily and rapidly. Only with liquidity does size make a direct positive impact. Size is also an important *contingency factor* in the overall design of the firm—an idea we'll return to in Chapter 8.

THE CHOICE OF MISSION

When we asked CEOs to describe their firm's mission (questions 6-9 through 6-12 above), we got a wide variety of answers. See Table 6–1.

Many CEOs describe their mission objectives with terms such as ''growth'' or ''expansion'' (mentioned by 31 percent of the CEOs); serving a particular geographic region (mentioned by 29 percent); profit (mentioned by 26 percent); offering ''the best quality'' (mentioned by 23 percent); and serving the customer (mentioned by 22 percent). Others include ''offering a unique product or service'' (18 percent); offering a ''full range'' of services or ''value-added'' products or services (16 percent); larger market share (13 percent); survival (12 percent); diversification (10 percent); employee-related goals (9 percent); being their own boss (5 percent); having

TABLE 6–1   Different Mission Statements and Their Frequency of Occurrence in the Study, Managing the Growing Firm

	CEO MENTIONED[a]	AT LEAST ONE MANAGER MENTIONED[a]
Mentioned the specific service	81%	58%
Growth/expansion	31	45
Serve a particular geographic region	29	19
Profit	26	47
Offers best quality	23	28
Serve the customer	22	38
Unique product/service	18	14
Full range of services/value-added	16	11
Market share	13	22
Survival	12	9
Diversification	10	15
Employee related	9	12
Be own boss	5	2
Have lowest price (discount)	3	5
Society related	3	6

[a]Columns do not add up to 100 percent because of multiple mentions by many respondents.

the lowest (or discounted) price (3 percent); and society-oriented goals (3 percent).

We find that some types of mission may prove more profitable than others. Let's explore some of these.

Market Share as a Primary Mission: A Recognized Profit Maker

Firms whose primary mission includes the aim of expanding market share tend to be more profitable, especially a year or two later (called a *lagged* effect). This lagged effect makes sense, since a company's mission only reflects the *intent* to enlarge market share. The emphasis on market share is especially predictive of profitability for the largest firms in our study—those between 50 and 500 employees. Of course, not all firms in our study require larger market share to be successful. But results reported on by Buzzell and Gale show a clear linkage. They find that among companies with *less than 10 percent* of the market share, only one-quarter of the firms have a return on investment (ROI) exceeding 20 percent, whereas three-fourths of firms with *more than 40 percent* of market share exceed 20 percent ROI.[2]

Quality as a Primary Mission: Another Profit Booster

Firms whose primary mission includes offering the best quality are likely, on a lagging basis, to be more profitable. Quality is gaining attention as a long-term or strategic issue, both by researchers and practicing managers.[3] Increasingly, committed companies are proving that quality does not have to cost more. Indeed, many find that better quality actually reduces production costs associated with scrap and return rates for defects. It also reduces marketing costs by increasing repeat customers and/or referrals—the least expensive lead sources a firm can have because they are free. This concept is beginning to sweep the automobile industry in particular. Poor quality suppliers are simply eliminated. Many CEOs share with pride the fact that they had obtained Ford's Q1 rating or GM's Mark of Excellence.

Quality is not just an issue among manufacturers, however. One very successful wholesaler we interviewed says:

> I'm tough when I buy. I can't squeeze too much. We pay our bills the way they want: 5 days, 10 days, whatever. We import our own merchandise from Taiwan. But I don't want call-backs [because of] bad goods. I want trouble-free products. I'll pay a slightly higher cost to get products with good warranties. . . . I don't want some guy walking in my store toting a broken garbage disposal with garbage dripping from it.

This wholesaler does quite well with his philosophy. He grew from about 4 million dollars to 13 million dollars in sales in six years, making a pretax net profit of 8 percent in his most recent year. He has had significant liquidity throughout this period.

Diversification: Not for Small Firms

Small-to-medium firms that focus on a unique product or service report better profits. Among firms with fewer than 20 employees, the least profitable were those offering a *full* range of services. In the middle third of firms (20–80 employees), those mentioning diversification as a goal are less profitable. We only see a reversal in this pattern as the firm surpasses 80 employees. The timing for diversification needs to be carefully planned.

Diversification can greatly complicate the work-flow task. One firm in our study is a data-processing firm serving FORTUNE 1000 clients. At one point, the CEO expanded by opening several out-of-state locations. He complained of tremendous resulting coordination problems. A year later, his company had successfully grown from about 250 to 280 employees, and from $12 to $14.2 million in sales, but had also dropped from break-even to a loss on sales of about 3 percent.

JPI was alert to the dangers of "overdiversification" while reviewing acquisition candidates. While some larger firms achieve economies of scale with marketing programs, technological development, and the like by broadening into related lines of products or services, even FORTUNE 500 companies can diversify poorly. Companies have finite resources (especially brains) and must focus to be effective. "Diseconomies" are realized when diversification is too broad.[4]

Companies cannot afford to be all things to all people. One way to avoid "destruction by centrifuge" is to tie diversification to an overall strategy. JPI focused on just two industries but eventually chose to divest plumbing parts in favor of engine components alone. Then it continued diversifying into different engine-market segments—OEMs and various international aftermarkets. A large proportion of the acquisition candidates reviewed at JPI were inappropriately diversified. One of the elements in JPI's turnaround strategy included the careful examination of the product mix for those firms that it acquired and the elimination of products and services that didn't make sense. This strategy proved extremely profitable and, incidentally, eventually made JPI a very appealing acquisition candidate when the founder decided to sell the firm. After all, it's easier for buyers to evaluate a focused seller.

Picking a Price-Competitive Niche: It Depends on Your Size

Your customers and competitors have a big influence on strategy. In mature industries, price is relatively important. Demand is highly *elastic* (i.e., demand fluctuates depending on the price). And in the automobile industry, customers increasingly demand both price and quality. Where a firm offers a unique product or service, price is usually far less important.

We find CEOs faced with more intense price competition are less pleased with their market strategy—especially the way in which they set company direction. But CEOs faced with high quality demands, but not necessarily at the lowest price, rate their direction-setting strategy as more effective. In short, CEOs rate most highly a niche that allows them to concentrate on producing the unique, high-quality products and services for which they are well paid, no doubt providing them not only with monetary rewards but with a sense of pride and accomplishment.

Whether price competition actually hurts growth and profits depends upon the size of the firm. Among the firms with fewer than 20 employees, firms in price-sensitive industries report slower growth and less profit than firms that are not. Yet we find just the opposite in firms with over 80 employees. These firms are more profitable than their counterparts in industries that are not price sensitive—confirming the general rule that larger firms can compete more effectively on price, even if they are not the deepest discounter. (Only three firms in our study mention discounting as a competitive advantage.)

Chaganti's research also shows no relation between discounting and profitability.[5] Chaganti's work is particularly relevant because it is based on 192 manufacturing firms with fewer than 100 employees. These results raise the question whether price discounting *ever* makes sense as a strategy for small firms, even in price-sensitive markets, and once again highlights the importance of quality.

How do successful firms avoid discounting? Some emphasize service. Others network. The CEO of an office-supply business was at a crossroads when we talked with him. National warehouse clubs and direct-mail businesses were intruding on his business. One way this CEO responded was to join a buying group, not only to save money but also to share ideas. This strategy proved successful enough that a few years later, the firm announced a large acquisition. It had done fairly well in the interim and was responding aggressively.

CHOICE OF NICHE

Market niche refers to the specific products or services you offer and/or the customers you serve. There are countless ways in which a niche can be defined. New markets are created or discovered daily. The way firms define their strategies affects their success in finding a good niche. Due to marketplace complexity and unpredictability, hitting the right success formula does take an element of intuition or luck, as many successful entrepreneurs admit. Nevertheless, in reviewing results from a large group of firms, certain patterns emerge.

We attempted to sample in roughly equal fourths from four historically rapid-growth industry sectors in our region: manufacturing, construction, wholesale, and business services. We ended up with 37 in construction, 40 manufacturers, 54 wholesalers, and 37 business-service firms. In construction, 25 of the 37 are in special trades, 8 in building construction, and the rest in other construction. In manufacturing, 11 of the 40 are in machinery, 8 in fabricated metal products, and the rest in wide-ranging products including food, furniture, printing, chemicals, plastics, stone and clay, steel, transportation, and specialized control instruments. In wholesale, 45 are in durable goods, the rest in nondurables. Within business services, the 37 firms span advertising, credit reporting and collecting, computer software services, and many other service areas.

For many analyses, we identified a *top-performer* group of 28 firms, based on profits and sales. The top performers were selected on the basis of a minimum of 5 percent annual profit and having at least doubled sales in a five-year period. The top performers span all four industry sectors, though construction and manufacturing are represented disproportionately. Top firms in construction span: residential construction; remodeling for retail chains; water- and sewer-utility subcontracting; plumbing and heating; specialized electrical for hi-tech applications; asphalt pouring; helicopter-based construction; and large-scale renovation. Manufacturers span:

an automotive stamping plant; industrial controls; tool design; metal fabrication; robotic welding; consumable pipe; metal finishing; coffee manufacture/wholesale; and kitchen- and plumbing-fixture manufacture/wholesale. In wholesaling, we found excellence in two companies: a carpet wholesaler and a plumbing and heating parts supplier. And four business-services firms—an advertising agency, blueprint and photocopy firm, metal testing laboratory, and an industrial marketing-research firm—round out the list.

One unique aspect of these top performers distinguishes them: About half list the automobile industry as a client. About one-third serve the automobile industry exclusively. This is not what conventional "wisdom" would suggest! It indicates the size and strength of mature, "stodgy" industries as profit-generating *clients* for small and medium-growth firms, despite recent downsizing of American manufacturers. Of course, it would be valuable to revisit these companies after a few more business cycles!

HOW FIRMS SET A COURSE

So far, we have concentrated on the overall mission. How is a firm's market strategy developed? Table 6–2 on page 54 summarizes some of our findings pertaining to strategic planning in growth firms.

Two things stand out: First, the majority of successful CEOs we talked to do not write formal business plans. Secondly, many of the most successful CEOs tend to devise the company's overall direction on their own. Let's look at each of these aspects.

Most Small Companies Don't Have Formal Business Plans

The general lack of formal small-business plans is well documented. In a content analysis of published materials from 150 successful entrepreneurial firms in Chicago, Hills and Welsch find fewer than 2 percent use a business plan, and a mere 23 percent even give reference to a planning horizon.[6] Shrader and his colleagues concur.[7] In our study, only 2 out of 168 CEOs mention formal strategic planning. And only 5 firms mention *any* type of written business plan. Fewer than 20 percent have a formal mission statement.

Rather than formal business plans, in one-third of the firms direction is driven by simple customer demand, and in an equal number by the CEO's reading of trade journals and talking to people in the industry. About one in five hold planning meetings with their boards and managers. Still others use intuition. Interestingly, one-quarter of our top performers, compared with fewer than 10 percent of the remaining firms, use gut feel for setting direction.

Shrader and his colleagues ask small-business CEOs why they do not plan. Time is cited as a factor, as is the lack of skills and expertise. Most frequently cited is that planning is simply not appropriate: The firm is too small, too unpredictable, and "the CEO has a mental plan," anyway. Many researchers (including Shrader) assume that a lack of formal strategic planning is "bad."

TABLE 6–2   Strategies CEOs Use to Set Direction

	ALL FIRMS[a]		TOP PERFORMERS	
	REVIEW	DONE FORMALLY	REVIEW	DONE FORMALLY
Content Analyzed:				
The competition[b]	83%	28%	80%	26%
Organizational strengths and weaknesses[b]	83	35	80	40
Market trends[b]	82	25	84	22
Economic and social trends[b]	75	23	84	26

	ALL FIRMS[c]	TOP PERFORMERS
Who Sets Direction:		
CEO involved (with or without others)	98%	96%
CEO does it alone	54	54
Top managers involved (with or without CEO)	46	46
Others below top management involved	5	7
Top managers alone	2	4

	ALL FIRMS[d]	TOP PERFORMERS
Process Used to Set Direction:		
Driven by customer demand	34%	41%
Read magazines, talk to people	33	32
Gut feeling, intuition	11	23
Meetings	18	18
Planning in general	8	5
Written business plans	5	0
Marketing research	3	5

[a]Out of 168 firms. Adds up to more than 100 percent because most firms review more than one area.

[b]Estimate based on data from a partial sample. Not all CEOs were asked to distinguish formal from informal review.

[c]Out of 163 CEOs responding

[d]Out of 114 CEOs responding

Lack of planning should not be equated with a lack of knowledge or focus. Though few plan, Hills and Welsch report that 90 percent of their firms cite market, product, and industry knowledge as success factors. And 77 percent of the firms mention sticking to a given mission as a key to their success.

In our own study, CEOs emphasize the importance of knowing their environment and their organizations. Eighty percent or more analyze competition, market demand, and technical trends and organizational strengths and weaknesses. Three-fourths review economic and social trends. All these factors are building blocks for strategic planning. As Table 6–2 shows, only 25–35 percent of the CEOs queried review each of these areas on a formal, systematic basis—roughly the same as in the top-performing group. So it seems the information that would go into a strategic plan is gathered. It just doesn't get typeset.

The CEO Usually Sets Direction Alone

Of course, without writing down a plan it is difficult to have staff share in design of the strategic plan or in its execution. Is this bad? We find a large number of CEOs carry out these functions on their own, anyway.

Table 6–2 summarizes who sets direction. The CEO sets direction exclusively in over half of the firms we studied—among top performers, too. Which is better—direction setting by the CEO alone or in participative fashion? Based on much of the recent popular management literature, more heads would seem better than one. But not here. In other analyses, we find companies that select or design products and services participatively and set direction for the firm more participatively report *less* steady growth and *lower* profits. This holds for all the size ranges we looked at—fewer than 20 as well as between 80 and 500 employees.

We are not the first to document the limited role subordinates play in setting direction. Alpander and colleagues find small-business owners act on their own when addressing the firm's most critical problems. Those who do not involve others are much more likely to be satisfied with the outcome of their decision than those who do.[8] Our study goes one step further, suggesting that solo decision making is not only more appealing to the CEO, but also more effective.

There are exceptions. A successful manufacturer of fabricated metal products says his success is because of, not in spite of, its participative approach. His strategy is market driven. He gets his information directly from the sales staff. The firm places a high priority on innovation and is not afraid to spend money to keep the company on the cutting edge. The special role of sales people is also reflected in responses by the various managers. The sales manager notes more involvement with setting direction than does the production manager. This firm has about 100 employees and grew from about $8 million in sales to $20 million in sales from 1983 to 1988, generating high profitability throughout.

Another president—one of the few not also chairman—runs a very profitable wholesale firm. The president has a BA in marketing—and is not a family member. A ''managers' committee'' sets direction. It is comprised of the president, top managers, three board members, and the chairman (whose family owns the firm). It is not clear that this format is the key to the firm's success. The president mentions frustration when trying to bring about productive change during fast growth. He especially senses the conflict and differing views between himself and the chairman/founder. Even though the firm performs well, he often feels great resistance to change by the chairman and by employees.

The founding/visionary CEO must be very cautious about delegating direction-setting responsibilities. Most aspects of business management can be taught. But our observations and experience suggest something truly unique sets successful entrepreneurs apart from the rest of us—that knack for sensing a business opportunity. A successful CEO must have the courage of conviction, taking the time to persuade others—recruits, existing employees, bankers, investors, suppliers, and anyone else needed to realize this vision—that he or she is on the right track. In the end, the CEO must articulate the goals and mission and take the initiative. No committee can pull it off as effectively.

HOW DIRECTION IS SET CHANGES WITH TIME

About 40 percent of firms studied report changes in how direction is set since start up. Firms reporting changes usually indicate planning has become more formal, less intuitive, less customer driven, and has more emphasis on organizational assessment and written plans.

Common Triggers for Change

Growth in employment is the most commonly mentioned reason for changing the approach to market strategy. A new president, desire to improve efficiency or control, decreased profits, desire to increase profits, and increased competition are also cited. Many reasons refer directly to market demand: The customer base had changed, the firm had been dependent on one customer, or customers weren't paying their bills. Sometimes CEO attitudes simply evolved.

EFFECTIVE MARKET STRATEGY: INFORMAL
AND INTUITIVE

Business schools have sustained criticism in recent years for not focusing enough attention on creativity and strategy. Dr. Deming, a well-known quality guru, argues that poor quality comes from too much emphasis on analysis of short-term financial results and number crunching in general.[9] In spite of this, most assume that CEOs with more extensive business education will develop more effective strategies. Our results show just the opposite. CEOs of top-performing firms with 80–500 employees have *less* education than those in the poor profit-growth group. Firms with a greater number of college-trained specialists report slower and less steady sales growth. These findings could be chalked up to chance. But other results of our study clearly point to the value of less formal/more intuitive styles of thinking in overall direction setting—styles not generally emphasized in typical MBA programs. Formal planning can nonetheless be very useful if balanced with intuition and gut feeling. The next section describes how this blend of formal planning and intuition were contributing factors in JPI's success.

FORMULATING STRATEGY AT J. P. INDUSTRIES *(JPI)*

The market strategy at JPI was specifically stated in each of its annual reports:

> J. P. Industries is a unique entrepreneurial growth company. It was founded with a strategic plan to acquire, develop and manage underperforming manufacturers of industrial and consumer durable goods.[10]

In creating its competitive edge, JPI strove for recognized product quality and customer confidence in reliable service at reasonable prices—not necessarily the lowest price. A well-trained knowledgable sales force, readily accessible to potential and existing customers, was emphasized.

Quality . . . at a Reasonable Price

From 1985 to 1989, JPI's export sales grew from $1 million to $50 million, while many American manufacturers were outsourcing, downsizing, and *hollowing* (putting domestic labels on foreign-produced goods), conceding critical chunks of even their domestic markets.

JPI's emphasis on quality began even prior to an acquisition. Targets were discarded from further consideration unless they had a solid reputation and customer loyalty. Product reputation was considered paramount because reputation is a much longer, more difficult turnaround than product-line pruning or debt restructuring. Ideal targets were those with high-quality products complementary to existing JPI products but which had been unprofitable due to bad management.

Trimming Unnecessary Lines

Weeding unprofitable lines was important for several of JPI's turnarounds. Many reasons exist for maintaining such "sacred cows," none valid. Sometimes the seller figured its customers wanted a full range of products. This dead weight makes "keeper" lines more expensive than they need to be. Many sellers had inadequate cost controls and simply didn't realize which lines were unprofitable. Some firms had sunk a large amount into research and development. Keeping or dropping a line should be made with overall strategy in mind. If an acquisition's product line fit the overall profile at JPI and could be made profitable, it was kept. Otherwise it was quickly dropped.

JPI's Vision: Part Experience, Part Intuition

JPI was guided by several elements: product quality, top service to customers, a dynamic and progressive internal environment yielding opportunities for employees to grow, and developing unique, complementary lines to fit the existing engine-component manufacturing business.

Dr. Psarouthakis, JPI's founder, explains how this vision came to be:[11]

"I evolved the initial focus of the business pretty much by myself—my knowledge, experiences, feelings, and intellectual projections of things to be—you might call the latter my gut feelings or intuition, although I certainly gained useful insights and honed my ideas by talking to friends and business acquaintances. My vision is an amalgam of rational and emotional, qualitative and quantitative, past and future. I trace my initial inspiration for JPI to a report I reviewed for my work as vice-president for planning and technology at Masco Corporation based in Taylor, Michigan. In particular, the report mentioned that as many as 70 percent of all manufacturing firms perform well below their actual capabilities. At the time, my job at Masco involved sifting through acquisition candidates in that narrow subset of highly performing firms. It was then that I began to muse about the advantages of purchasing underperformers myself and turning them around. These were in plentiful supply. The correct choices, I thought, could produce tremendous short-term gains. One can often purchase underperforming firms well below market value. Assuming I could correct basic management mistakes, I could make these firms profitable and realize tremendous gains. From the beginning, I held this vision in my mind. I could see my successful firm down the pike. Then I began to talk to a lot of people to synthesize the vision more clearly.''

The thought process documented here clearly shows the key role of creative insight in the development of JPI's initial overall strategy.

Maintaining Direction at JPI

Implementation of JPI's vision involved extensive formal planning, both on the technical side and the people side. Whereas the overall direction was an outgrowth of its founder's inspiration, maintaining it required the acceptance, cooperation, and support of everyone in the firm—both initially and after exponential growth. Duties were extensively delegated throughout the corporation but only in the context of the overall plan. The overall focus was maintained by monitoring specific parameters built into both the capital-expenditure plan and the operating plan.

SUMMARY OF KEY GUIDELINES

Here are some ideas to consider, in closing, that have worked for many of the top-performing companies:

- Emphasize quality, though its impact takes time to show up in bottom-line improvement.
- Set a goal of larger market share. But be patient. Results take time.
- Take ultimate responsibility for your company's direction. Firms ruled by committee do not generally perform as well as those with a strong leader and a clear vision.
- Avoid discounting, especially if your company is very small.
- Follow your instinct and intuition. Experience and instinct are not always quantifiable as independent variables inside neat formulas. Many firms in our sample—large or small—are driven to success by CEO intuition.

- Diversify cautiously. The smallest firms we studied had big trouble as they diversified. Even in large firms, diversification should probably be along complementary lines of the existing services or products.

NOTES

[1]Cecil J. Bond, *Hands-on Financial Controls for your Small Business* (Blue Ridge Summit, PA: Liberty Hall Press, 1991). For a much more sophisticated treatment, see John J. Clark, Thomas C. Chiang, and Gerald T. Olson, *Sustainable Corporate Growth: A Model and Management Planning Tool* (New York: Quorum Books, 1989).

[2]Robert D. Buzzell and Bradley T. Gale, *The PIMS Principles: Linking Strategy to Performance* (New York: The Free Press, 1987), p. 85.

[3]Buzzell and Gale. *The PIMS Principles,* pp. 103–34.

[4]For a further discussion of related versus unrelated diversification strategies, see Arthur A. Thompson, Jr. and A. J. Strickland III, *Strategic Management: Concepts and Cases,* 6th ed. (Homewood, IL: BPI/Irwin, 1992), pp. 169–78.

[5]See Radha Chaganti, Rajeswararao Chaganti, and Vijay Mahajan, "Profitable Small Business Strategies Under Different Types of Competition," *Entrepreneurship: Theory and Practice,* 13 (1989), pp. 21–35. In this article, Chaganti and colleagues also present relevant findings linking quality and product scope to profits.

[6]Gerald E. Hills and Harold P. Welsch, *High-Growth Entrepreneurial Ventures: A Content Analysis to Identify Common Strategic Factors* (unpublished working paper).

[7]Charles B. Shrader, Charles L. Mulford, and Virginia L. Blackburn, "Strategic and Operational Planning, Uncertainty, and Performance in Small Firms," *Journal of Small Business Management,* 27 (1989), pp. 45–60.

[8]Guvenc G. Alpander, Kent D. Carter, and Roderick A. Forsgren, "Managerial Issues and Problem Solving in the Formative Years," *Journal of Small Business Management,* 28 (1990), pp. 9–19.

[9]Rafael Aguayo, *Dr. Deming: The American who Taught the Japanese About Quality* (New York: Lyle Stuart, Carol Publishing Group, 1990).

[10]J. P. Industries 1985 Annual Report.

[11]We felt it made sense in a few places to move Dr. Psarouthakis's comments into quotation marks and present it in first-person singular form, especially where we wanted to underscore his own thoughts or behavior while heading JPI. This may be a little unconventional but we feel that our choice is a more accurate way to present such material than the alternatives.

CHAPTER 7

Building Profit Through Organization and Smooth Work Flow: Step 1—Division of Work

"What, you forgot to certify that check?"

"They forgot to send the parts air freight. Send the second shift home."

Your management style hasn't changed but things slip through the cracks a lot more than before. A customer cancels because he gets tired of waiting. Another customer returns an item because it isn't the expected quality. All firms face these problems occasionally; but if the frequency is unacceptable, you might be experiencing problems with work flow.

Work flow is a complex issue involving the ability to divide work among staff and put it back together again in a coordinated manner that meets goal. Work flow is made up of two components: division of work—both tasks and authority; and coordination—assuring that everyone's efforts and overall information fit together in a timely and efficient way.

Division of work is both *vertical* and *horizontal*. Vertical division refers to the distribution of authority: Who is involved with the decisions—input as well as the final decision. Horizontal division relates to assignments across tasks and functions—job classifications and duties assigned to each job.

ORIGINS OF THE WORK-DIVISION PROBLEM

Anybody can start a company. But a business doesn't become an "organization" until two or more people work together: Decisions then must be made about how work will be divided—and put back together.

With small groups of equal partners, people may virtually define their own jobs. But with growth, specialization occurs typically along functional lines, such as production, marketing, and administration.

One undesired side effect of specialization is more difficult coordination. When everyone does the same job, understanding each other is fairly easy. With specialization, people become less sure of what others are doing. Increasing attention must be paid to how smoothly different efforts fit together. The entrepreneur now takes on the potentially uncomfortable role of detail manager.

Increased size itself complicates the work-flow issue. Simple arithmetic illustrates this point. With two people, only one linkage exists—between those two people. Conversations between the two quickly resolve any work-flow questions. With three people, there are three possible relationships: Between person A and person B; between person B and person C; and between person A and person C. With 10 people, the combinations grow to 45. At this size, the CEO can still effectively act as a go-between to coordinate efforts. But at 20 employees, the number of possible relationships climbs to 120; and at 50 employees, it jumps to 1,225 pairs, not to mention the additional vast number of combinations possible among groups of three or more people. True, not every employee must deal with everyone else, but the need for organization and clear division of duties becomes rather obvious. Yet the complexity grows so rapidly that it catches many CEOs by surprise.

ASSESSING YOUR FIRM'S DIVISION OF WORK

Now that we have introduced the topic of work division, ask yourself the same kinds of questions we asked CEOs in our research. By doing this, you can begin to visualize the work-division component of the work-flow issue more clearly in your own company setting.

Question 7-1: Adequacy of information.   How adequate is the information you get from others *inside* your firm. Would you say it is:

[1] Extremely adequate
[2] Very adequate
[3] Fairly adequate
[4] Not so adequate
[5] Totally inadequate

Question 7-2: Role-assignment strategy.   How do you divide work? That is, how are roles assigned?

[1] Preset job descriptions for everyone (though not necessarily written down)
[2] Joint development of positions (the worker makes suggestions about what the job should include, but then management finalizes the role)
[3] A fairly loose approach in which individuals play a large role in designing their own jobs as needs arise.

Question 7-3: Communication of roles. How are roles and duties generally communicated to employees—by informal conversation, meetings, written job descriptions, manuals, on-the-job training, or what?

Question 7-4: Effectiveness of work-assignment strategy. Consider how you answered questions 7-2 and 7-3. How well do you feel your work assignment strategy is working out for you?

[1] Extremely well
[2] Very well
[3] Fairly well
[4] Not so well
[5] Not well at all

Question 7-5: Management-reporting structure. List job titles or one-sentence job descriptions for each manager reporting to you.

Question 7-6: Departmental structure. Which best describes the way you divide your work into different departments?

[1] Functional—by operational tasks (e.g., marketing, production, office, accounting, etc.)
[2] Geographically—by city or region
[3] By type of customer (e.g., account executives to handle different types of customers)
[4] By process (breaking down production into subcategories such as installation/assembly/service or graphics design/production/distribution)
[5] By product line
[6] By market channel (e.g., head of wholesale, retail, telemarketing)
[7] Some other approach not listed above

Question 7-7: Number of managers CEO delegates to. Count the number of managers and staff people reporting directly to you about whom you feel you can delegate *major* decision-making authority. That is, you could take a *two-week vacation* and that person's department would take care of itself.

For questions 7-8 and 7-9, choose one of the following answers:

[1] Extremely high specialization, with very little overlap between jobs
[2] High specialization
[3] Moderate specialization, with some overlap
[4] Low specialization
[5] Very low specialization, with a lot of overlap between jobs

Question 7-8: Specialization of nonmanagement. How specialized are jobs in this organization? Do people have uniquely assigned tasks?

Question 7-9: Specialization of managers.   How about lower-level supervisors and line employees? For instance, in a small young firm everyone may take turns making, selling, and installing a particular product. In a larger firm in the same industry, there are likely to be specialists: sales representatives, installers, and production people.

Question 7-10: Distribution of authority.   Look over the list of functions in Table 7–1 on page 64 (or review question WF-3 in Appendix B). Ignore percentages for now and glance at the different functions on the lefthand side. Consider who is closely involved with each of these functions. Consider the following groups—you may check more than one:

[1] Yourself (CEO)
[2] Top management
[3] Middle management or supervisors
[4] Nonsupervisory employees
[5] Board of directors
[6] Others

Question 7-10a: Delegation of authority by function.   You *delegate authority* in a particular function if you checked anything **but** [1] in question 7-10.

Question 7-10b: Participative decision making by function.   You decide *participatively* in a particular function if you checked [2], [3], or [4] above in addition to or instead of [1] above.

The following questions should be asked in a confidential employee survey. Skim them for now.

Question 7-11: Adequate authority is allocated.   I am given the authority I need to get my work done. I can make the necessary decisions or get a quick approval if needed:

[1] To a very great extent
[2] To a great extent
[3] To some extent
[4] To a slight extent
[5] To a very slight extent or not at all

Using these same answer choices, answer questions 7-12 and 7-13.

Question 7-12: How widely information is shared.   Information is widely shared, so those who make decisions have access to *all* available know-how. (People at all levels of a company will have some know-how of use to decision makers.)

TABLE 7–1   How Different Functions of the Firm Are Managed: Comparison in
Decision-Making Style Between Top Performers and Remaining Firms

	CEO IS NOT INVOLVED WITH DECISION (DELEGATION)		*CEO* AND OTHERS PARTICIPATE IN DECISION (PARTICIPATION)	
	TOP PERFORMERS	OTHER FIRMS	TOP PERFORMERS	OTHER FIRMS
Function:				
Market Strategy				
Set firm's direction	4%	2%	46%	46%
Sell products/services that you offer	30	28	78	80
How/when/where to expand the business including physical facilities	7	12	26	41
Work Flow				
Define job positions below top management	50	37	79	77
Make sure activities flow smoothly	18	31	68	80
Resource Acquisition				
Recruit personnel	39	38	89	83
Track information about products or services	25	20	64	62
Obtain financing	11	11	19	32
Obtain materials and services	43	49	82	84
Human Relations				
Motivate employees	21	27	89	88
Resource Allocation				
Monitor/control costs	4	19	54	72
Public Relations				
Public relations	15	22	50	66
Government relations	27	40	60	74
Relations with others in the industry	16	16	48	51
Technical Mastery				
Develop/train personnel	58	61	92	92
Monitor quality	37	33	78	84
Select/design products/services that you offer (market strategy, too)	19	16	54	67
Produce the products/services	81	66	96	96

Question 7-13: Appropriate allocation of decisions.   To what extent are decisions made at those levels where the most adequate and accurate information is available?

Question 7-14: Degree of delegation to managers.   How much authority does the president delegate to you in your own area?

[1] The president makes the key strategic decisions. My main responsibility is to carry them out.

[2] Strategic decisions are decided jointly with the president.

[3] I handle strategic decisions myself, going to the president only when I see a need for major exception to overall policy and direction.

[4] I handle all decisions independently.

Questions 7-1, 7-4, 7-11, 7-12, and 7-13 address how adequately work is divided. Table 7–2 shows median responses on these items and some comparisons between top and lower performers. For questions 7-4, 7-11, and 7-12, in particular, top performers typically score higher than the remaining firms.

The other questions address your overall strategy and actual division of work. We will discuss them in more detail later.

TABLE 7–2   Effectiveness of Division of Work: Some Comparisons Between Top Performers and Other Firms

	ALL FIRMS		TOP PERFORMERS	REMAINING FIRMS
	%	MEDIAN	%	%
Effectiveness of Division of Work				
Adequacy of inside information[a] (question 7-1)	73%	2.0	75%	72%
Effectiveness of work assignment strategy[b] (question 7-4)	26	2.0	39	23
Adequate authority is allocated (question 7-11)	74[c]	1.3	87[c]	72[c]
How widely information is shared (question 7-12)	52[c]	2.0	74[c]	48[c]
Appropriate allocation of decisions (question 7-13)	74[c]	2.0	78[c]	74[c]

[a]Coded [1] or [2] in question 7-1.

[b]Coded [1] in question 7-4.

[c]Based on averaged data for one or more managers in each firm. The table shows the percentage of company averages that are 2 or less.

THE IMPORTANCE OF DIVIDING WORK EFFECTIVELY

Our research shows that appropriate work division and information flow affect almost every aspect of operations. The only exception is public relations, which is not linked to division of work. Effectively distributing work and decision-making authority is linked to greater profitability, better recruiting, and improved allocation of both personnel and nonpeople resources, as well as to employee commitment. Firms that effectively distribute work also have greater mastery of technology and more rapid growth.

Work division and profits.   Firms with effective approaches for assigning work and good information flow are likely to be more profitable. Firms in which employees feel they have the authority they need to produce results also tend to show higher profits.

Work division and growth.   As mentioned in Chapter 6, effective work division is linked to sales growth rate and steadiness of growth. Adequate flow of internal information, not surprisingly, contributes to effective direction setting.

Work division is linked to better resource acquisition and human relations.   Sharing of information expedites the firm's ability to obtain needed resources: personnel, capital, suppliers, information from outside, and subcontractors. Adequate flow of information also goes hand in hand with effective recruitment. Sharing of information is more widespread in firms with high employee morale, commitment, and understanding of the firm's mission.

Information sharing should not be confused with delegation of authority. Delegation can actually hamper mutual understanding of values. However, the "proper" amount of authority (as managers see it) is linked to better integration of individual and group goals.

Work division is linked to resource allocation and technical mastery.   Adequate resource allocation and work division also go hand in hand. In fact, some researchers see work division as an aspect of the allocation problem.[1] Different aspects of work division are linked to different aspects of technical mastery. Information sharing is linked with technical performance. Proper allocation of authority is strongly linked to productivity—the firm's ability to fill orders and meet schedules. Adequate information flow is linked with higher levels of employee technical skills and technical performance.

TYPICAL APPROACHES TO DIVISION OF WORK

Vertical Division of Work—Assigning Decisions

Table 7–1 shows how CEOs assign authority for a variety of decisions, organized by the seven DSP issues. The most commonly *delegated* decisions—i.e., those in which the CEO is not involved even in final decision making—include production responsibility, followed by personnel training and job definition. Table 7–1 shows two-thirds of CEOs delegate production responsibility. Among top performers this percentage is even higher, with four-fifths delegating production responsibility.

About 60 percent of all CEOs delegate personnel training. And slightly less than half delegate the task of obtaining supplies and services. About half of top-performing CEOs delegate the task of defining jobs, compared with only about a third of the CEOs in remaining firms. But top performers are *less* likely to delegate government relations and the coordination task of making sure work flows smoothly.

Table 7–1's righthand column takes the same raw data but compiles them to reflect the percentage of firms allowing managers below CEO to participate (whether or not the CEO is involved). Table 7–1 highlights differences between delegation and participation. For instance, only a few CEOs delegate direction-setting entirely to managers (lefthand column), but almost half involve managers in some way (righthand column). Many other decisions heavily involve managers. Most discrepancies between top performers and the rest are probably not significant, but in a few functions the shifts are more marked. For instance, only 26 percent of top-performing CEOs involve subordinates in expansion planning, compared with 41 percent in remaining firms. More dramatic is the difference in monitoring and controlling costs: Only 54 percent of top-performing CEOs share this, compared with about 72 percent of CEOs in the remaining firms. And only about half of the CEOs in the top-performing firms share the public relations function, compared with about two-thirds of the CEOs in the remaining firms.

Table 7–3 shows other patterns distinguishing vertical division of work.

When asked how many managers the CEO delegates to, the typical answer is two or three managers. About one-third of surveyed CEOs (top performing or otherwise) delegate authority to four or more managers (see question 7-7). About 75 percent share authority jointly with managers. This climbs to about 90 percent of top-performing CEOs (see question 7-8).

Horizontal Division of Work—Assigning Tasks

Table 7–3 also shows how work is divided horizontally. In response to our questions about specialization, about 40 percent of all CEOs note that management jobs are highly specialized. But for nonmanagement, we see a stark contrast between top performers and the rest. Whereas 38 percent of all CEOs report high specialization of nonmanagement employees, this drops to only 12 percent among top performers, providing evidence of trends toward cross training and job flexibility.

We also looked at the types of specialists reporting directly to the CEO. About one-third of CEOs list each of the following management specialties: controller, production manager, sales manager, general manager, and office bookkeeper. Other frequently mentioned specialties include engineer, purchasing agent, quality control officer, account executive, project manager, and shop supervisor.

Division of work defines the firm's *departmentalization*—how work is separated into departments. The most common structure we found is the functional

TABLE 7–3   **Work Division Strategies Within the Firm: Overall and Among Top Performers**

	ALL FIRMS	TOP PERFORMERS
Vertical Division of Work		
CEO delegates to four or more managers[a]	32%	35%
CEO shares authority with managers[b]	74	91
Horizontal Division of Work		
Specialization:[c]		
of managers	43	35
of nonmanagement	38	12
Management Structure:		
Finance, controller	35	29
Production/plant manager/operations	34	36
Sales/marketing manager	32	29
General Manager	28	29
Office—bookkeeping	28	32
Engineer	11	21
Purchasing	5	18
Quality Control	4	11
Account/project manager	11	14
Shop supervisor/foreman	5	14
Department Structure:		
Functional	47	57
Geographic	15	11
Customer base	8	14
Process (breaking production into subcategories)	5	4
Product line	3	0
Market channel	1	0

[a]% of CEOs who delegate to four or more subordinates
[b]% of firms whose managers, on average, report joint decision making or even more autonomy in their roles ([2] or greater on question 7-8)
[c]Coded [1] or [2] in the question

form—with departments such as marketing, production, and accounting represented. Other than geographic- and customer-based departments, alternative structural forms are rare—whether among top performers or the others, even among the larger firms in our study.

How Role Assignments Are Communicated

How do you pass on information about job assignments? Table 7–4 shows the typical means used by CEOs in our study. The most common means to communicate roles is simply to tell people: Seventy-five percent cite this strategy; 86 percent of top performers do. Written job descriptions and meetings are next most common, but by only 27 percent of CEOs. Manuals and on-the-job training trail far behind as means for *assigning* work roles.

TABLE 7–4   Ways in Which Role Assignments Are Communicated

	ALL FIRMS	TOP PERFORMERS
Informal conversation	75%	86%
On-the-job training	9	4
Meetings	27	21
Written job descriptions	27	25
Handbooks	8	11

Specificity of Roles Assigned

Patterns for top performers and other firms were almost identical in response to question 7-2. About 40 percent indicate roles are present for everyone. Twenty-two percent develop roles and another 22 percent are fairly loose, allowing employees to work where needed and define their own jobs to a great extent.

SIZE DIFFERENCES AND TYPICAL CHANGES IN THE GROWING FIRM

About one-third of companies we interviewed note change in their strategy for assigning work since their founding. When we asked CEOs how their approach to assigning roles has shifted, 60 percent note a shift away from fairly loose self-directed roles, with only about 20 percent still using that approach. About 40 percent now use preset roles for everyone, compared with only 15 percent of the firms in the past.

A comparison of the smallest firms in our study (under 20 employees) with the largest (over 80 employees) suggests other likely changes growing firms may go through. Larger firms rely more heavily on the traditional chain of command, and the CEO is less involved with overall work flow. In these larger firms, CEOs delegate to more managers, hold more meetings, rely more on written guidelines and job descriptions, and less on informal conversations, to assign work and coordinate efforts. Larger firms are more likely to monitor quality, production, and costs and compare them to targets or goals. This reduces the need for direct CEO supervision.

Larger firms also have more levels of management. And CEOs of larger firms delegate to more managers and involve managers more in their own functional areas. In Chapter 8, we review which ways are linked to better coordination and higher profits.

Triggers for Change in Division of Work

Among the CEOs we interviewed, the most frequently mentioned trigger for change in work assignment stems from a need to manage work flow more effectively. Several CEOs simply wanted to define responsibilities more clearly. Others complained that they had a hard time administering policies, things were dropping through the cracks, or it was simply too time consuming and stressful for the CEO to manage the old way.

Eleven CEOs also mention growth or size as a factor. A few mentioned decreased profits the old way. Human relations issues were also mentioned. Distrust among employees, sibling rivalry, and employee problems triggered the need for change for these CEOs. Other changes inside and outside the firm triggered change, such as maturing staff, applicant pool changes, fewer employees, and change in ownership or in the attitudes of the CEO.

HEAT, INC.: EVOLVING ORGANIZATION DESIGN

Let's follow Heat, Inc., a high-growth Inc. 500 company, over a ten-year period.[2] This case illustrates the way the work-flow issue changes over time. In particular, the case underscores the dilemmas a CEO of a rapid-growth firm faces in knowing when and how to delegate.

Phase I: Heat, Inc.'s First Year

Heat, Inc. began as a way to create summer jobs for a group of friends. That fall, four of them—Ron, Gary, Bill, and Jim—decided to commit full-time effort to the firm. Heat, Inc. sold residential heating equipment. It started as a retailer, selling in-home. At first a partnership, the group soon decided a subchapter-S corporation status would better protect the firm from product liability and automatic dissolution if a partner left the firm. This also made it easier to raise equity. Roles were loosely defined at first. Everyone agreed that Ron should be CEO because the idea for the business was his. Everyone pitched in, selling and installing the product. Specific tasks were decided for the day over breakfast. The group met often to keep tabs. After moderate success, it became clear that the firm would need help—focused sales people and installers. Gary liked sales and seemed pretty good at it, so he became sales manager. Bill, a professional engineer, was the firm's first installation manager and also researched new products. Jim was a residential sales representative and soon took over development of a dealer network as the firm branched into wholesaling. As the principals spent more time on the road, an office manager was hired to handle telephone calls and administrative details. She was a self-starter, organizing the office in short order and even writing her own job description for a successor when she left.

Inside its formative year, the loose patterning of activities eventually firmed into a specific organization structure: with a president and office, sales, and installation managers reporting to the president and additional commissioned sales people and installation crew members reporting to them in turn.

Phase II: Heat, Inc. Expansion

Heat, Inc. experienced its first major crisis in work flow in the second year. As sales grew, installation bottlenecks arose and Gary, the sales manager, became impatient. Bill, the overloaded installation manager, tried to prepare contract proposals for government jobs at the same time. Both managers threatened to quit. Since they aimed their complaints at each other, Ron thought at first that the problem was just a personality clash. But a problem-solving session facilitated by a consultant made it apparent that many problems also stemmed from vague job definitions. The managers were unclear about each other's roles—even what the president's role was supposed to be.

In a first meeting aimed at resolving the conflict, the consultant led the group through two important steps before actually engaging in the problem-solving activity itself: (1) helping Bill and Gary realize that in spite of their differences, they both had the company's best interests in mind; and (2) moving the group of managers away from threats and other destructive techniques toward a win-win, problem-solving approach as the accepted way to resolve the conflict.

Gary, who had started the meeting announcing his intent to resign from the firm, eventually became positively engaged in the problem-solving process. The group, with Gary's active participation, identified a number of immediate and long-term problems. The short-term challenge was to free up enough of Bill's time to finish writing the proposal. Jim, another manager, agreed to help out in installations and Gary also agreed to be patient for a few more weeks. Another meeting was called to explore the roles of each key manager—how each perceived his own and others' roles. These meetings did not eliminate all problems, but teamwork evolved to the point where many issues did get resolved and work went more smoothly. Both Bill and Gary stayed on for another year and were successfully replaced by more experienced managers. The immediate crisis had passed.

The meeting format used for this crisis is referred to as the Nominal Group Technique (NGT).[3] It goes like this:

1. Ground rules are explained.
2. Everyone gets as much time as needed (typically about 20 minutes) to write down silently the list of problems, obstacles, or issues related to their work.
3. The list of problems is generated uncritically on newsprint—one idea per person at a time, to equalize participation.
4. After step 3 is completed, problems are critiqued, explained, or amplified, as needed, by anyone who wishes to comment.
5. The group selects which problem is most urgent or most important through consensus or through some voting procedure.

Once the day's issue or problem is selected, steps 2 through 4 are repeated for generating solutions to that particular problem. For the solution phase, it is usually helpful also to brainstorm the criteria to be used in selecting the best solution. Setting up a grid or a matrix of solutions by criteria is an effective discussion aid in selecting the best solution.

For many problems, additional facts may need to be gathered or other employees consulted before the best solution can be picked. On another occasion, the production people at Heat, Inc. met to discuss production problems. Unfortunately, the CEO was absent and many cost assumptions used in picking the ''best'' solution were incorrect. That choice had to be scrapped, leaving production people frustrated. In retrospect, it would have been wise to postpone a choice until all the facts could be verified—perhaps at the next meeting.

In spite of its limitations, NGT was used frequently at Heat, Inc. as a way to involve more employees in the decision-making activities of the company. It was a very effective tool, not only in resolving the problem between Gary and Bill but also in making less conflict-laden decisions, including site selection for relocating the business.

Phase III: Heat, Inc. Takes on Expanded Functions

As Heat, Inc. grew, coordination of efforts was also a continuing challenge. New managers and departments were added over a ten-year period, so that eventually the firm had managers for residential sales, dealer sales, marketing, installation, service, production, research and development (R&D), and bookkeeping, all reporting to the CEO.

Strains were felt between departments as they were added, as is common in functionally organized firms. Installation people often complained that the sales rep failed to include all anticipated problems installers would face on their job paperwork. Fingerpointing went the other way, too. This caused delays, increasing job costs and lowering profits. Scheduling was another sore point. Sales people did not get paid until their job was installed, but the backlog—considered desirable by the bean counters—sometimes created a wait of several weeks before a job could go in. New control systems eventually smoothed out information flow between sales and installations. Installation dates for jobs were posted and scheduled as sales came in. Sales representatives could review progress on their own jobs that way. The production manager also installed a giant job board for scheduling production of needed parts.

In this growth phase, then, management systems evolved to handle information flow and work flow through the firm. Mere assignment of roles was no longer enough to assure that work was done in a timely manner. Additional sytems assured these roles fit smoothly together.

Meetings for other purposes were also held—weekly meetings among installation and production people to discuss mutual concerns; annual meetings of all the employees to review the firm's overall mission and direction. Additional specialists were added: a purchaser/inventory controller, marketing assistant, and sales "captains" to assist the sales manager in training and motivation of subgroups of sales representatives.

Phase IV: Heat, Inc. Grapples with the Delegation Challenge

One critical issue Heat, Inc. faced in its ninth year (approaching 70 employees) was to redefine the CEO's role. Typically a hands-on, wander-around–type manager, working side by side with other managers, he occasionally bypassed their authority "to get the job done." The larger Heat, Inc. grew, the more this was resented.

The CEO was also increasingly challenged to keep track of all critical internal details as well as the changing market (in particular, a rapidly deteriorating business climate for the heating industries as oil plummeted to $10 a barrel in 1986—good for just about every industry but Heat, Inc.'s own).

Perhaps the biggest challenge at this stage faced by the CEO was deciding what and how to delegate without losing control of a company in treacherous waters. Many texts, including little gems such as *The One-Minute Manager,* today urge CEOs to delegate more.[4] But which decisions should be delegated, how, and to whom? The CEO of Heat, Inc. began to experience intense pressure from restless managers to delegate more at about the time this INC. 500 firm reached 70 employees. This pressure, ostensibly based on concern for the firm's overall performance, was also fueled by managers' needs for greater autonomy. The bright, articulate, but inexperienced MBA marketing manager eventually convinced the CEO to yield considerable autonomy. The pressure was intensified by a board of directors largely composed of middle managers—some of whom dated back to the start up as part owners. For a brief but tumultuous period, the CEO delegated most of his spending authority to the marketing manager, along with a promotion to chief operating officer. But he soon had to halt several major spending plans that he viewed as expensive and ineffectual. In hindsight, it probably would have been better to phase delegation in gradually, setting specific spending limits and specific criteria for how money would be spent. Better yet, a capital spending plan could have been devised, for which Ron could have retained final spending authority.

DELEGATION OF FUNCTIONS AT J. P. INDUSTRIES

Dr. Psarouthakis describes how he delegated functions at J. P. Industries (JPI):

"In the pre–start-up phase, I did everything—marketing, manufacturing, engineering, and finance. Since JPI grew by acquisition, it jumped in size more quickly than most start ups. The first acquisition put JPI at about $3 million in sales. At this point, I delegated most financial work to a chief financial officer (CFO), although I monitored all financial information myself. I continued to oversee marketing, manufacturing, and engineering but hired a legal consultant.

"Once JPI acquired its second company, marketing became more important. I hired a full time VP of marketing and a public relations consultant. I kept the CFO, but each plant had a controller and plant manager so that main-office bureaucracy remained low. I continued personally to oversee manufacturing and engineering at the corporate level and now became more involved with corporate development. When JPI reached $30 million in sales, I hired a VP of manufacturing. This freed me up to take on more personal involvement with public relations, strategic planning, and personnel relations. I continued to cover engineering and corporate development myself and still avoided a full-time attorney.

"The organization structure evolved further at about $50 million in sales. I continued to have a marketing VP and CFO. The vice-president of manufacturing now absorbed the engineering function and I hired a full-time attorney and vice-president of corporate development. These changes freed me up to spend even more time in strategic planning. I also spent an increasing amount of my time communicating to three constituencies—JPI's employees, the public, and the financial community.

"JPI grew with this simple central structure to over $300 million in sales, with 19 manufacturing operations in the United States and western Europe. Then the organization structure evolved once more. At this point, I had top management support in each functional area. I added a full-time communications VP and human resources VP. I had group vice-presidents of operations and had top staff handling community relations and government relations. Just before the firm was sold, I further evolved the structure to separate the president's office from the chairman's office—even though at the time I still filled both spots. The two executive VP's, group VP's, attorney, and CFO all reported to the president. The top managers in community relations, government relations, corporate development, and investment reported to the chairman's office.

"At each point in JPI's growth, my role changed as I took on new functions and omitted old ones."

DIVISION OF WORK: INNOVATIVE APPROACHES ARE NEEDED

Early on, the CEO must develop some alternative to direct supervision of each employee. Eventually, a totally new approach to coordinating efforts and directing work flow is required. Large firms often manage growth with bureaucracy. By developing standardized job descriptions, rules, and written guidelines, and by delegating daily responsibilities in the chain of command, the CEO of a slow-growth firm in a predictable industry can get by. But today, firms need a more flexible approach.

Although narrowly defined jobs and other characteristics of bureaucratic firms often reduce training needs and can speed up production, they can also lead to poorer quality, in part by creating demotivating jobs with minimal authority or feedback. In such organizations, workers are so far "upstream" from the end product that mistakes compound many times before the error is caught.

Today, pressured to deliver ever-increasing quality at lowered costs, many companies experiment with team training, problem-solving groups, and individual autonomy. Clear standards are still set and monitoring systems are still in place; but set rules governing everyday activity and confining job descriptions are minimized.

JPI CELL CONCEPT: AN INNOVATIVE APPROACH TO WORK DIVISION

JPI is one example of this new breed, having adopted the "cell concept" at several plants.

Cellular manufacturing put more responsibility for manufacturing in a cell of people. At its McCord Gasket division, a three-person cell carried out the entire assembly process. Under traditional batch-method manufacturing, workers take raw gasket materials and perform the first step. Then the part is batched and sent to the warehouse. Another department receives this batch and performs processing step two. The process continues until the gasket is complete, taking as long as five weeks. Under this old approach, literally hundreds of thousands of gaskets could be made before an error was caught. Cell-based manufacturing, on the other hand, allows a small team of workers to oversee the entire production process and allows them responsibility for their own productivity and quality—even including packing.[5]

The great advantage is quality control. Problems can be corrected quickly. Employees get more rewarding feedback on how well their workmanship is being received. It also provides a more complete cycle of events for workers, improving not only the meaning of the task but the quality of work, as well. These concepts have been well understood by psychologists for almost 30 years, but they are by no means fully accepted by manufacturers.

The cell concept didn't work right away at McCord because a lot of other systems had to change. The pre-existing labor agreement was based on individual classifications, preventing multiple work assignments—an essential prerequisite for the cell concept. Eventually these barriers were eliminated after tough labor negotiations. Employees also needed to learn statistical process-control techniques to monitor their own quality.[6] And material flows had to be adapted to fit the cell concept.

In JPI's manufacturing environment, clear role assignments were extremely important. As technology gets more sophisticated, shop-floor flexibility must occur in a planned manner. The cell concept was a good compromise because it expanded the roles of nonmanagement employees, built in more responsibility for quality control, and still assigned very clear requirements to the team as a whole.

These innovative approaches to work division were just as important as improved technology. McCord Gasket is a fairly old plant, but such low-cost changes greatly enhanced the performance of the division.

PARTICIPATIVE LEADERSHIP VS. ABDICATION

Management research from the 1950s forward abounds with recommendations urging CEOs to share decision-making authority with subordinates. This is an important theme. Delegating too little can cripple the CEO's ability to manage time. There is no way to "do it all." However, delegating can harm an operation, especially delegating to unprepared managers, as we saw in the case of Heat, Inc. One critical CEO skill is to determine which decisions to delegate, which to retain, and when. A growing theme in management literature is "abdication of leadership." At some firms visited for the research study, it didn't seem that the CEO was really the person in charge. Rosabeth Moss Kanter cautions against abdicating responsibility to set goals and measure results.[7] As observed by an insider in the 1980s, Wright describes GM's lack of focus because of a committee style of leadership. This was a period when GM lost both dollars and significant market share. Wright describes committee meetings covering minutiae and decisions not properly delegated down the hierarchy.[8]

Top managers at one of the worst-performing firms we visited were frustrated with the committee-style approach used by their CEO. This firm experienced rapid growth over a six-year period, to a peak of about $10 million in sales, but had been losing 3 percent on revenues in each of the last two years. Shortly after our interviews, the firm was acquired and the CEO retained as president of the newly formed division—at least temporarily. Shortly thereafter, the division lost its largest client and two-thirds of the staff was laid off. What went wrong? One long-time manager was quite comfortable with the committee approach. But other newly recruited top managers felt it was too time consuming. One commented, "Too much time is involved in information gathering [before a decision is made]. . . . There are both financial and morale costs in delaying decisions. The style of the president is a serious problem." It's not clear whether a tepid committee would cause the major account to bolt. But such managers may not excel at finding new business!

PARTICIPATIVE DECISION MAKING AT *JPI*

Participation at JPI meant employees had an opportunity to influence decisions affecting them. This should not be confused with democratic systems, in which everyone decides policy. The JPI manager in charge still made final decisions. Some researchers refer to this approach as *consultative*. But if the manager made a decision counter to employee input, he or she was obligated to explain why. The process dies if managers routinely go against worker input. This approach empowers the manager because he or she gets the best thinking of all available minds. When JPI introduced real management-style changes in its acquired plants, all of a sudden hundreds of process- and product-oriented employee suggestions were coming out of each plant, where a year before none had emerged.

Jim McAuliffe, the former vice-president of human resources at JPI, further illuminates:

"This approach required a lot of additional training of our employees. Everyone at JPI was taught how to run a meeting: setting agendas; problem-solving processes; reaching decision points. Training costs were kept down by using self-training materials with which supervisors and employees could lead their own discussion groups aided by professionally developed materials.

"An interesting thing happens when you teach an entire organization the problem-solving process. When a manager or supervisor tries to shortcut it, and thus perhaps prematurely settles on a solution, someone will say, 'You just shortcut the process.' And if your decision doesn't make sense, employees will also tell you. The problem-solving process is basic: Identify and agree on the problem; identify all possible solution alternatives and then evaluate them; and then choose the best solution. When you bypass such logic, everyone notices. We assume everyone knows how to solve problems, but the education of many adults never included these basics; so we had to teach them.

"This approach shouldn't be confused with rule by committee. Chain of command is still there. The person responsible is the manager or supervisor. Otherwise nobody makes a decision.

"Not everyone adopted the new approach and those who didn't often left— both human-resource and plant managers."

DIVIDING WORK: A GUIDING PHILOSOPHY

We further explore the work-flow issue in Chapter 8. Division-of-work decisions are becoming increasingly challenging. No longer do employees accept jobs stripped of all creative and decision-making authority, nor do they work well in an atmosphere where they are kept in the dark. Top-performing firms in our study typically foster an open atmosphere in which information and ideas flow freely. But the CEO retains a clear vision and closely oversees activity directly or, with growth, via chain of command.

NOTES

[1]Basil S. Georgopoulos, *Organization Structure, Problem Solving, and Effectiveness: A Comparative Study of Hospital Services* (San Francisco: Jossey-Bass, 1986). Georgopoulos includes role allocation among resource-allocation issues. Although theoretically both address distribution, the steps and strategies for each are much different. Theory, as well as empirical research, links work division much more closely to the coordination of effort. Thus, we combine them as work-flow issues.

[2]Heat, Inc. is not the real name of this firm. However, all other details of the case are based on a firm that one of the authors is closely familiar with.

[3]The Nominal Group Technique is most thoroughly described in Andre L. Delbecq, Andrew H. Van de Ven, and David H. Gustafson, *Group Techniques for Program Planning: A Guide to Nominal Group and Delphi Processes* (Glenview, IL: Scott, Foresman, 1975).

[4]Kenneth Blanchard and Spencer Johnson, *The One-Minute Manager* (New York: Morrow Publishing, 1982).

[5]Luther Jackson, "Industrial Evolution: McCord Gasket Makes the Leap to the Future," *Detroit Free Press,* September 12, 1988, sec. D, pp. 1, 8.

[6]A good technical introduction to statistical process control is Eugene L. Grant and Richard S. Leavenworth, *Statistical Quality Control* (New York: McGraw-Hill, 1980). A good nontechnical introduction is Rafael Aguayo, *Dr. Deming: The American Who Taught the Japanese About Quality* (New York: Lyle Stuart, Carol Publishing Group, 1990).

[7]Rosabeth Moss Kanter, "All That Is Entrepreneurial Is Not Gold," in the Manager's Journal, *The Wall Street Journal,* July 22, 1985, sec. A, p. 14.

[8]J. Patrick Wright, *On a Clear Day You Can See General Motors: John Z. Delorean's Look Inside the Automotive Giant* (Grosse Pointe, MI: Wright Enterprises, 1979), pp. 98–112.

CHAPTER 8

Building Profit Through Organization and Smooth Work Flow: Step 2—Coordination of Efforts

This chapter explains more about what we mean by coordination and how to plan for it. Coordination of efforts is the second of two key components of the work-flow issue. Once again, ask yourself the same kinds of questions we asked CEOs in our research as a way of visualizing the coordination challenge more clearly in your own setting.

ASSESSING COORDINATION OF EFFORTS IN YOUR COMPANY

▶

Question 8-1: CEO's strategy for coordinating efforts. Do you have a particular way of insuring that activities are coordinated and run smoothly in your firm—so people aren't running off in six different directions at once? If so, what do you do?

For Questions 8-2 through 8-8, use the following instructions. Here are some techniques sometimes used by firms to coordinate their efforts. To what extent do you use each technique? Choose one of the following responses if you want to compare your answers to CEOs we interviewed:

[1] To a very great extent
[2] To a great extent
[3] To some extent
[4] To a small extent
[5] To a slight extent or not at all

Question 8-2: Chain of command. Coordination depends on the chain of command—each level coordinating the level below.

Question 8-3: Employee's own judgments. Coordination depends on individuals using their own judgment about how to handle the problem, even at lower levels.

Question 8-4: CEO's direct involvement. Coordination depends on the CEO's direct involvement in the overall flow of work, even if it means bypassing middle managers.

Question 8-5: Written rules. Coordination depends on consultation of the policy manual, rule book, written job descriptions, or other written guidelines.

Question 8-6: Meetings. Coordination takes place through meetings to share plans and review progress.

Question 8-7: Informal conversation. Coordination takes place through informal conversation.

Question 8-8: Work standards. Coordination takes place by the establishment of clear standards for work—expected levels of performance in quality, productivity, etc.

Question 8-9: Effectiveness of coordination strategy. Considering your answers to questions 8-2 through 8-8, how well do you feel your strategy is working for you?

[1] Extremely well
[2] Very well
[3] Fairly well
[4] Not so well
[5] Not well at all

Question 8-10: Slipping through the cracks. How frequently do you feel things slip through the cracks because no one feels it is their responsibility to take care of the problem?

[1] Very frequently
[2] Frequently
[3] Occasionally
[4] Rarely or seldom
[5] Never

Question 8-11: Unnecessary work delays.   To what extent are there unnecessary (avoidable) work delays among people who work together?

[1] To a very great extent
[2] To a great extent
[3] To some extent
[4] To a small extent
[5] To a slight extent or not at all

Question 8-12: Monitoring systems.   This question may take several minutes to answer but is also one of the most important. Many firms use control systems to track their progress in meeting goals. Feedback control systems compare what is expected to what actually happens. For each of the items (a) through (i), listed below, choose one of these four answers:

[1] No monitoring is done at all.
[2] Standards are set but actual performance is not measured.
[3] Actual performance data are measured and standards are set, but decisions *are not* made on the basis of this information.
[4] A full system appears to be in place. Actual performance data are measured and standards are set, and decisions *are* made on the basis of this information.

HOW DO YOU MONITOR:

a. Quality of products or services you offer?

b. How much is completed, or which projects are to be completed within a given time period (productivity standards)?

c. The costs of making individual products or services (budgets against actual expenditures)?

d. Net profits associated with certain products or services?

e. Net profits for the firm overall?

f. How much material gets used in producing a particular product or service (inventory control)?

g. Level of sales for particular products or services?

h. Performance of individual managers or suprevisors?

i. Performance of nonmanagement employees?

Scoring: Give yourself one point for each [4] you have put down and add these points. (Total possible points = 9.) Save your individual answers as well as the total.

Question 8-13: Day-by-day plans.   On a day-to-day basis, to what extent is the overall work of the firm planned out—that is, what needs to get done is *spelled out* and *prioritized*?

[1] To a very great extent
[2] To a great extent
[3] To some extent
[4] To a small extent
[5] To a slight extent or not at all

Question 8-14: Written job descriptions.   Do you have written job descriptions for employees here?

[1] No
[2] Yes, for some
[3] Yes, for most or all employees

HOW *CEOs* RATE COORDINATION ADEQUACY

Questions 8-9, 8-10, and 8-11 measure coordination effectiveness and help identify the most constructive techniques for coordinating efforts in different types of firms. Table 8–1 shows how firms in our study responded to these questions.

About 28 percent of CEOs feel their coordination strategy works out "extremely well" (question 8-9). Half feel their strategy works out "very well." This question is an excellent predictor of profitability.

About 60 percent of managers and CEOs note that things slip through the cracks at least occasionally. Only 13 percent of CEOs note that things slip through the cracks "frequently."

Top managers other than the CEO say that "some" unnecessary work delays occur (question 8-11) in about 20 percent of the firms. This figure is higher, about 26 percent, at top-performing firms.

TABLE 8–1   Description of Coordination Effectiveness in the Firms We Studied

	ALL FIRMS	TOP PERFORMERS
Coordination Adequacy		
Effectiveness of coordination strategy (question 8-9)[a]	28%	37%
Things slip through cracks (question 8-10)[b]		
Managers' view	59	44
CEO's view	60	53
Unnecessary work delays happen (question 8-11)[c]	20	26

[a]Percentage of CEOs who feel their strategy is working out "extremely well"
[b]Rated between "occasionally" and "very frequently" (codes [1], [2], or [3])
[c]Rated by top management between "some extent" and a "very great extent" (codes [1], [2], or [3])

COORDINATION OF EFFORTS: THE VITAL LINK

How important is effective coordination of efforts? Based on our interviews and many other research studies, it is vital.[1] Coordination is linked strongly with profitability and cash flow. Rather than slowing down growth, well-coordinated efforts and growth go hand in hand. Firms with smoother operation, not surprisingly, report a better public image and also better technical performance, quality, and productivity.

In well-coordinated firms, we find that employee and organization goals are compatible, and employee morale and commitment are high. There is no way to "make" an employee work more effectively. Thus it is quite logical that coordination and human relations are intertwined.

Appropriate allocation of resources among departments and projects is also linked to smooth flow of work. Among firms in our study we also find a link between the firm's ability to obtain needed resources and the coordination of efforts. But we don't necessarily recommend it as the best approach. Some firms may actually be *too* successful at obtaining needed resources—overstaffing or oversupplying inventory to avoid work stoppages or delays. This "slack" or excess in resources may smooth work flow but may also cover up problems and generate more costs. Current management thinking is to steer away from slack as a coordination technique. The less slack, the more precisely each resource must be used. Although mistakes may have a bigger impact, they also show up more easily with less slack.[2]

HOW FIRMS COORDINATE EMPLOYEE EFFORTS

As important as coordination is, few management texts treat techniques or strategies in much detail. Though many authors simply refer to "formal" and "informal" techniques, our research shows it is important to separate these techniques according to *who* is involved with coordinating efforts, *how* efforts are coordinated (i.e., what medium is used), and *what* types of coordinating information are shared.

Table 8–2 provides a summary of how firms in our study coordinate efforts.

Who Coordinates Efforts

Organizations differ regarding who coordinates efforts. (See questions 8-2 through 8-4, and 7-7). Over 60 percent of CEOs rely heavily on employee judgments. Half use the chain of command and slightly fewer use direct CEO involvement. Thirty percent of CEOs say they physically wander around, monitoring field sites and observing events in real time.

Small-firm CEOs are more often directly involved with coordination. With growth, CEOs delegate through the chain of command. Formal orders flow down the chain, and requests or feedback flow back up. All sizes of firms vary in how often employees self-direct and self-coordinate. Self-direction depends mostly on professional training and work experience.

Direct CEO involvement comes in several forms. The CEO of a five-person

TABLE 8–2   **Description of Coordination Strategies in the Firms under Study**

	ALL FIRMS	TOP PERFORMERS	"LARGE" TOP PERFORMERS[a]
Who Coordinates Effort			
Chain of command[b]	52%	59%	64%
CEO's direct involvement[b]	43	63	45
Employees' own judgments[b]	63	63	64
CEO delegates to four or more managers[c]	32	35	na
How Efforts Are Coordinated			
Written guidelines[b]	14	19	27
Meetings[b]	61	67	82
Informal conversation[b]	73	82	64
Written job descriptions[d]	46	36	18
What Information Is Shared			
Day-by-day plans[e]	29	39	na
Work standards[b]	71	78	64
Monitoring systems[f]	61	65	na

[a]The largest one-third of the top-performing firms by employment size. All have more than 65 employees.
[b]Percentage of CEOs who rated use of this strategy "to a great extent"
[c]Percentage of CEOs who delegate to four or more subordinates
[d]Percentage of managers noting use of written job descriptions for "at least some employees"
[e]As rated by managers other than the CEO in our study
[f]Percentage of CEOs noting a full monitoring system for six or more of the nine areas listed.

construction outfit is on each job for its first three days. He knows what inspectors like and dislike. A manufacturer employing 25 walks around and also uses an open-door policy.

Chain of command is found in most top performers, large and small. In one such firm, the chief tool-and-die shop engineer meets weekly with all 17 employees, informing the president of problems and opportunities that emerge. A 300-person automotive supplier relies more on the chain than on CEO involvement. But the CEO still holds weekly staff meetings, in addition to daily interaction. He notes, "I don't dictate. We agree as a staff." Another manufacturer of 100+ employees says, "My job is to wander around the plant." He says he relies more heavily on direct involvement, though a reporting structure is certainly in place. In the past, departments communicated less. He finds his direct involvement offsets this problem.

How Efforts Are Coordinated

Firms also vary in how efforts are coordinated—whether by written guidelines, job descriptions, meetings, or informal conversation (questions 8-5, 8-6, 8-7, and 8-14).

Most commonly used and simplest is informal conversation among employees and managers. About 75 percent of CEOs use conversation to a great extent. About 60 percent rely heavily on meetings—more among top performers, especially the larger ones.

Almost half of managers use written job descriptions for at least some employees. But only 14 percent of CEOs indicate they coordinate effort through policy manuals, rule books, written job descriptions, or other written guidelines.

Top-performing CEOs of firms with over 60 employees more frequently mention meetings than other media. One manufacturing CEO with 70 employees used to coordinate directly. Now he has a formalized structure with scheduling and coordination meetings twice a week. Some have standing committees, both for executives and employees. A 70-person aluminum finisher CEO laments that he has little formal means to coordinate, just one weekly management meeting in which priorities are decided upon. But work flows well and the firm makes a decent profit. It's not clear that he really needs to be doing more than he already is—at least for now.

What Information Is Shared

Finally, coordination techniques vary according to the content of information conveyed (questions 8-8, 8-12, and 8-13). Does the firm coordinate by specifying daily activities, by enforcing work standards, or by more elaborate monitoring systems, measuring if actual performance is up to spec?

About 70 percent of our CEOs (almost 80 percent among top performers) use work standards to coordinate effort. Two-thirds have monitoring systems for at least six of the areas listed in question 8-12.

Twenty-nine percent of all CEOs spell out and prioritize daily activities, compared with 39 percent of top performers—although comments from the latter group make it clear that flexibility in planning is still critical. A construction CEO with 50 employees relies heavily on daily planning. His industry is "unpredictable":

> Each day, top managers meet to schedule the next day—and discuss where we are. We make a plan, a back-up plan, and a second back-up—three flexible plans. I post the schedule and review it with the foreman. Then I coordinate the different departments and monitor them constantly.

He has relied primarily on work standards for three years. Previously, directives ran through one foreman, creating an information bottleneck.

A small-agency CEO likes to rely on specially trained personnel and a monitoring system to coordinate efforts:

> We have a sophisticated system. We use a computer for tracking. Each account executive is responsible for their accounts. I stay on top of things, too.

A 14-person heating and cooling contractor likes his computerized system: "It keeps track of each person's productivity, costs, and sales. As that person sells we keep a constant review."

Coordination Techniques Across Industries

We find no significant differences in *who* coordinates efforts or *how* between various industries. We do find differences in what information directs flow: spelled out plans, standards, or monitoring. Business services typically use a wider variety of monitoring systems than those in other industries—seven altogether, compared with six for construction, and five in both manufacturing and wholesaling. Daily plans are used more in construction and manufacturing than in wholesale and business services ("2.5" compared with "2" on question 8-13).

Construction outfits use work standards to coordinate efforts the most, wholesalers the least. Manufacturers and business services are somewhere in between (1.5, 2.5, and 2.0, respectively, on question 8-8—if you're interested in comparing your answers).

This does not necessarily mean work standards are less appropriate for wholesalers. Wholesalers using work standards actually report *higher* profits than those who do not.

Summary

The most commonly used coordination techniques in small to medium-sized growing firms are informal conversation and work standards, followed by independent employee judgments and meetings. Written guidelines and daily plans are used far less than any of the other techniques. But some rely on them to a great extent.

Coordination by top performers differs in four ways from the norm:

- The CEO is more directly involved.
- People talk more with each other.
- The CEO plans more on a daily basis.
- Top performers rely less on written job descriptions to coordinate efforts.

CHANGE IN COORDINATING EFFORTS

Triggers for Change

Half of CEOs interviewed had changed their coordination approaches since start-up. Fourteen chalk it up to simple growth. But the majority of reasons relate to the need to improve work flow. About a dozen wanted better communication and/or smoother operations. Eleven say the old way was too time consuming and personally stressful. Other CEOs mention that things were dropping through the cracks, or they wanted more control.

Change in management—the CEO, managers, staff—spurred change in over a dozen cases. Geographic expansion, increased competition, mergers, and decreased sales—all requiring shifts in market strategy—can also trigger a change in coordination, as can an interest in increasing efficiency, productivity, and cost control.

Human-relations problems also trigger change. Such problems as sibling rivalry, unhappy employees and managers, and lack of employee commitment brought about change in other firms. Even changes in government regulations triggered change for one.

Changes in Who Coordinates Efforts

When asked if and how CEOs had changed their approach to managing efforts, most typically mentioned that as they grow, they rely more on chain of command and on delegation. At the same time, they have become less directly involved in actual work flow.

Some CEOs are relying more on group consensus and participation than before. A small but profitable wholesaler says: "I was a one-man show before." What triggered his change? "High blood pressure."

Changes in How Efforts Are Coordinated

Our interviews show a strong shift in how larger firms coordinate efforts: more written guidelines, written job descriptions, and meetings. Use of informal conversation dwindles, compared with smaller firms. CEO recollections are consistent: Several report greater use of written policies, handbooks, and meetings now than in the past. And several mention lessening use of intuition and informal conversation.

Changes in Content of Information Conveyed

Larger firms tend to use a wider variety of monitoring systems. When asked to describe changes within their firms over time, CEOs mention an increase in output targets, work standards, and written progress reports.

A successful 80-person contractor describes his shift as triggered by growth, poor communication, and a desire for smoother work flow. "We were forced to develop coordinated procedures. . . . Project managers now are on site to answer questions and assess progress. We have a job-costing system: I know exactly what material and labor costs we have—it's all in the computer."

Size vs. Growth: Are the Patterns of Communication Similar?

In comparing the changes CEOs report due to growth with cross-company comparisons of small and large firms, we find essentially the same patterns. CEOs in larger firms rely less on direct involvement and informal conversation, but more on chain of command, delegation, written guidelines, job descriptions, monitoring systems, and meetings. These shifts are similar to those mentioned by individuals in recollecting changes over time, with one addition: CEOs in growing firms report using work standards more than they did in the past.

BEST WAY TO IMPROVE COORDINATION
OF EFFORTS

To sum up, to improve coordination, the single most important thing you can do is to *establish clear standards for work and monitor how well actual performance meets those standards*. Monitoring systems and work standards contribute not only to coordination but to better cash flow and profits, as well.

CONTINGENCY FACTORS IN ORGANIZATION DESIGN

Certain coordination techniques are more effective in certain types of firms. Employment size, company age, sales-growth rate, degree of environmental uncertainty, industry type, and degree of diversification help determine the right mix of coordination techniques. These are called contingency factors because they can alter the impact that certain designs and techniques have on your firm.[3]

Before reading what we found out with respect to each of these contingency factors, you may want to answer the following questions. Then as we refer to these factors, you will have a better idea how your own company fits in.

ASSESSING CONTINGENCY FACTORS IN YOUR
OWN COMPANY

▶

Question 8-15: Employment size. How many employees work for your firm year round? Count each part-timer as half.

[1] 20 "full-time equivalents" (FTE) or less
[2] 21 to 50 FTEs
[3] 51 to 80 FTEs
[4] More than 80 FTEs

Question 8-16: Rate of sales growth. How fast has your firm grown during the past five years? Compute your firm's annual sales growth as follows:

$$\frac{\text{Sales}_{\text{most recent year}} - \text{Sales}_{\text{5 years ago}}}{\text{Sales}_{\text{most recent year}}} \times 100\%$$

[1] Any decline
[2] 0 to 28% total (not average) growth over five years
[3] 29 to 80% growth
[4] 81 to 150% growth
[5] 151% or more (The fastest we studied grew 1,234% in five years!)

Question 8-17: Age of firm.   How many years ago was your firm founded?

[1] Less than 5 years ago
[2] 5 to 10 years ago
[3] 11 to 20 years ago
[4] 21 to 38 years ago
[5] 39 years or more ago

Question 8-18: Industry type.   Which industry are you in? (We based our sort on the Standard Industrial Classification [SIC] Code available at most public libraries).

[1] Construction
[2] Manufacturing
[3] Wholesale
[4] Business services
[5] Other

Question 8-19: Diversification.   How would you describe your firm?

[1] Primarily a one-product or -service firm
[2] Carries a number of related products or services
[3] Diversified, with offerings requiring varied skills, information, equipment, and technology

Twenty-two percent of the CEOs describe their firms as single-product firms; 42 percent as offering related products; and 35 percent as diversified.

Question 8-20: Predictability.   Is it easy to predict what will happen six months to a year from now in your industry?

[1] To a very great extent (high predictability)
[2] To a great extent
[3] To a moderate extent
[4] Slightly or not at all (low predictability)

COORDINATION IN DIFFERENT TYPES OF FIRMS

Not surprisingly, larger and older firms tend to have better cash flow. More diversified firms and those less able to predict industry trends are likely to have more coordination problems. But the real significance of age, size, and so forth is as *contingencies*—that is, in the way they alter the relationship between particular coordination techniques and organizational effectiveness. In this section, we note the most appropriate use of each coordination technique or practice based on our data, taking these contingencies into account.[4]

Chain of command helps—especially in small and in older firms.
Chain of command is linked with better coordination for smaller firms, (under 20 employees) and with better profits and cash flow in firms older than 40 years. In no case does chain of command prove detrimental.

Employee judgments—useful in smaller, younger firms.
Using employee judgments to coordinate efforts is weakly linked with coordination adequacy, in general. But smaller and younger firms use it to good effect. And in no case is it harmful.

CEO direct involvement can help or not, depending on the type of firm.
In firms with high uncertainty, and more weakly among manufacturers, CEO direct involvement actually hurts profits and cash flow. The reverse is true in relatively predictable environments and in single-product firms. Thus, when the firm is especially complex, the CEO needs to delegate.

One can delegate to too many people.
CEOs who delegate to *many* managers have less adequate coordination than those delegating to a small number, especially in slow-growing, small, or single-product firms. It may be necessary in large conglomerates; but in small-to-medium companies, titles apparently are not cheap!

Written guidelines are rarely worthwhile.
Written guidelines are not particularly helpful in any subgroup we looked at. They are linked to poorer cash flow in younger firms (5–10 years of age). They may simply be unneeded, expensive, time-consuming recording devices of what the firm is doing. The only possible exception is in the firm that has had slow-to-moderate employment growth. In that instance, the use of written guidelines is positively linked to cash flow.

Job descriptions—a potential liability.
Job descriptions are negatively linked to both coordination and liquidity among medium-to-large and slow-growth firms (more than 80 employees or annual sales growth of 0 to 5 percent).

They introduce harmful inflexibility, and an excuse to avoid cross-training or to pick up slack in different work areas. They breed the saying, "That's not in my job description."

Meetings as problem solver or time waster—it depends.
Meetings among staff to coordinate efforts are likely to help profits and cash flow among construction firms. In the wholesale industry, meetings are actually linked to lower profits.

Meetings also link with better coordination in larger firms. Why the difference? Meetings can provide an unparalleled forum for bringing more brains together to identify and solve problems and come up with new ideas. They are also valuable if work requires close teamwork. But they are enormous time wasters if merely used to pass along directions and other information. You need to reflect on your own firm's needs to consider whether problems are complex enough or team effort intricate enough to select this labor-intensive and costly but creative approach.

Informal conversation: Don't drop it as you grow.   Our results support the adage, "Talk is cheap." Larger firms are *less* likely to rely on informal conversation. Yet, manufacturers and larger firms relying *more* on informal conversation have better coordination of effort and even better cash positions. In short, don't assume that the prevalent approach is necessarily the best.

Monitoring systems—a real winner.   We already saw that across all our firms, the use of monitoring systems benefits the firm. Monitoring of quality, costs, profits, and performance (both of management and nonmanagement) are positively linked with effective coordination for all companies. The more criteria are monitored, the better coordination is likely to be, especially in single-product firms, manufacturers, and younger outfits (under 10 years of age).

Daily plans: Use them in unpredictable settings.   Whether daily planning is effective depends on the predictability of events surrounding the firm. Though a costly waste where work is highly predictable, a top-performing CEO in a highly unpredictable environment uses daily planning religiously to achieve coordination of efforts.

Work standards are almost always a good idea.   As we mentioned before, setting work standards links strongly to coordination, profits, and liquidity for all companies studied. In smaller firms, work standards link especially well to coordination. Firms between 5 and 20 years old and those in unpredictable environments also achieve better profitability with work standards.

Some strategies are more widely applicable than others. You won't go too wrong using the chain of command, employee judgments, informal conversation, work standards or monitoring systems, regardless of your business. On the other hand, for some firms there may be such a thing as too many meetings, too much CEO direct involvement (or excessive delegation), too many written guidelines or too detailed a job description, depending upon the contingency factors noted above. The wrong choice may have a negative impact on not only work flow but profits and cash flow, too. One can find all approaches used, however—even among top performers. Each firm needs to sort out the best mix of approaches for itself.

TWO CASE HISTORIES

We have uncovered numerous tactics in these two work-flow chapters. Let's look at two concrete cases: a manufacturer and a business-services firm. Each firm is successful, growing, profitable. We keep actual names confidential, but the cases are real. Each firm's CEO developed a unique work flow approach.

XYZ Auto Parts

XYZ is a high-tech supplier of precision automotive parts. XYZ grew sixfold in just six years, from $2 million to over $12 million, with over 100 employees. Its recent net ROS averaged 16 percent, and its CEO rated the firm as having significant liquidity. It faces a very unpredictable and very competitive environment, in which price often threatens to squeeze out quality.

XYZ has a manufacturing manager, engineering manager, sales manager, controller, and purchasing manager. Its CEO talked about transition troubles when he grew past 40 employees:

> People didn't know each other. There was a lot of competition among employees. The problem had to be dealt with. With a paper trail, I set up a system of responsibility based on departments. I try to eliminate individual stardom. I have committees to investigate and make recommendations about areas from production to morale.

He feels his strategy works well. "Some [employees] . . . expected too much . . . [from this new system]. It took three years to get fantastic results. It was hard work."

Being only moderately involved in direct work flow, he relies a lot on employee judgments. Because of his committee structure, he is less dependent on chain of command. Clear standards of work are set and incorporated into formal monitoring systems for costs, profits, sales, quality, quantity, and performance. Though extensive monitoring and *paper trails*—written documentation of decisions and activities—are used for feedback, policy manuals themselves are almost nonexistent. Instead, focused meetings and informal conversations are used. Everyone in the firm is involved with day-to-day shop-floor decisions, including a joint role in defining their jobs. However, strategic decisions, such as setting performance standards and output goals, are made by the CEO and top managers alone. Managers there feel they have the right amount of authority to get the job done.

Other top managers concur with this approach, but some lament the shortage of trained talent. This may reflect the highly sophisticated training required and small recruiting pool. It is a common enough complaint among high-growth firms. To compensate, a number of training programs exist ad hoc, providing extensive guidance. Positive and negative feedback on performance is amply supplied.

XYZ's top managers feel committee-style management has given people more latitude and input. They also emphasize the key role of automation in tracking results.

LMN Tool-and-Die Company

LMN Machine Tool Company, a 50-year-old top performer with 200 employees, operates quite effectively without a lot of written rules and policies. In fact, it uses fewer rules now than when it was much smaller. Growing 40 percent, to $18 million, during six years in the mid 1980s, it averaged a 12–13 percent pretax net return on sales, proving that top performers don't have to be young. Similar to XYZ in that it operates in unpredictable, competitive waters, by contrast its customers place quality concerns solidly above cost.

Eight people report to the CEO: plant vice-president, finance vice-president, sales manager, marketing manager, plant operations manager, and three salesmen. There is very little overlap among top-management jobs. Geographic dispersion usually prevents the CEO from directly observing plant activity from corporate headquarters. So he stays in frequent phone and computer contact, making site visits once a month. He also holds a series of "goal vs. actual" meetings, bringing in someone else from the main office to increase contact between corporate and field offices. At LMN, chain of command, meetings, informal conversations, and standards—including extensively developed monitoring systems—are used to coordinate efforts.

Managers handle strategic decisions themselves, going to the CEO only for major exceptions to overall policy. Standards are more clearly defined, with more meetings than in the past. The CEO was very articulate about reasons for this shift: Before employees were not as happy and productive as they could be. A more frank and open climate was needed. Management and employees like their meetings. They have become more productive and produce higher quality, despite minimal feedback, and the fact that performance is not reviewed on a scheduled basis.

One of the managers notes: "Nothing is cut and dried. Every issue is looked at again. A lot of positive changes are taking place, things that . . . [make] day to day working pleasurable. . . . [but] there are two groups of employees: those who are older and don't want to change and those who are new and very trusting." Another manager on the current open style: "Communications are very important. I don't tell people, 'Here is your job, do it.' I tell them *why* they have been assigned a job. They feel better about their jobs this way and have a lot fewer questions."

WALKING AROUND: A COORDINATION TOOL AT JPI

J. P. Industries (JPI), in spite of its growth, retained many informal coordinating approaches we've described. "Walking around the plant" is of interest because of unique problems CEOs begin to face when using this technique. Co-author Dr. Psarouthakis describes how he could "wander," yet avoid bypassing his managers and undermine his chain of command:

"In addition to formal meetings and committees, I spent a considerable amount of time walking around the plants, talking casually with employees. However I learned early on how easy it is for comments of a CEO to be taken as orders or directives. One time, when I was on one of my plant 'walks,' I asked why a particular machine was in one corner of the room, rather than in another. Satisfied by the response the employee gave me, I moved on to another area of the plant. About a month later, I happened to return to the same plant, only to find that the machine had been moved to the new spot I had pointed to in my query. Apparently, the mere questioning about the particular issue was misinterpreted and action was taken.

"I learned from this experience to make sure employees knew when I was only asking a question, and that I did not wish them to take action unless they were later asked to do so by their own supervisor. In this way I could wander without creating ambiguity and disruption in the chain of command. I was very careful to maintain the chain when it came to executing orders. This is a critical component in making employee-input and -involvement programs effective. Otherwise, people go off in multiple directions and lose focus.''

SOME GUIDELINES FOR BETTER COORDINATION OF EFFORTS

Designing the "best way" to coordinate effort may be one of the hardest exercises the CEO of a fast-growth company faces. Growth causes conflicting pressures to adopt a more bureaucratic approach with less informal discussion, when the exact opposite need is manifested. Group problem-solving techniques are increasingly being introduced to handle greater complexity and to avoid the stifling tendency created by bureaucracy. This is such an important theme, we return to it again in Chapter 13 to see how such approaches have been introduced to improve quality in the organization. For now, please consider the following suggestions in devising and revising your coordination techniques.

1. Establish work standards and set up monitoring systems to compare actual performance with goals. Work standards alone are useful almost everywhere. Even better are systems to monitor how closely you are meeting those standards. Any company, large or small, can do this efficiently with computers. Search for "canned" software that caters to your industry.

2. Use meetings and teams while maintaining control. Most successful large firms in our study grew toward increasing use of meetings to (A) review actual output versus the objectives, and (B) jointly problem solve on issues ranging from productivity to morale. Meetings are usually a good way to help enforce work standards, along with a lot of informal conversation, even in larger firms.

3. Be careful what you delegate and to whom. Employee involvement is not the same as authority abdication. Delegating too much is a recurring nightmare. XYZ corporation is a good role model: Decisions about daily operations are extensively shared in a committee that reports to the CEO. But the CEO makes performance-standards and direction-setting decisions, looking for top management concurrence. The CEO must maintain this control. In smaller firms, direct observation of work and more formal monitoring seem to work equally well, though CEOs notice that a monitoring system frees up a lot of their time for other things.

4. Review your written policies. By law, personnel departments are increasingly required to document policies to protect themselves against wrongful discharge suits and discrimination suits. It would be foolhardy to suggest eliminating policy manuals altogether. However, few firms actually rely on these written guidelines to coordinate work. They coordinate "people to people," not "people to paper."

5. Watch your written job descriptions. Growing firms should especially be wary of written job descriptions. Worse than ineffectual, their presence can foster an attitude of "it's not in my job description," allowing work to slip through cracks. Even large firms, such as JPI, work hard to eliminate job classification systems from outmoded labor contracts because they are a serious limiter to innovative programs. If you're planning written job descriptions, think twice.

NOTES

[1]Robert A. Cooke and Denise M. Rousseau, "Problems of Complex Systems: A Model of System Problem Solving Applied to Schools," *Educational Administration Quarterly,* 17 (1981), 15–41. B. B. Longest, "Relationships Between Coordination, Efficiency, and Quality of Care in Hospitals," *Hospital Administration,* 19 (1974), 65–86. W. H. Money, D. P. Gilfillan, and R. Duncan, "A Comparative Study of Multi-unit Health Care Organizations," in *Organizational Research in Hospitals,* eds. S. M. Shortell and M. Brown (Chicago: Blue Cross Association, 1976). Robert I. Sutton and Larry H. Ford, "Problem-Solving Adequacy in Hospital Subunits," *Human Relations,* 35 (1982), 675–701.

[2]Jay Galbraith, *Organization Design* (Reading, MA: Addison-Wesley, 1979). Galbraith presents three alternatives to slack in coordinating efforts: creation of self-contained tasks, investment in vertical-information systems, and creation of lateral relations. Zero-based inventory models and continuous inventory flow also urge a reduction in slack as a work-flow strategy. See for instance: Michael Umble and Mokshagundam L. Srikanth, *Synchronous Manufacturing: Principles for World-Class Excellence,* (Cincinnati, OH: South-Western Publishing Co., 1990).

[3]Almost all introductory management texts discuss contingency theory. See for instance, John R. Schermerhorn, Jr., James G. Hunt, and Richard N. Osborn, *Managing Organizational Behavior,* 4th ed. (New York: John Wiley & Sons, 1991), pp. 8, 315–35. One of the best-known works on the topic was done by Paul R. Lawrence and Jay W. Lorsch, *Organization and Environment* (Boston: Graduate School of Business Administration, Harvard University, 1967).

[4]See Lorraine Uhlaner Hendrickson, "Size, Growth, or Uncertainty: What Matters in Design of the Firm?" *Proceedings of 1990 International Council for Small Business Conference,* Washington, DC, June 7–10, 1990.

CHAPTER 9

Acquiring Personnel, Capital, and Supplies

Next we turn to resource acquisition. This chapter explains more about what we mean by resource acquisition and how to plan for it. As in previous chapters, we begin with a survey drawn from our study. By answering the following questions, you can begin to visualize resource acquisition more clearly in your own company setting.

ASSESSING YOUR RESOURCE ACQUISITION STRATEGY

Ask yourself and key managers the following questions.

Questions 9-1 through 9-6: Ability to obtain resources. Use the following choices to compare your firm's responses to those in our study for questions 9-1 through 9-6:

[1] To a very great extent
[2] To a great extent
[3] To some extent
[4] To a small extent
[5] To a slight extent or not at all

TO WHAT EXTENT IS YOUR FIRM ABLE TO OBTAIN
EACH OF THE FOLLOWING IN ORDER
TO OPERATE EFFECTIVELY

Question 9-1: Managers and supervisors

Question 9-2: High-quality nonmanagement people, especially in the technical areas

Question 9-3: The right supplies, equipment, and materials

Question 9-4: Subcontractor services

Question 9-5: Capital

Question 9-6: Information about products, services, competition, government requirements, or other information from outside the firm

Question 9-7: CEO's strategy for recruiting managers.   Do you have a particular way of finding your *key people:* managers and/or technical personnel (i.e., do you always build from within? Where do you look if you have to go outside?)

Question 9-8: Effectiveness of recruitment strategy.   How well do you feel your way of finding key people is working out for you?

[1] Extremely well
[2] Very well
[3] Fairly well
[4] Not so well
[5] Very poorly

Question 9-9: Adequacy of outside information—CEO.   How adequate is the information you are able to obtain from sources *outside* the firm (such as new technical developments in your industry, information about competitors, suppliers, vendors)?

[1] Extremely adequate
[2] Very adequate
[3] Fairly adequate
[4] Not so adequate
[5] Not adequate at all

These questions measure your ability to acquire needed resources. Table 9–1 provides a summary of results for all firms in our study and comparisons of top performers and other firms.

Among these established firms, obtaining capital, supplies, and even outside information is far less of a problem than recruiting both management and nonmanagement staff. For this reason, although we cover all aspects of resource acquisition briefly, we place special emphasis here on recruitment. Table 9–1 shows a very similar pattern among top performers and the remaining firms, with two possible exceptions: Fewer top-performing CEOs complain of problems with their recruitment strategy (question 9-8), and slightly fewer report problems with obtaining capital and outside information.

TABLE 9-1 Comparison of Top Performers and Remaining Firms on Resource Acquisition Effectiveness

	ALL FIRMS	TOP PERFORMERS	REMAINING FIRMS
	$n = 165^a$	$n = 28^a$	$n = 137^a$
Ability to Acquire:[b]			
Managers and supervisors	36%	32%	37%
Nonmanagement people	33	35	32
The right supplies	88	91	88
Subcontractor services	73	74	72
Capital	71	87	69
Information	65	70	64
Adequacy of outside information (CEO's view)[c]	56	64	54
Effectiveness of recruitment strategy[d]	35	50	32

[a]Actual size varies, depending on missing data.
[b]On questions 9-1 through 9-6, [2] or better—"great extent" or "very great extent."
[c]Rated [2] or better, "very or extremely adequate" on question 9-9.
[d]Rated [2] or better—"very well" or "extremely well," as rated by the CEO, on question 9-8.

WHAT IS RESOURCE ACQUISITION AND ITS ROLE IN SUCCESS?

Organizations transform *inputs* into *outputs*—finished goods or services. Inputs include personnel, material, capital, and information. Their importance varies with the type of firm. In manufacturing and wholesaling, the availability and quality of suppliers play significant roles. In some service firms, where the major investments may be computers and ideas, the supply problem is trivial but successful recruiting is paramount. In very young firms, capital is often the key shortage, along with problems in recruiting new managers.[1]

During the life of the firm, challenges to obtain different inputs will vary. Working-capital problems do diminish with size, but management recruiting problems and supplier problems tend to increase. For this reason, we focus most attention in this chapter on recruitment strategies. Materials that provide guidance on obtaining both debt and equity financing are plentiful.[2]

Failure to find needed resources means a firm has less latitude, resulting in difficulty coping with smooth work flow, human relations, and resource allocation. However, this shortage of resources does not necessarily hurt profits or cash flow— nor public image, technical performance, or quality.

In fact the only resource linked to profits is capital. But the lagged effect we find in our study suggests that, if anything, profits *provide* capital availability, rather than the reverse. And what profits do for capital, sales growth does for recruitment. The CEO of a highly profitable and rapidly growing automotive-supply firm describes how growth helps his ability to get needed talent:

> I reach out to people I know. I look for responsible dedicated people who want the same things I want. Lately I have been hiring from within. In the past I had to hire from the outside. Growth makes it easier to find talent inside the company. I identify the firm's needs a few years ahead of time in order to train managers.

While staff is important, a well-run organization can compensate for staff shortages in various ways. Consider the case of an Italian wine importer in the Netherlands who lost his chief financial officer. When he couldn't find a suitable replacement, he simply took up the slack by working more hours himself. Nevertheless, the CEO now has more limited time to consider other components of his business.

In sum, although resource acquisition poses a challenge, resourceful management practices can often compensate for deficiencies, at least in the short term. Remember also that the Japanese have made a virtue of "deficiency," forcing suppliers to deliver no more than is needed and just in time. The real challenge in managing this area is not only to acquire enough of everything but to avoid obtaining too much.

HOW FIRMS TYPICALLY ACQUIRE KEY PERSONNEL

Recruitment is often a "nail-biter" for growing firms. We interviewed CEOs extensively about strategies to keep key spots filled. Most use a mixed strategy of both promoting from within plus hiring from outside. Table 9–2 summarizes CEO strategies.

The smallest firms sometimes rely on family members or co-owners for top-management slots. Second only to promoting from within as a source of recruits is the tactic of networking. Business acquaintances—including customers, competitors, bankers, CPAs, members of boards, vendors, and consultants—are tapped. The use of vendors is especially interesting. They call on many competing companies in the same industry and get to know everyone on their route. Bad news and opportunity both travel quickly. Disgruntled but talented employees often make connections this way.

Advertising, be it local classifieds or national trade publications, is mentioned by only 15 percent of the CEOs we interviewed. Recruitment agencies are mentioned only 12 percent of the time. About the same proportion welcome walk-ins. About 7 percent of CEOs recruit on college campuses for management positions.

Why aren't recruitment agencies used more? For some, agencies have backfired badly. Many recruits brought in to one firm with the help of executive-search firms came with very different outlooks, corporate cultures, and expectations, influenced by previous work in much larger firms. The new recruits were more

TABLE 9–2   Strategies Presidents Reported Using to Find Top Managers

	n	%[a]
From Family/Within:		
Look within their firms	82	49
Top management are owners	6	4
From family	14	8
Subtotal:	102	61%
From Networking:		
Others in the business	14	8
Acquaintances in general	13	8
Competitors	5	3
Customers	2	1
Consultants	2	1
Banks, CPAs	2	1
Board of directors	1	1
Vendors/suppliers	1	1
Subtotal:	40	24%
From Advertising:		
Ads, nonspecific	17	10
Ads in local papers	6	4
Ads in trade magazines	1	1
Ads in national other than trade	1	1
Subtotal:	25	16%
From Recruitment Agencies:		
Government-run agencies	2	1
Local employment agency	4	2
Executive search firm	3	2
Other agents, nonspecific	11	7
Subtotal:	20	12%
Miscellaneous:		
Recruit on college campuses	11	7
Outside, generally	18	11
Walk-ins	11	7
Grapevine/employees	5	3
Personnel department	1	1
Unions	1	1
Subtotal:	47	30%

Sample size = 168

[a]Adds up to more than 100 percent because many firms use multiple strategies for finding managers.

"career-oriented," much less loyal, and much more political than the veterans from the firm's start-up. A clash soon developed as a result of these two very different styles. The senior vice-president, long with the firm, describes this tension:

> Our pending merger, as well as recent organization change, has contributed to tension in the firm. We grew very fast in the past and then hit a plateau. We brought in senior management from other firms with a more mature structure. A conflict has emerged between old and new managers—the new managers bringing in more traditional approaches and more sharpened political skills. In the past two years, we have experienced employee morale problems [and] productivity difficulties [while] making the new professional step.

The follow-up here is very sad. After the merger, the perennial mainstay client bolted. A majority of staff had to be laid off. One can't blame the loss of clientele on recruiting alone. But the politics and divisiveness brought on by the dual culture didn't help.

CHANGE IN RECRUITMENT STRATEGY

Three-fourths of our firms report using the same recruitment strategy that they always have. Most likely this reflects a continuation of some, but a shedding of other, less workable approaches. Having run businesses ourselves, it's hard to imagine that at least some experimenting among strategies didn't take place. The most common reasons for change include the need to professionalize and upgrade management, company growth in size, response to a distrustful climate and the maturing of management staff. The shifts go in two directions: Some CEOs recruit more outside, others more from the inside. Of those shifting to the outside, some had no top managers before and thus had to look outside the firm. Others mention a move away from family hiring. Of moves to internal promotion, the strategies dropped include advertising, networking with competitors, employment agencies, and networking among friends.

WHICH RESOURCE ACQUISITION STRATEGIES
ARE BETTER?

Many of our CEOs were vocal about their preferences and dislikes for one recruitment strategy or another. Most popular is promoting from within. Only 7 percent of those providing input about this complain about this approach. But not everyone is completely satisfied. One CEO critiques his current inside hiring strategy:

> When hiring from outside, it is difficult to reorient. When hiring from inside, you often don't get fresh ideas. Candidates inside the company tend to be young. It is difficult to get a good balance of maturity and experience among managers.

A top-performing kitchen and bath wholesaler grew from $4 million to $13 million in five years, realizing a pretax net of 8 percent return on sales (ROS). He echoes concerns, however, about the need for fresh ideas when sticking to the inside approach:

> We've always promoted from within, but I will probably change to outside input. . . . I think it's time to get some fresh ideas. When you promote from within, they only do things your way.

This conflict is echoed by a small remodeler of 20 employees, that grew from $500 thousand to $1.3 million over six years, averaging a 7.5 percent pretax net ROS. He expresses intense ambivalence about the best way to fill top spots:

> I brought people up through the ranks, but I can't do it anymore. It takes too long. On the other hand, I'm afraid to get top managers from the outside. Our firm is in a small town. I'm worried about information leaking to competitors. I hired a friend three years ago from the outside, but I'm afraid to hire any more.

This said, the CEO notes that he still hires applicants from the local tech center.

Relationship Between Recruiting Strategy and Growth/Profits

Preferences aside, which recruitment strategies work better? Table 9–3 compares the recruitment strategies of top performers with the rest of the pack. Two-thirds of the top performers promote from within, compared with slightly less than half of remaining firms. Top performers rely less on advertising, except for those in high-tech industries. In all other categories, use is about the same.

TABLE 9–3 Comparison of Selected Strategies for Management Recruitment Between Top Performing Firms and Remaining Firms

	TOP PERFORMERS	REMAINING FIRMS
	%[a]	%[a]
Promote from within	68	47
Managers are family members	7	11
Networking with friends and acquaintances	18	18
Advertising	14	23
Agencies	11	14
College campus recruiting	7	4
Walk-ins	11	12

[a]Due to multiple responses, and other categories which have been omitted, the totals do not add up to 100 percent.

PROMOTING FROM WITHIN: ADVANCE PREPARATION

Promoting from within is more successful when planned in advance. This topic was discussed in The President's Forum, a roundtable of CEOs sponsored by Eastern Michigan University's Center for Entrepreneurship. CEOs there underscored the importance of hiring top-flight people even for junior positions. The group cited two common errors: Hiring for the short term; and keeping individuals long after they prove incapable of individual growth.

The field of human-resource management also offers useful guidance. Simple forecasting techniques, referred to as *human-resource forecasting,* can be used to project types of personnel needed over a coming period, just as with cash or inventory.[3] This is done, though less formally, by some CEOs we interviewed. Through such forecasting one can spot deficiencies early. Individual career paths can be designed for longer-term employees. New recruits can be hired and others trained for more senior positions. On-site seminars and courses at the community college or local university can help prepare future junior executives. For targeted employees, job rotation is also a valuable training tool. Recruiting for key personnel can be a time-consuming frustrating activity. Firms planning ahead are likely to have a pool of talent when they really need it.

College recruiting combines well with internal promotion. For many CEOs we spoke with, college recruiting works well with a strategy of promoting from within. College graduates usually lack job experience, but are often willing to start at lower wages than more experienced recruits. A top graduate can quickly pick up needed skills on the job and bring in fresh ideas. They are also apt to have fewer preset notions than someone brought in from another firm. Thus, clashes based on experiences with contrasting corporate environments are minimized. Whether they prove to be valuable long-term investments probably depends on the complexity of your business and your resources to train them.

OTHER MANAGEMENT PRACTICES ASSOCIATED
WITH BETTER RECRUITMENT

Our interview data suggest that certain management practices may make the firm more or less appealing to a top-management recruit. For instance, firms basing incentives on seniority and salary rather than on performance are able to recruit technical personnel more easily. Along similar lines, CEOs who place a high value on quality also have an easier time recruiting nonmanagement personnel. But firms that monitor productivity have more trouble recruiting than those that don't. You figure it out: Do recruits prefer firms that let them lounge about? Perhaps. Or maybe people are attracted more to a philosophy of craftsmanship than to number crunching. Recall that in Chapter 6 we reported on a trend among CEOs themselves consistent with this latter argument.

Recruits are also attracted to firms with clear standards, a monitoring system for costs, and an emphasis on profits. These findings probably support your own experience: Top-flight managerial applicants investigate well before agreeing to join. Poorly organized operations are less attractive to most prospects. Of course, some are attracted by the sheer challenge of a turnaround.

Though not always helpful for coordinating efforts, as we saw in Chapter 8, written job descriptions are an aid in the hiring of specialized personnel. Firms in which employee roles are clearer also have an easier time filling nonmanagement positions. Perhaps applicants can zero in on these jobs more quickly. Or this clarity may help managers sift more quickly through the applicant materials, knowing what they are looking for.

One final tidbit: Firms with office managers have an easier time recruiting. No doubt the office manager provides a means for screening incoming leads, whether solicited or not. Or perhaps the office manager is a one-person grapevine.

RESOURCE ACQUISITION STRATEGIES AT JPI

J. P. Industries (JPI) developed its own strategies for obtaining needed resources, including recruitment of personnel, capital, and outside information. Although JPI had become a large company, many strategies and rationales for those strategies are still quite similar to those of the CEOs in our study.

What JPI Looked For

JPI had a recruitment strategy with two components: filling immediate needs; and filling anticipated long-term needs. As with many successful firms in our study, JPI promoted from within whenever possible. As part of their job responsibilities, supervisors and managers were routinely asked to identify internal people with promotion potential, so that when a need arose, information was readily available. If a function was weakly managed, the firm would start looking for a stronger person, but kept the weaker person in the slot until a replacement was found.

In the hiring and promotion processes, managerial or people skills were heavily emphasized. A one-page list of criteria was developed, including oral and written communication, ability to relate to others, ability to work as part of a team, sense of responsibility, and willingness and ability to take initiative. Formal personnel-selection test techniques were not used. Rather, many of the characteristics that such tests identified were determined, instead, through conversation and observation of on-the-job behavior. Outside interests and activities were also considered, such as hobbies and community activities.

Dr. Psarouthakis describes how he selected key managers for JPI: "I preferred to hire and promote innovators rather than people I would label as 'traditionalists.' I would observe the reactions of people during daily corporate activities—in meetings and conversations with me and others. When a corporate manual was issued that attempted to define a new culture for JPI, the innovators tended to react more favorably and openly to the new directions. In order to determine who has initiative, it is vital to allow free discussion. Note, though, that there is also a danger of innovating too much. There are times for action and the setting of clear direction at the top. Overall, a balance needs to be maintained, providing, on the one hand, enough freedom so that initiative can be identified and fostered and, on the other, a time for clear direction and focus.''

Why JPI Preferred Hiring from Inside

Because observation was important in measuring management talent at JPI, internal candidates were considered first.[4] It often takes six months to figure out if someone is working out in a particular job. In this amount of time, many small companies can be killed by incompetence. By promoting from within you have the luxury of observing them in a junior role first.

Even though much of JPI's growth was through acquisition of poorly performing companies, the JPI managers still found that they could locate good people who were already working in each of the companies JPI acquired. The exceptions were the positions of general manager and controller, which were almost always filled from outside the newly acquired division. Even these recruits, however, were generally obtained from employees in other divisions. Vacancies that could not be filled from the inside were typically filled by means of networking or through placement consultants.

Networking

John Psarouthakis describes his own approach to networking:

''I devote a great deal of my time to networking with colleagues in my industry, in the business world, and in the academic communities. I find that my volunteer activities not only help me to keep informed of what is going on in the outside world but also help in recruiting talent. To stay current, I serve on various university advisory committees and keep up informally with professors at many different institutions. Sometimes I attend symposia or am asked to speak, where I learn from others. These are also good ways to obtain recruitment leads. I have gotten leads from people I know in the same industry, and peers in other or similar companies have provided recruitment leads. Professional associations and their related conferences are also useful contact spots. In the past, when an internal candidate cannot be found, I tend to consider candidates brought in via networking more seriously than those with equal credentials but who are unknown to my circle of acquaintances. This way I can get a report from a known source, who has actually observed the applicant at work.''

Use of Placement Consultants

JPI found placement consultants very helpful in seeking recruits for positions requiring quantitative skills. Positions in manufacturing, engineering, and accounting were at times filled in this manner. Placement consultants were used less often for positions requiring the types of management or people skills described earlier. For the same kinds of reasons, JPI management rarely used advertising, because it generally failed to provide applicants who could be observed in their prior work environment by a credible source.

When to Let Go

One management practice that reinforced the recruitment practice was the maintenance of a high-quality pool of employees within the firm. As observed by many other CEOs of growing firms, some employees do not grow with the firm. Regarding those employees, JPI managers were asked to consider whether the employee had reached his or her limits and whether or not the company had given that employee adequate opportunity for growth. Often, more limited responsibilities would be assigned. It usually wasn't necessary to fire such employees. They would eventually leave of their own volition. The same kind of issue also arose with consulting firms with which JPI contracted. When it became apparent that JPI outgrew what a particular legal or accounting firm could offer, JPI management phased the firm out gradually—giving it explanation and notice well in advance, so that it would not be surprised when it had lost the account.

Strategies for Obtaining Capital at JPI

JPI used a combination of equity and debt in major acquisitions. Since banks are usually more conservative than investors, if the bank felt the asking price for a particular company was too high, we accepted this as useful feedback. Each time JPI sought additional funds, the need was carefully scrutinized. Did the firm really need more capital at that time or should it slow down its growth instead? In the ten years before its sale to British conglomerate T&N plc, JPI raised a lot of equity on the public stock exchanges, first on NASDAQ and then on the New York Stock Exchange. Timing is critical in the decision to go public. Investors change tastes. With emphasis on automobile-related parts, the appeal of JPI's stock to the public was tied closely to ups and downs in the automobile industry, regardless of JPI's specific performance. But even when certain industries are unattractive to the public stock investor one can still often find large private investors.

Strategies for Obtaining Outside
Technical Information

Networking was very important, also, in obtaining updated information in the manufacturing area and research and development. Salespeople, with the latest brochures and product descriptions, provided a lot of information about what was new.

Psarouthakis describes other ways in which technical information was obtained at JPI:

"While CEO, I associated with many university and independent research centers. For instance, I learned about new technical innovations affecting my industry, when I was serving on the board of directors for the Industrial Technology Institute, based in Ann Arbor, Michigan.

"We also encouraged our employees, as well, to belong to outside groups. In more technical fields, attendance at relevant conferences is also informative. At JPI, employees from both the marketing and engineering areas attended conferences regularly.

"Sometimes, however, detailed outside information can be overemphasized. When I first started the company, I didn't need to do expensive or sophisticated market research. In determining whether or not to acquire JPI's first stamping plant, we knew that the plant did only a few million dollars in revenues in a multibillion-dollar market. We didn't pin down the exact market share that we could obtain. But we did a lot of legwork, talking to potential customers who could be served by the plant, to determine their real needs and what uniqueness we could offer.

"Competitor information can be challenging to get. Of course it is illegal to spy, but you can often deduce a lot about what your competitor is thinking and doing by that firm's reaction to your own program. Gathering customer reaction to the competition's products and programs is also quite useful. Other ways that you can learn about your competitors are by analyzing product brochures and their annual reports."

GUIDELINES IN ACQUIRING RESOURCES

Resource acquisition involves a firm's ability to obtain people, capital, supplies, services, and information it needs to operate smoothly. Although firms often get by with less, too little slack can generate too much work overload and stress. Our interviews with CEOs and personal experience point to a number of avenues through which to acquire resources. However, strategies may have to change over time. Some firms grow too quickly to groom personnel from the inside. Others may need to recruit from the outside, anyway, to get fresh ideas and approaches. Resource acquisition, especially recruitment, is easier when:

- A positive climate exists among employees
- Quality is emphasized
- Work is more predictable
- Roles are clearer, more specialized, and even written into job descriptions
- Standards are set and followed
- Seniority is rewarded among nonmanagement personnel

Promoting from within is not only a strongly favored avenue—it works better, too. Entry-level recruiting on college campuses works out well in combination with internal promotion. On the other hand, recruitment agencies and advertising can be troublesome, especially for locating nontechnical recruits.

CONCLUSION

Although frustrating, recruiting does not have direct impact on profitability. But failure to recruit can slow the growth of the firm. Successful recruiting certainly eases the CEO's task and improves the flow of operations. The relationship between recruitment and work flow goes both ways. Potential candidates are attracted to a firm with clear work standards and work roles. In turn, firms that are able to recruit key personnel report better coordination of effort and smoother flow of work.

Morale is another two-way street. Firms with a positive team climate report an easier time filling vacancies. And firms more able to recruit tend to report better morale.

Management specialists are beginning to look more intensely at the pitfalls of *too* much slack, which can mask defects in operations. Appropriate resource acquisition involves a balance that avoids getting either too much *or* too little of what is needed.

NOTES

[1]Guvenc G. Alpander, Kent D. Carter, and Roderick A. Forsgren, "Managerial Issues and Problem Solving in the Formative Years," *Journal of Small Business Management*, 28 (1990), 9–19.

[2]For further reading on manpower planning and human resource forecasting, see Michael Armstrong and John F. Lorentzen, *Handbook of Personnel Management Practice: Procedures, Guidelines, Checklists and Model Forms* (Englewood Cliffs, NJ: Prentice Hall, 1982).

[3]"ABCs of Borrowing," U.S. Small Business Administration, Management Assistance Support Services, Management Aids Number 1.001. (Copies of aids are available from SBA, P.O. Box 15434, Fort Worth, Texas 76119). This publication provides a useful overview of steps required to obtain a loan from a financing institution. See also John R. Thorne "Alternative Financing for Entrepreneurs," *Entrepreneurship: Theory and Practice*, 13 (1989), 7–9. This article presents many creative ways to obtain capital through debt or equity. And a good basic text that covers this topic in a nontechnical and clear fashion is Robert L. Anderson and John S. Dunkelberg, *Entrepreneurship: Starting a New Business* (New York: Harper & Row, Publishers, 1990).

[4]There are very good reasons why managers prefer to observe the work of the people they hire and promote. Work samples (also referred to as job-sample tests and job-sample performance tests) tend to have the highest validities and reliabilities of all selection approaches. John M. Ivancevich and William G. Glueck, *Foundations of Personnel: Human Resource Management*, 4th ed. (Homewood, IL: BPI/Irwin, 1989), p. 290.

CHAPTER 10

Maintaining Human Relations with Growth

In this chapter, we examine the human-relations issue. But first, you may want to browse through the following questions to focus your thoughts on human relations in your own company.

ASSESSING YOUR HUMAN-RELATIONS STRATEGY

Goal Integration

Questions 10-1 through 10-5 examine *goal integration*, the degree to which organizational and individual needs match or mesh with each other. Though more appropriate to ask in a confidential employee survey than of yourself, you may want to skim through them anyway. For each of the five questions consider:

**TO WHAT EXTENT DO EACH OF THE FOLLOWING
DESCRIBE YOUR FIRM?**

[1] To a very great extent
[2] To a great extent
[3] To some extent
[4] To a small extent
[5] To a slight extent or not at all

Question 10-1: Clear understanding of company objectives.
People have a clear understanding of company objectives.

Question 10-2: Self-centeredness of employees. Everyone looks out just for themselves, rather than doing what is best for the firm.

Question 10-3: Intention to leave. Employees think about quitting.

Question 10-4: Insecurity of employees. People feel insecure about their place in the company.

Question 10-5: Lack of understanding of objectives. People lack understanding of where the firm is heading.

Question 10-6: Morale. For lower-level employees, how would you rate their morale, job satisfaction, and commitment to company objectives?

[1] Very high: Top 2% of the industry
[2] High: Within top 10%
[3] Well above average: Top 25%
[4] Above average: Top one-third
[5] Average: About the middle
[6] Slightly below average: In the top two-thirds
[7] Well below average: Bottom one-third

Question 10-7: Consistency of mission. To assess how consistent your view of the firm's mission is with those of your managers, follow these four steps:

Step 1: What do you see as the firm's primary mission, including products and services offered, and anything else defining its main direction and purpose? (Refer to question 6-11.)

Step 2: Give this same question to your managers. Ask them to record their answers without discussing it first.

Step 3: Now compare the consistency of CEO and manager answers. Are they:

[1] Word for word (reads like the same mission statement)
[2] Same content, though different words
[3] Substantially the same (50–75% overlap of key issues)
[4] Some similarity (25–50% overlap in key issues)
[5] Very slight overlap (5–25%)
[6] Totally different

Question 10-8: Types of values emphasized. As CEO, do you emphasize certain values that you feel are especially important to the success of the business? What are they?

Question 10-9: Consistency of values.

Step 1: Without discussing your opinions, ask managers: "Does your CEO or president emphasize certain values he or she considers especially important to the firm's success? What are they?"

Step 2: Compare manager and CEO answers and rate their consistency. Are they:

[1] Word for word (reads like the same statement)
[2] Same content, though different words
[3] Substantially the same (50–75% overlap of values)
[4] Some similarity (25–50% overlap in values)
[5] Very slight overlap (5–25% overlap in values)
[6] Totally different (no overlap in values mentioned)

Question 10-10: How effectively values are shared.   If you answered *yes* to question 10-8, ask yourself: Do you have a particular way of sharing values with your employees? If so, how well does this technique or strategy work?

[1] Extremely well
[2] Very well
[3] Fairly well
[4] Not so well
[5] Not well at all

TABLE 10–1   Human Relations Effectiveness for Top Performers and All Firms Combined

	ALL FIRMS		TOP PERFORMERS
	MEDIAN	%	%
Clear understanding of company objectives (quest. 10-1)	3.0	31[a]	44[a]
Self-centeredness of employees (quest. 10-2)	4.0	16[b]	13[b]
Employees think of quitting (quest. 10-3)	4.0	22[b]	17[b]
Insecurity of employees (quest. 10-4)	4.0	19[b]	22[b]
Lack of understanding of objectives (quest. 10-5)	3.7	31[b]	26[b]
Morale (CEO view) (quest. 10-6)	2.0	57[e]	71[e]
Morale (Management view) (quest. 10-6)	3.0	28[e]	36[e]
Consistency of mission (quest. 10-7)	4.0	6[c]	18[c]
Consistency of values (quest. 10-9)	4.0	12[c]	29[c]
How effectively values are shared (quest. 10-10)	2.0	36[d]	50[d]

[a]Answered [1] "to a very great extent" or [2] "to a great extent"
[b]Answered [1] "to a very great extent;" [2] "to a great extent" or [3] "to some extent."
[c]Percentages of firms where at least two-thirds of the managers share the same content if not the identical language.
[d]Percentage who say the strategy is working out "extremely well."
[e]Morale rated within the top 10 percent in the industry.

Table 10–1 shows how firms in our study stack up in human relations. For some measures, the percentages for all firms are very similar to those for the top firms. The sharpest contrasts are in questions 10-1, 10-6, 10-7, 10-9, and 10-10. Employees have a clear understanding of company objectives (to a great or very great extent) in 44 percent of top-performing firms compared with 31 percent of all firms. Morale is also better at the typical top-performing firm—rated in the top 10 percent of the industry by 71 percent of top-performing CEOs, compared with 57 percent for all firms combined. Based on question 10-7, at 18 percent of the top-performing firms but only 6 percent of firms as a whole, at least two-thirds of the managers share the same content if not the identical language in describing the firm's mission (though both are low percentages!). CEOs of top-performing firms also have an easier time conveying values. Similar values are reported by the CEO and managers in almost 30 percent of top performers, but in only 12 percent of all firms combined (question 10-9). Finally, 50 percent of top-performing CEOs feel their values are shared extremely well, compared with only 36 percent for all firms combined (question 10-10).

WHAT IS HUMAN RELATIONS?

Effective human relations refers to the extent individual employees are willing to accomplish overall organizational objectives.[1] We refer to *willing* here rather than to actual *doing* because many other factors come into play, in addition to employee predilection, in determining actual performance—appropriate fit of skills and talents, accurate expectations, sufficient tools and assistance, and other factors beyond even the firm's control. Though they overlap somewhat, we look at five components of human relations effectiveness: 1) morale—overall job satisfaction and commitment of employees; 2) goal integration—consistency of organization and individual goals; 3) a consistent view of the mission by CEO and managers; 4) a consistent view of values; 5) how effectively values are shared.

The human-relations movement can be traced back to the Hawthorne experiments in the 1930s.[2] Hawthorne researchers were originally interested in effects of light and noise on worker productivity in a sewing-machine factory. Their unexpected results showed no correlation between illumination and worker output. In some trials, the darker it got, the more workers produced. Obviously, light levels alone were not affecting performance. Though a number of alternative explanations existed, they all pointed to ''people'' factors. The results of the Hawthorne experiments and others by Roethlisberger and associates triggered systematic research into the connection between employee attitudes and performance.

The human-relations movement can also be traced to motivation theorists, including MacGregor, Likert, Herzberg, and Maslow—all of whom looked beyond the economic models of work behavior to more complex psychological needs workers desire from the workplace.[3] These needs include praise, recognition, power, accomplishment, and pride from a job well done.

Our growing understanding of human behavior underscores the importance of providing opportunities for people to fulfill individual and organizational needs simultaneously. Without this link, the firm will experience increased absenteeism, turnover, vandalism, grievances, strikes, and litigation. Where human relations is poorly managed, people may quietly sabotage their work efforts or simply work in a sloppy manner. Worker attitudes are also linked to the quality of output. Committed employees feel more pride of workmanship. How do firms foster such pride? As many have discovered, no amount of pleading or threatening will improve employee performance as effectively as positive approaches. Today's workers may not be better educated, but they certainly have higher expectations than their forebears and most won't work for money and job security alone. Empowering employees and managers to make decisions is far more effective than "idiot-proofing" jobs.

Despite 35 years of field research pointing to the worker's importance in the overall company success, a major beating by the Japanese is what finally made this sink in. Ironically, much of Japan's success is traced to a U.S. citizen, Dr. Deming. Known for his work in statistical process control, Deming's philosophy is grounded in early motivation theorist Douglas MacGregor and his Theory Y view of workers. Theory Y asserts that the employee *wants* to do a good job, and does so when given the chance.[4] We now see more American companies implementing Theory-Y human-relations concepts, adding new twists as they go. McDonald's has demonstrated that these ideas even work in Russia!

IMPORTANCE OF THE HUMAN-RELATIONS ISSUE

As we showed in Chapter 5, human relations is an integral part of the Dynamic System Planning Model. We find links to most indicators of organization effectiveness, including profitability, sales growth, work flow, public relations, and technical mastery. Human relations is also linked to resource acquisition and resource allocation. In short, it is intertwined with all the other issues.

Morale and profits are linked.   The relevance of human relations has been debated over several decades, because its effects are delayed or lagged—a phenomenon Likert first noted in the 1950s. These results are less apparent in cross-sectional studies—those that test ideas by comparing people or companies at the same point in time. Lagged effects clearly show up in our own study, reinforcing Likert's long-standing claims that morale and profits are linked.[5]

Growth boosts morale.   Our findings further suggest that rather than straining relations among people, rapid growth may be a boost to morale. It is much more exciting to be part of a success.

Human relations is linked with work flow, company image, and productivity.   Not surprisingly, firms with better human relations report smoother work flow, too. Employees can serve as ambassadors of goodwill—or harbingers of ill will. Poorer morale is reflected in a worse reputation. Of the different components of technical mastery, productivity is most closely linked to human-relations effectiveness, including morale and goal integration.

Human relations is also clearly linked with resource acquisition and allocation. But we lack the right kind of data to pin down whether smooth human relations
is the cause, or the effect, of good resource acquisition and allocation. We might
guess, though, that when people have the right resources to work with, they do their
jobs more easily and encounter fewer frustrations.

CHARISMA, CORPORATE CULTURE, AND SHIFTS IN HUMAN RELATIONS

Charisma and Emerging Firms

Practitioners are increasingly aware that good human relations involves more
than just assuring a rewarding environment. Leadership theorists, such as Bass,
point out distinctions between "reward-based" (or transactional) and "charismatic" (transformational) leadership.[6] Charisma is personal magnetism that goes
beyond the mere doling out of rewards. We have all felt it, that person with something special who makes others excited to join their projects, willing to work harder
to please them, simply to be near enough to feel that same exuberance and magnetic
energy. Many founding entrepreneurs have such qualities.

Some, like former U.S. President Ronald Reagan, and Chrysler Chairman
Lee Iaccoca, have such strong magnetism it can even be conveyed across electronic
media. But most entrepreneurs are more like former President Lyndon Johnson.
You had to be face to face with him to sense his charisma.[7] Charisma is one factor
that explains the willingness of many employees to work for less money in a smaller
firm. But charisma wears off somewhat as the firm grows. The CEO becomes less
visible and involved in daily activity, and routine sets in. Though the exact point
varies from firm to firm, the 70–100-employee range seems to be critical. At that
point, many CEOs lament that lower-level employees no longer understand the
firm's mission or why the CEO started the firm. Some CEOs even experience pain
at "losing" the sense of family. Now they have just another company.

You may say, "But I have an open-door policy. Employees can walk in
whenever they want." But when your firm gets past a certain size, the employees
are *afraid* to walk in. For many employees, especially newly hired ones, the CEO is
often a distant, disconcerting symbol, not unlike the caricatures of tycoons found on
television. The "boss" or the "big cheese" is never someone you just walk up to
and start a conversation with, no matter how close in age or how friendly.

Corporate Culture—the Replacement for Charisma

It's easier to maintain that old charisma with the inner circle—top managers,
investors, the board, and even nonmanagement people who started out with you.
What can you do to give new employees the same enthusiasm and loyalty? This is
the human-relations challenge. Consciously building a "corporate culture" is a part
of this—making sure these new people know who you are, what you stand for, and
why you built the company. "Corporate culture" is the company's underlying suc-

cess philosophy and value system, plus the means for communicating those beliefs. Those beliefs are disseminated by word and deed, even reflected in the physical environment.[8] What is said and done when an employee makes an honest mistake? What are the sayings managers and CEO put on the wall? What kind of condition is the work space in? All these provide clues to the underlying culture.

Where does corporate culture originate? Some case studies suggest values derive from the CEO. But corporate culture is also built up by a string of previous presidents and owners. In a strong corporate culture, consistent values are reflected in behaviors, employee attitudes, and even policies and structures throughout the firm. In a weak culture, CEO values are not apparent past executive suites. In this vacuum, subcultures evolve in different departments that can conflict and confuse. In acquisitions, the blending of two existing corporate cultures is a predictably major challenge.[9]

CHOICE OF VALUES

Table 10–2 presents a broad range of values CEOs emphasize. Customer service and honesty are mentioned most often by CEOs and managers alike. Fostering good

TABLE 10–2   Frequency with Which Values Are Mentioned by Participating Firms

	CEO MENTIONED	AT LEAST ONE MANAGER MENTIONED
	%	%
Customer service: good customer relations; value-added service; follow-up on complaints	39	49
Honesty; integrity among employees and with the customers; fairness to customers	29	41
Quality	28	34
The organization meeting the employee's needs: morale; respect for employees; fairness; job satisfaction	20	18
The work ethic: productivity; attendance; getting the job done; motivation	15	33
Efficiency of business practices: proper execution of tasks; timely delivery; do it right the first time	10	32
Good teamwork and communication	8	17
Professionalism, in general	5	13
Cleanliness; clean living; other personal lifestyle issues	5	10
Image: reputation of the firm	3	2
Making money; making a profit	2	12
Loyalty to the firm; longevity	1	8
Improving employee skills; education; creativity	1	8

employee relations through mutual respect and fairness is mentioned by one in five CEOs and managers. One-third of managers note their CEO stresses the work ethic—productivity, attendance. Yet only one-sixth of CEOs mention this. Efficiency of business practices—proper execution of tasks, timely delivery of goods, doing it right the first time—is mentioned by a third of managers, triple that of CEOs mentioning it.

About one-third of managers and 28 percent of CEOs mention quality as a value. Managers also mention certain values more frequently than CEOs: especially values such as good teamwork and communication (17 percent of managers compared with 8 percent of CEOs), professionalism (13 percent compared with 5 percent), personal lifestyle issues, including clean living (10 percent compared with 5 percent), making a profit (12 percent of the managers compared with 2 percent of the CEOs), loyalty (8 percent vs. 1 percent), and improving employee skills (also 8 percent vs. 1 percent). Table 10–2 provides more detail on these findings.

Values at Top-Performing Firms

Table 10–3 highlights similarities and differences in values held by CEOs in top-performing and remaining firms. One difference stands out. Fully half of top performers explicitly mention quality. Only 22 percent of the rest do. This supports other work heralding a "quality revolution," with roots in consumerism, demand, and global competition. Companies, and even countries, that cannot deliver the right quality services and goods are driven to the rear quickly.

TABLE 10–3   Comparing the Values of Top-Performing Firms with Those of Other Firms

	TOP PERFORMING FIRMS ($n = 28$)	REMAINING FIRMS ($n = 140$)
Quality	52%	22%
Customer service	32	41
Honesty; integrity among employees and with customers	21	28
Meeting the employee's needs; good morale	25	16
Cleanliness; clean living; other personal life issues	11	4
Efficiency; timely delivery; doing it right the first time	11	9
The work ethic; productivity; motivation	7	15
Good team work	7	8

HOW FIRMS SHARE VALUES AND GOALS

Overview of Different Value-Sharing Strategies Mentioned

Table 10–4 summarizes the approaches that CEOs in our study use to share values and goals. A fairly large number (42 percent) don't use *any* strategy to share values. Of those that do have a strategy, the most common approach is simply to talk about it, mentioned by about 32 percent. Another 25 percent bring up value issues secondarily at meetings. Seventeen percent incorporate their values into hiring practices or social activities. Only 6 percent devote company-wide meetings to values.

Other strategies to share values include newsletters, memoranda, open letters, and bulletin board notes, handbooks, manuals, and codes of ethics. Only a small number provide a distinct formal statement of corporate values.

TABLE 10–4   Strategies CEOs Report Using to Share Values

	n	%*
Informal conversation	31	31.5
Bring up value issues as secondary agenda of meetings	25	25.5
Hiring practices, social activities	17	17.3
Company-wide meetings	6	6.1
Meet with managers	6	6.1
Others; combinations	13	13.5
	98	100.0

*Percentage only out of those having a strategy (*n* = 98), not the entire sample.

EFFECTIVENESS OF HUMAN-RELATIONS STRATEGIES

Several management practices predict effective human relations.

Lack of a clear reporting structure is linked **with poor morale.**
Who reports to you? The typical CEO has no trouble answering this question. But 20 percent of CEOs we talked to hemmed and hawed trying to answer who reported to them, suggesting an underlying fuzziness in their reporting structure. We kept track of this after awhile and found fuzzy thinking is linked to lower morale and more poorly integrated employees.

Let them know the score.   The more positive (and negative) feedback employees receive about their work, the better is morale and the better integrated employees are likely to be.

People like to keep score. They wouldn't rush out at 5:01 PM to play golf, or baseball or to bowl if they weren't allowed to keep score. Many employees get frustrated because nobody at work lets them know how they're doing, individually and as a team. Try playing baseball where you can't count the runs or, worse yet, to bowl with a blanket hiding the pins. Yet many CEOs jealously guard simple company success measures.

People also want to know what they are expected to do. Otherwise, it's like playing a game with no rules. Firms relying on standards, a chain of command, and meetings also have better morale. As with feedback, these practices help people know more clearly what is expected of them and, in turn, improve morale.

Talk with employees.   The best strategy is the simplest: Talk with employees. CEOs and managers at more successful firms talk about work expectations, about jobs to be done, about values that the CEO feels are important, and about the firm's overall objectives. Firms relying more heavily on informal conversation, rather than on formal means, to coordinate work efforts and share values also tend to have better morale and better integration of employee and company goals.

Using informal and formal means of communicating values and other information isn't an either/or situation. The most effective firms use both to be sure the message gets across.

Build trust.   It may be a cliche, but some firms do have a much better atmosphere or climate than other firms—showing trust, cooperation, and creativity. In these firms, politics are downplayed. In such firms, not surprisingly, morale is higher; and employee and firm goals are more closely integrated.

Building trust is the CEO's responsibility—no one else's. This is usually simple when the firm is small. With growth, the distance between CEO and junior people increases, leading to distrust, unless active steps counteract it.

How to achieve clearer firm objectives.   An important step toward goal integration is a clear understanding of company objectives. A firm's careful determination of training needs develops employees who are clear about overall objectives. A reward system that consistently recognizes better performance also helps.

The importance of consistency.   The old adage "it's not what you say but what you do" applies here. If the company says it emphasizes quality and yet condones sloppy work and allows defective merchandise to be shipped, the words will have little effect. In many Ford plants, anyone can stop the assembly line to nip a quality problem in the bud. This was unheard of in the past. CEOs can also reinforce values such as quality via performance reviews. People should be evaluated on criteria consistent with company values and missions. This is easier said than done. Managers told to emphasize quality but evaluated on quarterly profits will emphasize the short-run, when the two objectives clash. Beware also the common tendency of choosing what is *easiest* to measure (e.g., gross sales) rather than what is most clearly tied to the firm's objectives (gross or net profits, or market share).

How top performers share key values.   Among top performers, several CEOs reinforce desired values via hiring practices. The CEO of a small construction firm looks for and hires long-term people. He notes that "most understand [the firm's mission and objectives] automatically by now."

Hiring is mentioned by another profitable and rapid-growth construction CEO. The company has only 38 full-timers, hiring over 500 temporaries and subs during peak season. His number one goal is to make a profit. He shares this goal by computing the percentage profits generated by *each* job. He adds, "Everyone who stays gets cost conscious this way."

But profit isn't his only value. "I try to maintain the job stability of the full-time people." He also emphasizes consideration of other employees, noting, "we try to maintain a friendly, warm feeling on the job site. We provide extra services to employees such as car loans or little incentives like occasionally getting off early. To maintain a sense of community, loyalty, and shared values, "we keep pumping them—directly communicating with everyone in the field. Once a week I call them."

Another large (80 +) top-performing construction firm makes high-tech electrical installations. The mission is to be recognized as a real force in that market niche. The CEO encourages employees to take classes and sends out complimentary letters from customers with their paychecks. He also holds quarterly meetings between supervisors and manufacturers' representatives who demonstrate the most up-to-date equipment. Integrity and honesty are his top values. He expects a real commitment from his people. He communicates these values verbally and also through the policy manual.

The CEO of a small successful tool-and-die firm encourages equality and respect: "I treat them like people. I try to joke with them. I let them know I need them. Then they'll work for me."

One simple way to convey values is through signs. On the wall in the front office of another successful tool-and-die firm three signs read:

> Bad planning on your part doesn't constitute an automatic emergency on my part.
> There are three kinds of people: Those who make things happen, those who watch things happen, and those who wonder what happened.
> When all else fails, read the instructions.

In this firm, quality and initiative seem crucial. The CEO communicates these values by talking about them and by sharing articles in trade magazines. A lot of customers visit the firm and he asks them to let employees know how important quality is. Customer expectations are a powerful motivator.

A top performing 90-worker automotive-stamping plant CEO notes that raw growth is not his primary objective, but rather a by-product of doing the job well. He communicates this mission by example and talking informally: "We try to operate as family. I don't like the word 'boss.' I encourage everyone to . . . use the Golden Rule. This is the most important business slogan, because I am always in a constant battle. People come from different backgrounds." When asked about values to share, he picks "quality, mutual respect. A person's job has nothing to do with their worth as a human being.'' He shares these values by having a company relations committee and by setting an example.

A top-performing plumbing wholesaler stresses profitability as the number-one mission, communicated via a company newsletter reporting on sales and gross profits. Customer service is an important value. In addition to discussions at regular sales meetings, a president's newsletter shares anecdotes describing how attention to detail makes the firm more successful. Twice a year, the president meets with each branch, reviewing expectations and how well the company is hitting goals. To sum up his philosophy about customer service, he states simply: ''Everyone has an ego. But the customer is always right.''

In contrast to the upbeat messages of these top performers, languishing firms often transmit negative vibes. A food manufacturer tells his people they ''can't advance by usurping power.'' When asked how he shares these values, he notes, that ''I try to impress on them that we have survived.''

CHANGE IN THE APPROACH TO FOSTERING SHARED VALUES

Only 20 percent of CEOs we studied have changed their approach to sharing values since start-up. Typically, these were the largest firms. Recall that almost half of the CEOs modified their work-flow techniques. In fact, of all issues, CEOs were least likely to report change in how they communicate values.

Changes in value sharing.   With company growth and maturation, CEOs tend to rely less on talking with employees or pointing out problems as they arise. Instead, more meetings are held to discuss values, at either general meetings or at those specially set to discuss the firm's mission. Other ''innovations'' include newsletters, memoranda, open letters, and manuals. Fewer social activities are planned than before. Approaches remain simple.

Triggers for change.   The change in approach to sharing values is usually triggered by growth or by specific people-related problems, poor employee performance, a climate of conflict and distrust, a desire for better communication, or a desire to have more career-oriented employees. With the old approach, one CEO noted that employees weren't being productive enough, lacking interest both in their jobs and willingness to cooperate. Another mentioned that with the old approach, it was difficult for new hires to fit in. CEOs also mention a desire to improve quality, increase efficiency, lower costs, or just ''improve operations.'' One simply acted on a consultant's suggestion. This is an exception, however. Few CEOs change for change's sake alone. Finally, some changes were due to turnover in top-management.

RETAINING COMMITMENT TO MISSION WITH GROWTH

Customer service is mentioned as a key value by one-third of CEOs. Yet walking into any service-oriented business today—the grocery store, the shopping mall, the print and copy shop—how many times have you run into employees who figured they were doing you a big favor just to be there? If too demanding, you might even be steered to a competitor! (You want faster service? Why don't you go to. . . .)

In contrast, the typical founder is keenly aware of customer requirements: No customer—no sales; no sales—no business; no business—no job for you *or* your employees. Simple enough? So why don't these employees realize that if customers stop walking into their store, they are out of a job? What went wrong here?

Although it is easy to blame lower-level employees, they are not the only ones at fault. In many companies, low-level jobs are mindless and demeaning. Little is done to include employees in problem solving and decision making. A we–they attitude is fostered between management and worker with separate dress codes, cafeterias, bathrooms, and parking spaces. One successful CEO emphasizes the importance of mutual respect and equality among employees: "A person's job status has nothing to do with his or her worth as a human being."

Employee complacency is further bred by a gross misunderstanding of private enterprise by most of our population and is reinforced by negative media stereotypes that hound the American public. For most couch-potatoes, the CEO isn't the dedicated, risk-taking entrepreneur depicted in business magazines, but a tycoon or distant figurehead taking advantage of everyone in sight. Even among supervisors, many lack understanding of the term *profit* and how to interpret a financial statement. So they think a 26 percent gross profit heads straight into your pocket.

The need for practical business education is widespread. Without it, employees can't be expected to share the CEO's commitment to profit. If you question this assertion, run a little experiment. Ask your employees how much profit they think your firm makes and what profit means. The answers may surprise you.

BUILDING CULTURE AT J. P. INDUSTRIES

Dr. Psarouthakis was keenly aware of the human-relations challenge at J. P. Industries (JPI). He describes his approach to building culture: "People need to know *why* they work, what their company stands for. People like to belong in an environment with clarity of mission and direction, and they like to feel that they are participating in something worthwhile."

Economic Education at JPI

"The first step is training in economic basics. If you want committed employees, those who understand the link between profits, growth, and their own well being, you have to aggressively counter ignorance of free enterprise and negative business stereotypes. An economic education program was set up at JPI to teach employees that profit is simply the gain needed to satisfy three groups: investors, employees, and customers. All three must be satisfied in order for a company to remain viable and strong. The entrepreneur who discovers a new niche not only gains personally but also generates new capital for society—new jobs for employees and the 'multiplier-effect' of paychecks being spent in the community. Not all investor profit is spent on personal whimsy. Employees benefit differentially from re-investment depending on the firm. They may receive better job security, pay raises, bonuses, or a direct profit share.

"Economics education also reviews income-statement and balance-sheet basics so employees grasp the relationship between sales, operating expenses, and gross and net profit."

Quarterly Meetings on Mission

"At JPI we frequently discussed our central purpose and each employee's role in it, including the way that progress was to be achieved. We recognized that people want to know if they are achieving the appropriate results: Internally, are employees achieving quality; and externally, is the firm being recognized for this? Employees need to know whether the firm is growing and meeting its goals—including the achievement of quality objectives and the financial health of the company.

"Communicating information on a frequent, planned basis was an important key to assuring employee motivation and allegiance. Although initially I held quarterly meetings with plant employees, as we expanded into multiple divisions, other senior executives reviewed our status with all employees at formal, quarterly, plant-wide meetings.

"At the update meetings, employees also had the opportunity to ask questions. If answers were not available on the spot, every effort was made to get back to employees on a particular issue. These meetings were an important way to track company progress as the company rapidly grew in size. The specific questions themselves helped zero in on problems. A lot was also gained tuning into the underlying attitudes that questions sometimes conveyed, the emotion with which questions were asked, and even the body language used. How attentive employees were, side comments people might make and other cues provided valuable input about how much employees cared about the business and their general commitment.

"When no longer able to run all the quarterly meetings myself, I handled the expansion in two ways. First, to assure uniformity of style and content, I ran an update meeting with each senior executive who took over this task. Second, I continued to visit each plant, although on a less-frequent basis—every 12 to 18 months—in order to maintain direct feedback from each location.

"The impact is not quite the same when a CEO cannot visit a plant directly. Other senior executives have to work harder to maintain morale. People like to see the CEO show up—it provides an opportunity for them to influence the CEO directly. But by taking senior executives along and letting them participate early on, I succeeded in creating a fairly smooth transition to the time when it became simply impossible to visit every location every quarter. If the CEO is *too* visible, a company can almost create a personality cult out of its CEO. This is not healthy, because it is not transferable—a real drawback when you no longer run the business. I always tried to plan for when I would no longer be readily available. Keep this in mind if you ever plan to sell your business or even pass it along to family successors.''

Employee Involvement at JPI

"I also gave each plant the opportunity to set up a formal committee of elected representatives—between 5 and 16 employees. Such committees usually addressed training programs, ways to augment skills and education, and the need for improvements in the plant. This gave many employees a way to participate, to get involved in improving things. It helped to create an atmosphere of pride, commitment, and involvement.

"We introduced more elaborate employee-involvement programs at some plants, but this was entirely up to the plant manager. We did not feel that elaborate programs worked well if imposed from above. For example, all plant managers were introduced to the 'Scanlon Plan,' a plant-wide improvement program involving employees in suggestions and profit sharing.[10] Initially, one manager was eager to try it. Before the plan could work, we provided an economic-education training program, as noted above. The committee eventually fashioned a profit-sharing program that was adopted by some other plants, as well.'' (We describe more details about this program in Chapters 13 and 14.)

Other Ways to Boost Trust and Morale

Dr. Psarouthakis mentions using some of the same techniques for both coordination and morale boosting: "I would walk around the plants to find out what was going on. Although this was valuable for identifying problems, it was also useful in building trust. Job enrichment and the cell concept were other work techniques that also built employee morale and commitment.''

Performance Evaluations at JPI

The performance evaluation was an important tool in clarifying expectations and motivating employees. Every effort was made to state work expectations clearly. JPI top managers reviewed discrepancies between actual and expected performance regularly with employees. The cause of a discrepancy was discussed—whether due to lack of skills, understanding, motivation, or cooperation from others, or from nonemployee problems. A two-pronged strategy was always followed: Recognition and reward for those performing well and analysis of the causes of low performance. A joint decision was made about how to correct underperformance. If problems persisted, eventually formal actions would be taken—actions that were always in keeping with relevant labor-law and union-contract guidelines.

"Better Makes Us Best"

One way JPI fashioned a strong corporate culture was with its motto, "Better makes us best.'' To reinforce the motto—the company philosophy of success—it was discussed at company meetings. A manual, later published as a book, was circulated to all employees.[11] "Better-makes-best" examples were crafted as short vignettes illustrated with cartoons throughout the book. We produced it in bound-book format because this has more lasting impact than monthly newsletters and other "reminders."

Though simple, this motto conveys the message that employees should never stay at a plateau. Even a slight improvement in performance day by day means the firm will rise to be the best in the industry. Continuous improvement should be in service of the overall objectives and mission clarified quarterly at update meetings and in other communications.

Dr. Psarouthakis explains the motto further: "I purposely picked the word *better*, rather than *best*, because superlatives are often vague and/or impossible goals. *Best* also suggests the possibility of remaining at a particular plateau—at the best level. The term *best* sometimes also implies the best of some group, thus setting an external standard relative to other people or firms. I used the term *better* to signal that employees should focus on an internal standard, relative to themselves, which is easier to identify and grasp. Asking employees to try just a little harder and do just a little better, gives them an easier-to-manage, bite-size grasp of the specific goals they are to achieve."

Building Trust at JPI

Trust is critical: You need to be up front with people. Honesty can be conveyed in many ways, but in a corporate environment, it includes openness about the company's status—whether things are going well or poorly. One must create a level of confidence and believability.

This becomes more difficult as the firm grows. The CEO needs to be not only sincere, open, and consistent, but also up to speed about what is going on. If not, you can come across as being insincere, even though you don't mean to be. Of course you can't know everything going on at every moment, but you need to be accurate about what you talk about—not only objective things but also the atmosphere within the firm and key issues of concern. If you have been too busy to keep up with these issues, employees are likely to misinterpret what you say and think you are trying to pull a fast one—to 'bamboozle' them. This is where a lot of CEOs lose credibility when the firm grows, and this loss often takes them by surprise. It is a lot of hard work, but to maintain trust you have to do your homework and keep track of what is on your employees' minds.

Another way to build trust is to avoid adversarial relationships between plants and the corporate office. This is achieved simply by not getting angry if a problem arises. People have to have the confidence that they can tell problems to top management without repercussions to them or their supervisors. In short, people have to be allowed to make mistakes. This problem-solving orientation did a lot to build trust and openness of communication at JPI.

If people communicate freely in a trusting atmosphere, performance issues can surface rather than be disguised. This is why trust plays such an important role in assuring quality.

Blending Corporate Cultures at JPI

Gary Reed, a former executive vice-president of JPI, describes in more detail how, when acquiring a firm, JPI worked to blend the old culture with the new: "Mentoring and role modeling were key elements in training the new general managers at different plants. Usually the existing general manager was removed and a top JPI manager ran the firm for three to six months, training a new plant manager. Most were hired from the inside since they could work with the JPI executive to learn how things were now to be done. JPI executives usually felt the plant manager was ready to take over when he started managing the way they would manage.

"Much of what new managers learned was JPI culture: assumptions about how things need to be run in order to succeed. Part of JPI's success was its consistency in introducing these beliefs into firms as they were acquired:

- Successful managers are action oriented—they get out and walk around the plant to find out what is going on.
- Changes are engineering based—with careful planning and technical considerations reviewed.
- Each plant needs good cost accounting and internal controls.
- Hourly people need to be involved in quality improvements.
- Management must delegate responsibility throughout the plant.
- The general manager must be prepared impromptu to answer detailed questions from the CEO.

"At one point, an attempt was made to hire an extra corporate manager to help train plant managers. But his management style clashed with JPI's. He did not get involved with details. He tended to have a more autocratic style and he was used to working at a large bureaucratic firm that always went by the book. We let him go because he was unable or unwilling to change to fit JPI's culture.

"In another case, JPI bought five or six plants and promoted one inside engineer to general manager without the extensive training that new managers usually went through. Things went along pretty well until the first business downturn, and JPI corporate managers discovered that things were not nearly as good as they appeared. In spite of profits, a lot of scrap was being generated and there was workforce unrest. Managers were unhappy, and there was a lot of turnover. Finally the general manager was replaced by another inside manager who had already demonstrated his compatibility of management style in running another JPI plant. The replacement was demanding but he delegated responsibility, he got the hourly people involved and turned the plant around.

"Because of a very limited corporate staff (just 23 main-office employees for a $400 million company), it wasn't always possible to send someone in to train a new plant manager. When this happened, problems would often arise. At one plant, the existing manager was kept on. The plant manager said the right words to corporate, but the plant was run exactly as it had been under the previous owners. They had a hierarchical organization, and the plant manager believed he shouldn't get involved with certain things. He would just sit in his office, have staff meetings, and get all of his information from what was told to him. More successful managers would spend half their time on the shop floor. This way the manager picks up a lot of feedback from hourly people.''

These were just some of the things JPI did to maintain trust, develop commitment, and maintain morale among employees: holding regular quarterly meetings on objectives for *all* employees at *every* plant; involving employees in all aspects of work process and quality; redesigning jobs according to the ''cell'' concept, walking around the plants, developing a motto and corporate handbook to reflect JPI's corporate culture; and staying on top of employee concerns. Dr. Psarouthakis notes: ''This was not done overnight and many changes are still in process, even though I am no longer with JPI. But focus on these concerns was a big factor in JPI quality improvement and cost reductions.''

SOME GUIDELINES FOR EFFECTIVE HUMAN RELATIONS

Resolving ''people'' issues during growth is as important as product development. Human relations sails along fairly smoothly until the firm hits 70 to 100 employees. Suddenly human relations becomes critical, more important than work flow or market strategy. Because most firms in our study were at or under this size, few had developed a plan. JPI provides a good example of steps you can take to manage the human relations issue effectively. Building trust, developing clear direction, and providing feedback to employees—all elements of JPI's strategy—are reflected in our findings. Many applications work in smaller firms, too.

Here are some ideas to consider that have worked for other CEOs of growing companies:

- Be clear about the organization's structure. Clearly assign responsibilities to both managers and employees.

- Maintain a clear chain of command. Don't bypass managers by giving orders directly to employees.

- Set up clear performance standards. Let employees at all levels know how well they are achieving those standards.

- Foster a positive climate: one of trust, cooperation, and innovation, rather than a political one.

- Structure jobs and supervisory duties so employees get positive *and* negative feedback: The ''cell concept'' at JPI and performance evaluation systems are good examples.

- Give employees clear role definition; it should be easy to know when the employee is doing well.

- In successful firms, employees share confidence in the CEO. He or she is viewed as a wise leader, who knows what is best. So become more knowledgeable about events outside the firm and inside the minds of employees.

■ Periodic update meetings are effective for sharing information about values and mission.

■ Take the time to talk to employees one on one, to learn and to share philosophy, values, and mission with them.

NOTES

[1]Georgopoulos refers to this as *social-psychological integration*. See Basil S. Georgopoulos, *Organization Structure, Problem Solving, and Effectiveness: A Comparative Study of Hospital Services* (San Francisco: Jossey-Bass, 1986). But since Lawrence and Lorsch use the term *integration* to mean work-flow coordination, we thought the term *human relations* would be less confusing. See Lawrence and Jay W. Lorsch. *Organization and Environment* (Boston: Graduate School of Business Administration, Harvard University, 1967). More recently, we labeled this issue *employee relations*.

[2]Frederick J. Roethlisberger, *Management and Morale* (Cambridge, MA: Harvard University Press, 1941). Frederick J. Roethlisberger and W. J. Dickson, *Management and the Worker* (Cambridge, MA: Harvard University Press, 1939).

[3]Most introductory texts in organization behavior still review these theories. One might refer, for instance, to James L. Gibson, John M. Ivancevich, and James H. Donnelly, Jr., *Organizations*, 6th ed. (Homewood, IL: BPI, Irwin, 1988), pp. 102–35.

[4]Rafael Aguayo, *Dr. Deming: The American Who Taught the Japanese About Quality* (New York: Lyle Stuart, Carol Publishing Group, 1990).

[5]Rensis Likert, *New Patterns of Management* (New York: McGraw-Hill, 1961).

[6]Bruce J. Avolio and Bernard M. Bass, "Transformational Leadership, Charisma and Beyond," in *Emerging Leadership Vistas*, eds. J. G. Hunt and others (Lexington, MA: Lexington Books, 1988). For further reading on leadership theories, see Bernard M. Bass and Ralph M. Stogdill, *Handbook of Leadership: Theory, Research, and Managerial Applications* (New York: The Free Press, 1989). For a creative new approach to leadership that takes corporate-culture building into account, you may want to read Peter B. Smith and Mark F. Peterson, *Leadership, Organizations, and Culture* (Newbury Park, CA: Sage Publications, 1988).

[7]For those who encountered Lyndon Johnson only on television, it is hard to appreciate the charisma he wielded in face-to-face encounters, which explains much of his enormous success in getting legislative bills passed while in the Presidency. Robert A. Caro, *The Years of Lyndon Johnson* (Alfred A. Knopf: New York, 1982) discusses Johnson's political life.

[8]Peter J. Frost and others, *Organizational Culture* (Beverly Hills: Sage, 1985). See also, for an excellent introduction to corporate culture, Terrence E. Deal and Allen A. Kennedy, *Corporate Cultures: The Rites and Rituals of Corporate Life* (Reading, MA: Addison-Wesley Publishing, 1982).

[9]Price Pritchett, *Making Mergers Work: A Guide to Managing Mergers and Acquisitions* (Homewood, IL: Dow Jones-Irwin, 1987).

[10]Carl F. Frost, Jack H. Wakeley, and Robert A. Ruh, *The Scanlon Plan for Organization Development: Identity, Participation and Equity* (East Lansing, MI: Michigan State University Press, 1974).

[11]John Psarouthakis, *Better Makes Us Best* (Cambridge, MA: Productivity Press, 1990).

CHAPTER 11

Putting Resources to Best Use: Allocating Dollars, Material, and Personnel

When should you add staff or equipment as you grow? How do you make spending decisions? Do you have a spending plan? These are resource-allocation questions.

ASSESSING YOUR RESOURCE-ALLOCATION STRATEGY

Ask yourself further:

Question 11-1: Resource-allocation strategy. Do you have a characteristic way of allocating dollars, equipment, material, and personnel support? For instance, do you always budget? Do you use the "squeaky-wheel method," or some other approach?

Question 11-2: Effectiveness of your resource-allocation strategy. How well does this strategy work?

[1] Extremely well
[2] Very well
[3] Fairly well
[4] Not so well
[5] Not well at all

Question 11-3: Lag in financial information. What is your reporting period (monthly, quarterly, etc.)? How many days after the end of the reporting period do you typically obtain your financial statements?

Question 11-4: Budget accuracy.   In general, how *accurately* can you project your budget, in percentage terms (i.e., within 5 percent, 10 percent, etc.)?

For questions 11-5 and 11-6, use the following answer choices.

[1] To a very great extent
[2] To a great extent
[3] To some extent
[4] To a small extent
[5] Not at all

Question 11-5: Adequacy of allocating people.   To what extent can your firm assign people to the right departments in the right numbers (so that one department isn't understaffed and another department overstaffed)?

Question 11-6: Adequacy of allocating material.   Can your firm allocate equipment, dollars, and materials so all work groups (departments, projects, crews) have sufficient resources to operate?

▶   Questions 11-2 through 11-6 all measure some aspect of resource-allocation effectiveness: How well people and material are allocated across departments; the quality of budget information (how quickly and accurately you get it); and the effectiveness of the allocation strategy (how well it is working). Table 11–1 shows the median response for all firms and how CEOs in top-performing firms and those in remaining firms compare. For each measure, top performers report more success. Almost half (46 percent) feel their resource-allocation approach works extremely

TABLE 11–1   Some Comparisons Between the Top Performers and Remaining Firms

	TOP 28	REMAINING FIRMS	MEDIAN (ALL FIRMS)
	%	%	
Resource-allocation strategy effectiveness (quest. 11-2)[a]	46	26	very well
Receive financial statements in 10 days (quest. 11-3)	75[b]	46[b]	10 days
Spending within 5% of budget (quest. 11-4)	80[b]	59[b]	5 %
Adequacy of allocating people (quest. 11-5)	65[c]	47[c]	2.2
Adequacy of allocating material (quest. 11-6)	72[c]	43[c]	2.3

[a]Rated [1] Extremely well
[b]Percentages out of those who budget
[c]Percentage who responded with a [2] "to a great extent," or better.

well, compared with only a quarter (26 percent) of remaining CEOs. Sixty-five percent of the managers in top-performing firms feel their firms assign people correctly to a great or very great extent ([1] or [2] on question 11-5) compared with only 47 percent in other firms. Similar contrasts (72 percent vs. 43 percent) are reported for material allocation. The quality of budget information is also better. About three-fourths of top-performing CEOs get budget information within ten days of the close of a reporting period and are able to set budget within 5 percent accuracy, compared with only about half of the remaining CEOs. These examples illustrate the results we found—that effective resource allocation is a key aspect of overall firm performance.

IMPORTANCE OF RESOURCE ALLOCATION

Two firms have $100,000 in start-up capital. One spends most of it on a new office set up: Brand-new furniture, an up-to-the-minute phone system, and a large yellow-page ad. The other starts out in his basement, uses half to purchase inventory and the rest on a slick mail-order catalog. How does one make spending decisions? How do you track what you spend? These are important aspects of the resource-allocation issue.

Overview

Companies able to allocate appropriately needed supplies, capital, and personnel are more likely to be profitable. They manage work flow better, acquire resources more easily, maintain smoother human and public relations, and master technology more adeptly. The only aspects of the Dynamic System Planning Model not linked to resource allocation are cash flow and market strategy. Proper identification of individual talents and provision of proper tools have both long been recognized as keys to higher performance.[1] Our study verifies these links.

The link between appropriate allocation and morale reinforces Theory-Y views of employees. Most want to do a good job but need the proper tools and assistance to do so and may be frustrated if not given a fair opportunity to succeed. You can't ask someone to build a house without hammer and nails! Let's turn now to the ways CEOs report allocating resources.

HOW FIRMS ALLOCATE RESOURCES

Who Budgets and Controls Costs

In most firms CEOs are heavily involved in tracking and controlling costs. As Table 11–2 shows, managers are often involved, as well, though less frequently in top-performing firms. Though not asked specifically of all CEOs, comments by many imply that final spending authority is usually reserved for the CEO. A few share the final decision with a board of directors.

TABLE 11-2   Comparisons of Some Resource-Allocation Strategies Between Top Performers and Remaining Firms

	TOP FIRMS	REMAINING FIRMS
Monitoring systems for:		
Net profits—overall	69%	71%
Costs	71	73
Net profits—by product	81	75
Inventory	74	58
Sales	44	61
Some sort of budgeting process mentioned (excludes job costing)	50	28
Managers participate in monitoring and controlling costs	54	72
CEO involved with monitoring and controlling costs	96	81
CEO makes cost decisions *alone*	46	28
Uses a CPA firm:		
in general	85	77
for taxes	62	48
for financial statements	73	58
for auditing	31	42
for general advice	27	31

Note: Percentages reflect percentages of firms in each group that indicate use of each of these approaches for allocating resources.

Table 11–3 summarizes comments about the *process* of allocating resources—how the allocation decision is made. One-third use informal methods alone—filling informal or oral requests daily as needs arise, adding numbers up in their heads, or responding to ''squeaks'' (managers' requests or obvious needs) with spending decisions. ''Market-driven'' CEOs do whatever it takes to satisfy customers.

TABLE 11-3   Strategies CEOs Use to Allocate Resources

	n	%
Informal Means		
Squeaky wheel	55	38
Market-driven	11	8
Subtotal:	66	46
Formal Means		
Formal budget	40	28
Financial analysis other than budget (job costing, break-even analysis, etc.)	20	14
Planning other than financial (formal requests by managers, targets, goals, etc.)	18	13
Subtotal:	78	55

n = 143

Note: Some responses did not fit into either category and some CEOs mentioned both informal and formal means.

As Table 11–3 also shows, of the nearly 80 company CEOs describing a more planned approach, only 40 describe what we might consider *formal budgeting*— that is, defining spending limits in advance and tracking expenditures in all catego- ries of the business. Among the remaining 38 companies using a planned approach, responses are split fairly evenly between some other type of formal financial analy- sis (such as job costing or break-even analysis) and a more qualitative approach (such as setting goals or targets, or requiring formal requests by managers).

Financial Indicators—What Is Tracked

CEOs were asked which financial indicators they use to track success (see Table 11–4). Table 11–4 also contrasts percentages of top-performing and remain- ing firms.

Most commonly mentioned is sales. Over half of top performers watch sales closely, but only about one-third of remaining CEOs do. In most other areas, per- centages are fairly similar: Gross profits are mentioned by 21 percent—trailed by net profit (19 percent), cash flow (19 percent), and accounts receivable (18 percent). Costs were mentioned by 14 percent, accounts payable or bills owed by 8 percent, year-to-date (YTD) budget comparisons by 7 percent, and inventory by the same percentage. Five percent mention the assets/liabilities ratio. Only 4 percent mention ROI (return on investment). A wide variety of other indicators are mentioned by a handful of CEOs: interest payments; depreciation; production rate; customer pat- terns; variance in schedules; retained earnings; employee income/payroll; break- even point; and finally, an accounts-payable–to–accounts-receivables ratio.

Some items overlap, accounting for lower frequency of mention. The wide di- versity of responses is interesting in and of itself.

Do CEOs who use certain indicators perform better than others? Yes—for some indicators. For instance, CEOs who track sales report a higher five-year sales-

TABLE 11–4 Percentages of Firms That Use Certain Financial Indicators for Success

	ALL FIRMS[a]	TOP FIRMS[a]
Financial Indicators for Success:		
Sales—general or by product	39%	54%
Gross profits	21	21
Net profits	19	25
Cash flow, cash in bank, working capital	19	14
Accounts receivable	18	14
Costs	14	15
Accounts payable, bills owed	8	2
Budget, year-to-date comparisons	7	6
Inventory	7	11
Assets/liabilities ratio	5	11
Return on investment	4	7

[a]Percentage of CEOs who indicated use of each indicator for tracking performance of the firm.

growth rate. Tracking cash flow has a positive lagged (delayed) effect on profits. Finally, firms tracking YTD comparisons to budget are likely to have a more adequate allocation of material across groups and departments.

RESOURCE-ALLOCATION STRATEGIES AND EFFECTIVE MANAGEMENT

How Well Resource-Allocation Strategies Work

CEOs leading single-product firms are usually happier with their resource allocation than CEOs of diversified firms. But although accounting systems are much more complicated to set up and monitor in diversified firms, it is not always a problem. Three out of five top-performing, diversified manufacturers note that their formal budget systems are working out extremely well.

Financial "Info-lag" and Accuracy of Reports

Delays in financial reports are excruciating. The biggest factor in not getting timely and accurate financial reports seems to be participative management! Involving people takes time and can create errors. Where authority is delegated to a larger number of managers, and where the CEO is less involved with monitoring and controlling costs, financial reports can be delayed and contain more errors. But involving employees in cost control can help you to discover many important formerly hidden cost-saving ideas. Review your approach to monitoring costs and see whether everyone is properly trained and motivated. Appropriate tools (e.g., computers) also help get the job done quickly and correctly.

Allocation of People and Materials Across Departments

Use of chain of command, meetings, and standards, in addition to coordinating efforts, also expedites the adequate allocation of people. Positive feedback helps, as does the use of a CPA and a clear reporting structure—the latter two for proper allocation of materials, especially.

HOW TOP PERFORMERS ALLOCATE RESOURCES

Table 11–2 also compares the monitoring systems set up by top firms and the remaining firms. Similar to other firms, two-thirds to three-quarters of top-performing CEOs monitor net profits (overall and by product or service) and costs. Possibly because more manufacturers are part of our top-performing group, 74 percent of top performers monitor inventory, compared with 58 percent of remaining CEOs. The biggest contrast is in sales. Surprisingly, only 44 percent of top performers set performance targets for sales, compared with 61 percent of remaining firms.

A few other comparisons are worth noting. Top performers are more likely to use a CPA for help with financial statements (75 percent, compared with 58 percent), but fewer use CPAs for auditing purposes (31 percent vs. 42 percent). And managers at top firms participate less. Half involve managers in cost control, compared with three-quarters of CEOs in lower-performing firms. One of the most notable contrasts is the use of budgeting. Fully half of the top performers budget, compared with 28 percent of remaining firms. Looked at by size, among the 11 top firms with 65 + employees, 9 have a formal budget. The remaining 2 are headed that way. Even among top performers, however, of those with fewer than 65 employees only one-third of the CEOs mention any sort of budgeting.

How Top-Performing Manufacturers Budget

Manufacturing CEOs seem to have the easiest time with budgeting. Of top performers, none of the five firms under 25 employees budgets. All but one of the 65 + -employee firms do. A CEO of a 15-employee firm notes: "We need to watch the books carefully." Another of the same size comments, "We put resources where they are most needed. We figure the line burdens (expenses) for each job." A third small manufacturer sets up a simple break-even analysis to start each year: "I set targets, profit sharing, bonuses, capital items, a wish list, and sales volume we need to break even. I review the break-even plan to see if it allows us to do all these things." A 17-person manufacturer shares some of his frustrations with more formal budgeting:

> In the past, I used capital budgets, but no one seemed to listen. I allocate resources on an as-needed basis. If we require it, we get it. We delay expenditures to the last minute. But people spend money and wait to see if I'll stop them. It requires a lot of involvement of my time. But the old system was meaningless because no one understood budgets but me.

Among larger manufacturers, responses change markedly. All these CEOs describe fairly sophisticated accounting systems as far back as they can remember. A CEO of a 250-person firm comments:

> We use budgeting. We do a year-end projection. I do a five-year plan, too, but the industry is very volatile. We also carry out cash-flow planning, reviewing monthly cash needs and required borrowing.

Another successful 300-employee manufacturer comments, "We budget with monthly reviews so if we have to, we can make adjustments." An 85-employee manufacturer states: "We computerize everything—financials, accounting, inventory, sales."

A 100 + -employee manufacturer takes requests from department heads into account when budget building. But even with a budget, "we are still fairly conservative. We pay as we go—taking things one step at a time."

How Top-Performing Wholesalers Budget

Of two wholesalers in our "top 28," the smallest one (with 21 employees) uses a formal budget, but also eyes the purse strings: "I watch every cent. Anyone can ask me directly if they need new equipment and supplies."

A family-owned 75+ wholesaler just changed from a "seat of the pants" approach:

> We use a formal budget now. We have a monthly managers' meeting to compare how we are doing against budgets. Next year we will target expenses and aim for specific objectives.

How Top-Performing Service Companies Budget

The smallest business-service firm in our "top 28" uses "squeaky-wheel and gut-feel." But a 22-employee placement service already uses computers to track accounts and check profitability. A 25-employee CEO adds: "We have extensive budgets. I can plug into it daily. We budget by the job. It has always been done this way."

And a 130-employee CEO sits down with his son to discuss budget needs: "We just put air conditioning in. It cost $100,000, but it helps improve working conditions."

How Top-Performing Construction Companies Budget

Construction CEOs seem to struggle the most with formal budgeting procedures, frequently citing difficulties. The smallest outfits report the least trouble. One with 14 employees notes,

> I take inventory. People order what they need. We discuss large purchases as a group. We're not impulsive. . . . This is the first year for setting [sales] goals, budget, and costs for minor projects like trucks, people, etc.

Even a five-person construction firm has a budget and goals. Its CEO further comments,

> Last year we sold $1.5 million and had a reserve of $5,000. I see to it that we earn funds to build up reserves and lines of credit. Reserves dictate the risk.

And a top-performing 15-employee construction CEO makes computerized year-to-date budget comparisons. He adds: "The best investment we ever made is that computer. It saves the work of 4–5 people."

A CEO from a 32-person firm notes that budgeting is difficult. Instead:

> We allocate based on direct requests. The CEO monitors expenses. The foremen understand the range. We monitor and determine costs per job.

Another 50-person construction CEO comments,

> Our allocation decisions are market driven. We put assets in divisions that are selling. We don't do budgeting based on a monthly computation but on what our position is. We go by a bottom-line job-cost analysis and look at sales and net profit.

And a CEO of a 40-employee firm that peaks at 450 employees during the busy season, comments:

> We are trying to move toward budgeting. In the past we used the squeaky wheel. The trigger is that we have moved to a more competitive market with tighter margins.

The biggest construction firms we looked at (65+ employees) seem to struggle the most with the allocation process. Only one likes his budgeting system. He attributes much of his success to computers:

> We use a formal budgeting process. In the past it was more seat of pants. Growth has triggered this change. We have computerized everything. I get weekly reports for budget, inventory, accounts receivable, and accounts payable.

But another 65-employee construction firm is still making the transition to budgeting:

> We're in between. Now that we have cash, we give some to charity, some to debt retirement, and some to capital improvements. In the past, we used the "squeaky wheel" entirely because we didn't have the funds for all those things.

If anything, budgeting gets harder with growth. An 80-employee CEO admits: "It is difficult to cope with major changes on a short-term basis. It is hard to budget. We hope to have a budget goal by next year."

These comments suggest that many construction firms need special software and methods to accommodate job-cost approaches in the contracting industry. More generally, computerized systems are praised by top performers in a wide range of industries and in both small and large firms.

CAPITAL-SPENDING PLAN VS. BOTTOM-UP ALLOCATION

Though formal budgeting is useful, equally important is *how* you decide what goes into that budget. Joseph Bower studied resource-allocation processes in detail at four large firms.[2] All four have budgeting systems, differing in how they fit with the rest of the firm. Two have *capital-spending plans* devised at the top and drawn from an overall strategic plan. The other two use a *bottom-up* approach—requests from middle managers are approved further up the line. Managers who "squeak" the loudest are likely to get a bigger share of these budget "pies."

Though Bowers' study was based on large public corporations, his caution against bottom-up planning is applicable to growth companies. In firms large and small, middle and lower employees won't see spending impacts as clearly as the CEO—especially when managers are assigned to narrow functional areas, such as sales or production. This doesn't mean communications should be cut off. Bowers recommends that middle managers identify funding needs in their areas, which are then factored into the big picture. In sum, spending shouldn't be a "go, no-go" decision on a specific item but carried out in light of the firm's overall mission and current direction.

CHANGES IN RESOURCE ALLOCATION

In simpler organizations, the owner keeps a checkbook, saves receipts, and hands them to a bookkeeper for year-end taxes. Allocation is ad hoc. Money is spent on items of the most immediate importance. As employees are hired, different people advocate expenditures, often "at the last minute." In this squeaky-wheel approach, whoever makes the loudest and longest noise often gets the most.

Few experts advocate totally ad hoc approaches. At some point, advance planning is seen to be necessary. How big can you get before you need a change? Most top-performing firms have converted to a formal budgeting system by the time they hit 60 or 70 employees. Others have had a budgeting system for the firm from Day One. In all, about 22 percent of all CEOs in our study had made some change in their resource-allocation approach since their start up—a small number compared with 50 percent who made changes in coordination strategy. Most shifts are away from "squeaky wheelism," toward formality. However, one small firm abandoned a formal system because managers were not quite ready for it. All in all, budgeting is a central component of success but may require training of your managers if they (or you) lack a business background. With proper training it's never too early to start.

Triggers for Change

The most common trigger for changing resource-allocation strategy, is the desire to improve profits and control costs. Many also mention company growth as a trigger. Third is interest in better time management, especially of the CEO's time. A few CEOs note that "now they finally have some cash to allocate." There "isn't much point in budgeting when cash is tight," they say.

A change in leadership triggered a new approach for a few. Others wanted improvement in existing staff.

RESOURCE ALLOCATION AT J. P. INDUSTRIES

The approach to resource allocation at J. P. Industries (JPI) clarifies and reinforces many of the points we've made.

Capital-Spending Plan vs. a Budget

For some companies, the budget merely extrapolates from the recent past—5 percent across-the-board increases in sales, expenses, and other line items. At those firms, a plan is often written, after the fact, to justify the numbers in the budget. But at JPI, the strategic plan always came first, based on the questions: Where are we going? How will we get there? What staffing will we require? and What investment in technology will we need? The capital-spending plan followed from the strategic plan. The capital-spending plan, in turn, dictated the budget.

The plan doesn't have to be terribly formal, since formality can kill the essence of a plan when a document takes on a ''God-given'' quality. JPI action plans often *looked* incomplete; yet they were adequate to accomplish the company's goals. It wasn't the detail, but the direction, that was important. Based on the plan, management knew where money should be spent and how much the company could afford.

Plans for each JPI division always included sales forecasts, cost forecasts, budgets, plans for purchase of supplies and raw materials, an investment forecast for equipment or other major capital expenditures, and personnel costs. Planning was always done 12 to 24 months ahead. When the company was a year or two old and doing $5 million annually in sales, the CEO made most of the decisions. As the firm expanded to about 500 employees and $50 million in sales, he began to delegate spending—but *only* in the context of the capital-spending plan. Managers at different levels were authorized to spend *up to* a specific dollar amount.

The wheel squeaks when planning is not done well. It reflects last-minute reactions, problems, or needs. In real life, you can't plan and anticipate everything. Relying too heavily on the squeaky-wheel approach, however, means that *personality* can enter too heavily into the picture. One person may be more articulate or forceful in expressing needs, although these may not generate the best overall allocations. Politics can be very damaging to a company and often enters into the picture when the squeaky-wheel approach is used. In very small firms, CEOs may have a plan in their heads and be able to integrate complaints or pressures without losing overall focus. This becomes increasingly difficult to achieve with growth.

''Compansion'' at JPI

Increased staffing is one of the major expenses faced by growing firms. Whenever a division of JPI was in a growth pattern, that growth was tested first with overtime. If the growth was sustained, then overtime was gradually reduced and full-time people were added gradually. Temporary help was not used except for clerical staff. This approach was used so systematically at JPI that the term *compansion* was coined to symbolize how employment could be compacted and expanded to minimize disruption. If growth is not steady, then you don't want to hire and lay off. It is destabilizing and distracting.

Traditionally, a firm makes sales-growth projections and then starts hiring. If the sales goals aren't met, a costly staffing expense exists, along with legal and moral layoff issues. ''Compansion'' reduces this problem. At the Grand Haven

Camshaft division of JPI, automated technology was introduced that initially shrank employment and made the plant more capital intensive. It also kept staffing growth down over time. As the division quadrupled sales from about $10 million to $43 million in seven years, employment only doubled.

Monitoring Systems at JPI

Every week, quality, actual pricing (including discounts), cash flow, and certain ratios were monitored at JPI. One key weekly ratio was direct versus indirect personnel costs. *Direct* and *indirect* were defined in a rather unique way: Only those people actually making products on the line were direct. Tool makers, foremen, maintenance inspectors, or any others who weren't actually making parts to ship out the door were left out. In the marketing/sales area, direct costs of sales personnel were compared with indirect advertising, brochure, and market-research costs. This way JPI could quickly spot where it might be getting top heavy in overhead (indirect costs).

A minimum target was set for direct hours.   Direct hours were never allowed to drop below 55 percent of all hours worked. This simple ratio greatly augmented the company's ability to maintain productivity levels. Simple observation doesn't help, because you can see people working in the plant but they may not be producing product. Maintenance people often do things that could be postponed. But a plant depends on a certain level of daily output to make a profit. If two direct laborers didn't show up, the manager would put a maintenance person or foreman on the line to run the presses. JPI could do this because people were cross trained. At some of the plants, this involved a training program and an extensive renegotiation process with unions. You can overemphasize the productivity side at the expense of quality, of course; but that is another issue for the plant manager.

Cash was watched closely.   The flow of cash was also monitored closely at corporate headquarters. Monthly income statements, balance sheets, cash flow, and major investment projects were all studied carefully to compare how much was spent. JPI's CEO always kept control of the purse. Spending authority was delegated only up to a certain dollar amount. CEOs who delegate this area entirely, even to the company treasurer, may get a big surprise. The treasurer is really an assistant to the CEO and should handle daily needs—but not have ultimate spending authority.

Even when the president delegates up to certain expenditure levels, *intent* should be reviewed before money is actually spent. That way, if cash is diminishing, he or she knows exactly where to go to hold the line. Many CEOs confuse delegating with abdicating. Participative management is helpful in many areas but in allocating resources, the president must maintain clear control—making day-to-day decisions via policies and plans set only from the top. This philosophy was central to JPI's success.

The CEO should never be afraid to step in and review the progress of a plan, especially if it involves a major portion of the budget. Once, a JPI senior manager had been allocated about $500,000 to launch a marketing campaign for a particular product line, including new brochures and other printed material. On paper, it looked reasonable, but the plan wasn't followed and bills began to pile up more quickly than expected. The CEO detected the problem in the normal course of review of staff spending, but it should have been caught much sooner by the division head. The project threatened to go close to $1 million over budget. As it was, it still went $500,000 over. The moral? Delegate, but monitor frequently to make sure spending stays on course.

Inventory Control at JPI

How much capital should be tied up in safety stock? In classic manufacturing texts, the concept was that either too much or too little inventory was a bad thing. The new ideal, borrowed and adapted from the Japanese, is that of zero-based inventory management.[3] Ideally, everything should move at the level of demand and be kept no longer than needed to manufacture a product. Every time material stops somewhere along the line, it creates a discontinuity and costs money. The goal is to see how fast material can move along, and in the most continuous flow possible. These were ideals that JPI aspired to. One can no longer remain competitive and allow a pile of semiprocessed or raw materials to lie around just to keep feeding the line.

Achieving the minimum inventory goal without creating manufacturing and sales disruption requires education and much more communication among managers, sales people, and purchasing agents than the old system. It is not mathematically complicated. It involves talking to people on the line.

This approach was especially challenging on the plumbing side of JPI's business, because the rest of the industry had not yet adapted to this approach. In the plumbing business, there is typically a huge warehouse cost. Products "turn" anywhere from 3 to 18 months. Bypassing middlemen, JPI could save up to 30 percent of the costs of finished goods.

"Making Budget" at JPI

A few JPI plant managers instituted the Scanlon Plan on a plant-wide basis. One of these said, "I made budget last month, and that is because I have 400 people working on it." He had been able to harness the total commitment and energy of his people to keep costs down, while maintaining high production and quality levels—thus, "making" his budget. It should be pointed out, however, that employee involvement in identifying cost-saving ideas is somewhat different from employee participation in a capital-spending plan. The latter is always set at the top and employees are then engaged to achieve the plan, *including* areas where costs could be saved in executing the overall plan.

Recap of the JPI Allocation Approach

At JPI, allocation of resources was driven by a capital-spending plan established and monitored closely in keeping with the overall business plan. Though spending was delegated at certain levels, it was never delegated completely. The principle of "compansion" minimized overstaffing and layoff swings. Zero-based inventory levels were set as goals. Though employees were heavily involved in how to execute the plan most efficiently and with the least funding, the overall plan itself was set at the top.

GUIDELINES FOR ALLOCATING RESOURCES

The message seems pretty clear. Although it might involve a lot of extra work and might even require a computer, a formal budgeting system based on a capital-spending plan is probably needed once you get past 60 to 70 employees—simply because of the sheer volume of required decisions. Lay out what you need to spend to accomplish your goals and set parameters, making it possible to delegate mid-range decisions to your managers without jeopardizing the whole purse.

Setting up a formal budget system or a capital-spending plan is beyond our scope. Helpful resources abound that describe basic guidelines.[4] Although it takes time and money, initially, several firms in our study are exuberant about the level of control a good computer-based system provides. The widespread availability of user-friendly, low-cost computer software and hardware today makes it accessible to just about every business.

Experience at JPI and research by Bowers underscore the importance of developing a capital-spending plan based upon overall mission and direction for the year. The budget should not be a mere extrapolation of last year. If you plan to add a new product or service, consider the investment in research, technology, advertising, and training required to roll it out.

As CEO, you should never lose sight of your cash. You may delegate certain dollar amounts for specific expenses, but routinely review these to assure the money is properly spent. Here are other guidelines for allocating resources effectively:

- Implement a formal budgeting system in line with the way your firm operates.

- Invest carefully in appropriate computer software and hardware.

- Include input from your managers; but beware of "squeaky wheels," especially as the firm enlarges. The squeak may represent parochial needs, which crowd out strategic ones.

- Using your insight is okay when the firm is small, but it is never too soon to implement formal budgeting. If you have inexperienced managers, they will need training and incentives to use more formal systems.

- Monitor critical areas on a periodic basis, comparing actual to expected performance: profits, costs, sales, inventory, quality, productivity, and others.

If you have little background in accounting, that shouldn't stop you from making a plan. You may need help to set up a computerized system, but the investment is well worth it.

Although the exact transition point varies, budgeting is a helpful addition as you pass 60 employees in size. It will free up time to address far trickier public, government, and human-relations issues that typically crop up shortly thereafter.

NOTES

[1]Most basic organization behavior texts underscore the importance of providing appropriate tools and other resources for assuring job performance. See for instance, John R. Schermerhorn, Jr., James G. Hunt, and Richard N. Osborn, *Managing Organizational Behavior,* 4th ed. (New York: John Wiley & Sons, 1991), pp. 104–8.

[2]Joseph L. Bower, *Managing the Resource-Allocation Process: A Study of Corporate Planning and Investment* (Boston: Harvard University, Division of Research, Graduate School of Business Administration, 1970).

[3]A great introduction to zero-based inventory control that is nontechnical and very readable is Richard J. Schonberger, *Japanese Manufacturing Techniques: Nine Hidden Lessons in Simplicity* (New York: The Free Press, 1982). For further reading, see also, Richard J. Schonberger, *World-Class Manufacturing: The Lessons of Simplicity Applied* (New York: The Free Press, 1986). A much more technical book on the topic is: Michael Umble and Mokshagundam L. Srikanth, *Synchronous Manufacturing: Principles for World-Class Excellence* (Cincinnati, OH: South-Western Publishing Co., 1990).

[4]Cecil J. Bond, *Hands-on Financial Controls for Your Small Business* (Blue Ridge Summit, PA: Liberty Hall Press, 1991). Bond's book walks you through establishment of a business plan and a budget based on that plan, as well as pointing out problem areas and potential solutions for cash flow.

CHAPTER 12

Public Relations: Getting the Most Out of Your Firm's Environment

Public relations is the sixth organizational DSP issue you must directly and continuously confront to assure your company's success. This chapter explains more about what we mean by public relations and how to plan for it.

ASSESSING PUBLIC RELATIONS

Ask yourself and your managers the following question:

> **Question 12-1: Company image and reputation.** How do you rate your firm's public image and goodwill—your firm's reputation?

[1] Very high: Top 2% of the industry
[2] High: Within top 10%
[3] Well above average: Top 25%
[4] Above average: Top one-third
[5] Average: About the middle
[6] Slightly below average: In the top two-thirds
[7] Well below average: Bottom one-third

Forty-seven percent of the CEOs rate their firm's reputation among the top 2 percent of the industry! This is no doubt biased, though note the figure is even higher (64 percent) among top performers. Managers are slightly less biased, though not much. Twenty-five percent of the firms' managers put their firms in the top 2 percent in their industry. Note that, again, the figure is even higher for top performers—at 46 percent, suggesting that even though the scores are inflated, the trends are consistent with important performance criteria such as sales growth and profits.

DIMENSIONS OF THE PUBLIC-RELATIONS ISSUE

Most start-up firms follow a common sequence. Initially, the focus is on competitors, customers, and suppliers. With growth comes a broadening of attention to government regulatory bodies, the media, stockholders (including family), and the public at large. Relations with competitors and customer relations, for the most part, are an aspect of market strategy. Relations with suppliers are an aspect of resource acquisition. We lump the other categories together, as diverse as they are, because they are not a direct part of the buying–selling cycle.

Competitors warrant close scrutiny. They are a source of information and skilled transferees, and they may occasionally provide capital for joint efforts.

Likewise, government regulatory bodies demand attention, because the scope of their involvement in management issues (hiring, environment, health and safety, etc.) increases relentlessly at federal, state, and local levels within the United States.

The immediate community rarely goes unaffected and, therefore, must also be addressed. Besides the possibility of profound effects on the immediate community, the growing firm must recognize the public as a resource, valuable for such things as recruits and information.

About half of our firms are family owned, suggesting yet another primary factor to consider—family itself. Interpersonal dynamics among invested and noninvested family subgroups can introduce stresses. Books, journals, conferences, and institutes are being formed around the unique challenges of the family firm.[1]

A final consideration is the consumer public. Of primary importance is the firm's reputation. The long-term reputation of the firm is an obligation that knows little compromise. The very fabric of the firm—future employees, customers, and investors—is on the line.

IMPORTANCE OF THE PUBLIC-RELATIONS ISSUE

Based on our research, corporate image is a good predictor of effectiveness. Although not linked to profitability per se, firms with better corporate or public image tend, nevertheless, to have greater liquidity, steadier sales growth, smoother work flow, better acquisition of resources, more commonly shared values, and better morale. Good public relations is also linked with more effective allocation of resources and better mastery of technology—including better technical skills, performance quality, and productivity.

LINKS BETWEEN PUBLIC RELATIONS
AND MANAGEMENT PRACTICES

Although in our research study we treated other issues in the Dynamic System Planning Model with more depth, we did find some links between general management practices and improved company image.

The CEO: Involved with Public Relations

As Table 12–1 shows, about two-thirds of the firms involve managers in public relations, in general, and government relations, in particular. When the top 28 firms are compared with remaining firms, top performers are somewhat more likely to centralize activities related to government and public relations. Taken together, these findings suggest the importance of *direct* CEO involvement with these issues, whether or not other managers are involved.

Work-Flow Practices Linked with Public Relations

Employees who are clear about jobs and understand company goals can provide better service, thus fueling a firm's reputation. This common-sense notion is definitely supported by our interview data. Coordination techniques that work well to promote work flow—such as the use of work standards, conversation, and chain of command—also promote a better image and reputation in the community.

Companies that monitor profits and costs, comparing actual performance to set standards, also have a better reputation.

Corporate Values Linked with Public Image

Firms whose CEOs share specific values with managers, whatever the value, tend to have a better public image. Firms also tend to have better reputations where middle managers see quality as highly valued.

Summary

All these findings suggest that reputation is closely linked with successful management of throughput issues—especially work flow and human relations. Employees are emissaries of goodwill—or bad blood—throughout the community.

TABLE 12–1   Who Handles the Public- and Government-Relations Issues

	% INVOLVING MANAGERS		% WHERE CEO IS DIRECTLY INVOLVED	
	TOP 28	REMAINING FIRMS	TOP 28	REMAINING FIRMS
Public relations	50	66	85	78
Government relations	60	70	73	60

Image suffers when the CEO shuns a leadership role in this area and when employees are unsure of management expectations regarding reputation and image.

In short, the management of the reputation of the firm is integral to the overall management of the firm. It appears to be an outgrowth of effective work-flow management and human relations and is associated with many aspects of performance.

IGNORING THIS ISSUE IS COSTLY

One of the CEOs we interviewed heads a family-owned food-manufacturing firm with over 160 employees. It has been declining in profitability, losing about 2 percent pretax net profit on over $11 million in sales. The comments of its president illustrate the way in which human- and public-relations issues have become intertwined. He notes, "The energies of managers in the last ten years have been burdened by issues that have nothing to do with the goods produced. A great percentage of time is spent dealing with worker compensation, taxation, and union-negotiation issues. These have nothing to do with providing quality products. Direct labor as a percentage of sales has taken up an increasingly large percentage in recent years. Our involvement in government-related problems has also increased significantly— issues such as pension revisions and COBRA have been very significant for a firm our size, as have hazardous substances, which takes up all the extra time."

PUBLIC IMAGE AND GOODWILL AT *JPI*

Approaches taken by JPI are quite informative in this area.

At JPI, managers were made to realize they had responsibilities to both the community and to the physical environment. These include environmental, safety, discrimination and affirmative-action, local community, and broader educational issues—all of which JPI dealt with in one form or other. Many of these issues were not likely to be considered by CEOs of growth firms 20 years ago. Today, managers can't escape these issues—they can't manage in isolation. Public relations can be viewed as a form of two-way communications with the outside constituencies that affect and are affected by the company.

Relationship with the Local Community

At JPI, employees were strongly encouraged to participate in community affairs—in education, volunteer work, and donations. For instance, many employees were active in such organizations as the United Way, Red Cross, and Boy Scouts— especially in the smaller communities, where volunteerism is vital. JPI operated under the philosophy that it is good for the firm to be directly involved with the community, not only to foster general goodwill, which is certainly important, but also to stay in touch with events and changes in the community that might have impact on the firm. The geographical extent of the firm's community involvement may depend partly on the nature of the firm and of the community. Many divisions of JPI were located in small towns, so the area of involvement was often fairly well defined.

If a firm is in a community with about a thousand people and employs 200, everyone knows it's there. How that firm relates to the community is very important. For this reason, JPI encouraged volunteerism in its employees. Within reason, JPI employees could take time off; and corporate donations were also budgeted for the community. Although top management encouraged employees to be aware of community affairs, JPI didn't specifically pay or otherwise reward them for volunteering. In place of formal incentives, goals, and the like was a simple system of sharing hopes and expectations.

The Educational System and What Business People Can Do

Many business people in the United States share a growing concern for the educational system and the education of employees.[2] The reason for this concern and interest is that unskilled labor in manufacturing firms is a thing of the past. As with many manufacturing firms, at JPI the entry-level employees on the factory floor must have a better education than their predecessors—one that, in many cases, the public school system has not provided.

As the maxim goes, a work force who cannot read and write is not ready to work. Though JPI didn't go as far as companies that set up their own training schools, it did set up extensive networks with community-colleges to train employees in reading, writing, arithmetic, and basic computer skills. It went further, also, in requiring many employees to have more advanced skills, such as reading tables and graphs, relating variables and plotting them graphically, and more sophisticated computer skills.

Each firm is likely to respond in its own unique way to the education crisis. Regarding subject skills, a dialogue between business people and school systems is necessary so that schools understand the needs of business. After a painfully long hiatus, there are some signs that this is beginning to take place. Assuming schools are interested in their input, business executives can and should identify for the benefit of the schools and their students those skills that are important in the workplace.

One quality largely lacking in today's high-school graduates is a basic savvy of how business operates. Schools could be of great help by simply teaching a practical business vocabulary. But beyond this, schools really should convey economic principles and how the business enterprise is critical to the health of the overall economy and to improvements in the lives of individuals and families. Students need to be taught that businesses offer an opportunity not only to earn a living but to be creative and develop a career—that, in short, the firm can satisfy the needs of the aspiring young person.

These concepts are not really taught at any level in the educational system. Business is frequently characterized as a necessary evil rather than a potentially user-friendly, prosperity-generating machine for people to use creatively. In many high schools today, a lot of the most useful courses from the business perspective are offered only as electives, which limits their reach and impact on students. One suggestion would be for schools to sponsor monthly "guest seminars" featuring nearby firms and open to all juniors and seniors. Some schools do this, but only in a condensed one- or two-day program once a year.

Involvement is also important at the university level. Dr. Psarouthakis notes:

> My most active involvement has been at the university level. I find it helpful to tap new information and energy in academic life, as well as to contribute to it through my practical business experience.

Physical Environmental Issues

Today's CEO must be sensitive to environmental issues. Managers can no longer look at a particular issue independently and say, "Well that won't hurt anything." Environmental impact has to be part of the decision process. JPI had a director of environmental-control activities at the corporate level, responsible for reviewing its activities continuously from both an environmental and a safety perspective. JPI met and surpassed most environmental standards and developed programs to improve areas that needed it. In this way, JPI also kept abreast of new regulations. It was fairly unusual in the 1980s for a company the size of JPI to have a top-level person just for environment and safety. JPI was a pioneer in this area. Even JPI's acquisition candidates were evaluated from an environmental perspective. This wasn't just for philanthropic reasons, of course. An acquisition candidate with a poor record poses serious liability risks and other unforeseen costs.

Jim McAuliffe, former JPI vice-president of human resources, elaborates on the other safety-related approaches there:

> One component of the physical environment that we watched was inside the firm itself. The philosophy we followed at JPI was, if there is an environmental-safety or health problem, fix it immediately. We never allowed money to be an excuse for not fixing such problems.

JPI also used positive reinforcement techniques—referred to as "Safety Bingo"—to encourage safety. For instance, rather than punish workers who had an accident, a bingo game was introduced. For every day an employee went without a lost-time accident, he or she got to fill one square of a bingo card. If an accident occurred, the game started over. The first person in the plant to fill a card would receive two free tickets to Hawaii.

Equal-Opportunity and Affirmative-Action Issues

At JPI, the vice-president of human resources was responsible for compliance with equal-opportunity guidelines. JPI took all steps necessary to inform employees and applicants that it was open to hiring, independent of color, sex, race, religion, and so forth. JPI allocated staff and resources to stay on top of these issues and even received an award from the NAACP one year for its hiring practices. Eliminating bias and achieving a better balance racially, ethnically, and gender-wise was openly discussed with JPI managers. Prejudice was confronted head on and, in hiring practices, was viewed as an obstacle to obtaining the most competent person for the job.

Relationships with Shareholders

JPI also focused heavily on shareholder relations, another important aspect of public relations. JPI addressed this issue extensively but it is beyond the scope of this book to describe in detail.[3]

The Importance of Reputation in JPI Investments

The reputation of any division of JPI in the larger community was also an extremely important factor in decision making. When JPI first considered a firm for acquisition, it wouldn't even touch the firm if the firm's public image were negative. JPI managers looked at customer service, how the acquisition candidate treated its employees, how it dealt with the environment, the quality of its products, safety issues, its financial reports, and how the public viewed it, in general.

Role of the CEO in Government Relations

Although in small companies, the CEO is more likely to handle government relations, other employees become involved as the firm grows. JPI had a lobbyist at the state level, part time, to keep abreast of legislation affecting the business. Government is a big part of our society—politically, economically, and socially. Thus, a firm can't operate in a cocoon—but it can't spend all its time on this, either.

The CEO should see government relations as another area of information to consider and decide how to get input on it. Although JPI eventually kept an expert on retainer, smaller companies probably need not do this. But they do need to stay in tune with what is going on locally, at least. What geographic area the firm must deal with—local, state, regional, or national—depends on the nature of the business. Even a small firm may have to keep track of certain trends at the federal level if part of its business involves national defense. It is helpful for the CEO to circulate and see what is going on, but there should be a sense of proportion: Top management should know about changes affecting the business but not to the point where no time is left to manage.

Anticipating Governmental and Public Issues

Management cannot anticipate everything; but trying to do so may ultimately prevent a lot of unpleasant surprises. One high-growth company facing litigation had to spend an enormous amount of time on environmental issues—in this case an accusation of improper toxic-waste disposal. Even though the firm was eventually proven innocent, the management and dollar drain was enormous. Anticipating as many issues as possible allows management to prioritize, spending more time on planned activities, rather than on fighting fires. This is preventive maintenance. If you wait to stop production until something breaks, then you end up with more downtime. Similarly, waiting for a lawsuit before instituting affirmative-action policies or establishing recycling and toxic-waste policies is courting disaster. These issues can no longer be viewed as optional. They are fundamental to sound planning and growth and were guiding principles at JPI.

MANAGING PUBLIC RELATIONS

Let's sum up. In public relations, the CEO should consider:[4]

■ *Educational issues.* Businesses today face increasing difficulty locating employees with appropriate skills and motivation. Improvement in the entire educational system, public or private, would greatly offset burgeoning recruiting and training costs. CEOs must evaluate their level of involvement with the educational system. The discrepancy between graduate skills and business needs can no longer be ignored.

■ *Environmental issues.* Today, a drawn-out lawsuit can cripple a business for years, even if the business is guiltless. Efforts demonstrating to the community that a company is making every effort to maintain the environment may avoid costly liabilities.

■ *Safety issues.* Federal and state governments have become increasingly involved with health and safety issues. Once again, awareness and active management of these issues can avoid expensive surprises.

■ *Equal employment and affirmative-action issues.* Increasing government involvement in hiring, firing, promotion, and salary setting—especially when it involves race, sex, age, ethnic origin, and handicapped status—means even smaller firms must be aware of basic requirements. Ignorance of these complex laws is no excuse. Firing low performers can be especially problematic. Many management consultants today offer guidelines for appropriate personnel practices if you need help. Proper guidelines can reduce the chances for litigation from former employees as well as improve relations with existing employees.

■ *Good-neighbor policies.* As United States-based Japanese firms have discovered, active involvement in local community activities often pays rich dividends. Involvement in local charity and youth activities not only helps the community, it helps the company stay in tune with local changes influencing the firm later on.

The very young firm may ignore some of these issues for a while; but untended, they could result in major disruptions. How they are addressed will vary. State and local government offices often have helpful materials covering regulations in the environmental, personnel, and safety areas.

NOTES

[1]*Family Business Review,* a quarterly journal written for both managers and researchers, published by Jossey-Bass since 1988. The Family Firm Institute sponsors this publication, national conferences, regional study groups, a newsletter, and an information center on family firms. Their address is P.O. Box 476, Johnstown, NY 12095.

[2]A recent study of Michigan business executives is very revealing:
   ■ 91 percent report a gap between employee education and skills needed for their jobs.
   ■ Nearly 60 percent would pay higher company taxes if it guaranteed improvement in public educa-

tion—this at a time when state taxes are at an all-time high, an incumbent protax governor was defeated, and the state legislature has frozen property-tax levels. Advocating tax increases for education here suggests the extreme level of perceived need.

- More than 58 percent of those polled said they were willing to help directly, whether by offering jobs to qualified students or by providing speakers or other expertise.

These results were gathered in a poll of Michigan business executives conducted by Macomb Community College's Center for Community Studies for Durocher and Co. and BDO Seidman in 1991 and reported in *Crain's Detroit Business*.

[3]For further reading of sharehold relationships, see Alfred Rappaport, *Creating Shareholder Value: The New Standard for Business Performance* (New York: The Free Press, 1986). More recently, we shifted investor relations to the resource acquisition issue, since it represents a strategy for obtaining external capital.

[4]As noted in the introduction, more recently, we labeled this issue *community/government relations*. Furthermore, in family businesses, the family may be thought of as an overlapping but external system to the organization itself. The presence of the family unit may also factor into how the other six organizational DSP issues are managed. Take, for example, the resource acquisition issue: The family system may influence how hiring is done or how equity investments are handled in the firm (e.g., preferential treatment for family members).

CHAPTER 13

Technical Mastery

Technical mastery is the seventh and final organizational DSP issue you must directly and continually confront to assure your company's success. This chapter explains more about what we mean by technical mastery and how to plan for it. Ask yourself the same kinds of questions we asked CEOs in our research, so you begin to visualize technical mastery more clearly in your own setting.

ASSESSING TECHNICAL MASTERY

**FOR QUESTIONS 13-1 THROUGH 13-4, USE THE
FOLLOWING ANSWER CHOICES:**

[1] Very high: Top 2% of the industry
[2] High: Within top 10%
[3] Well above average: Top 25%
[4] Above average: Top one-third
[5] Average: About the middle
[6] Slightly below average: In the top two-thirds
[7] Well below average: Bottom one-third

Question 13-1: Quality. How do you rate the quality of service you provide, products you make, or projects you carry out? (If a wholesaler, consider the quality of customer services and order-filling accuracy.)

Question 13-2: Productivity. How do you rate your firm's productivity—its ability to complete projects or fill orders on schedule?

Question 13-3: Technical skill.   How do you rate the technical capability of your staff—their potential or skill, not necessarily how they actually perform?

Question 13-4: Technical performance.   How do you rate the technical performance of your staff (how well they actually perform)?

Question 13-5: CEO activities to master technology.   In which activities do you participate to keep up with technical developments in your industry? (Check all that apply.) Do you:

[a] Read trade or other business magazines that might have news relevant to your industry
[b] Attend trade-related shows or conventions
[c] Actively network with members of your trade association
[d] Serve on committees for your trade association
[e] Take seminars related to your industry

Table 13–1 shows how the firms stack up on technical mastery. Of course as self-reported ratings, they are probably inflated, CEOs being even more generous than their managers. But as a quick yardstick, you can use these norms to compare with your own answers. Both CEOs and managers rate technical skill and

TABLE 13–1   Percentages of CEOs and Their Managers Who Rated Their Firms in the Top 2 Percent of Their Industry in Technical Mastery

	ALL FIRMS		TOP PERFORMERS
	MEDIAN	%	%
Quality of Product or Service			
(question 13-1) rated by:			
Managers[a]	1.7	37	52
CEO[b]	1.0	60	71
Productivity			
(question 13-2) rated by:			
Managers[a]	2.0	28	41
CEO[b]	2.0	48	57
Technical Skill			
(question 13-3) rated by:			
Managers[a]	2.0	12	18
CEO[b]	2.0	33	32
Technical Performance			
(question 13-4) rated by:			
Managers[a]	2.3	9	14
CEO[b]	2.0	30	39

[a]Percentages of firms where at least two-thirds of managers rated their firm in the top 2 percent of their own industry.

[b]Percentages of CEOs who rated their firm in the top 2 percent of the industry.

performance lower than they do quality and productivity. About one-third of the CEOs and one-tenth of managers rate their employees' technical skills and performance in the top 2 percent. But half the CEOs put their firm in the top 2 percent for productivity. Sixty percent rate quality in the top 2 percent. Top-performing firms are even *more* highly rated by their CEOs, however, especially in quality and productivity. Though the percentages are lower, the patterns of management ratings are similar for quality and productivity.

WHAT IS TECHNICAL MASTERY?

Technical mastery refers to the firm's product and service know-how. Do key people in the firm understand related vital processes? Can the company provide output in enough quantity and quality to satisfy customer needs? Can it provide needed technical improvements and changes?

Technical mastery includes four components: employee technical *skills;* managerial and lower-level technical *performance;* the *quality* of goods and services produced; and *productivity*—the quantity of goods or services needed to keep up with customer orders.

TECHNICAL MASTERY:
A KOREAN INTRODUCTION

The hub of the microwave-oven industry shifted from the United States to Korea during the 1980s. Samsung Corporation, a diversified giant, was known in the United States at that time only for its personal computer equipment. According to a study by Magaziner and Patinkin, when Samsung Corporation first attempted to enter and lead the microwave-oven market, it couldn't even build one.[1] The first prototype actually melted on a Samsung engineer's kitchen table. Once a prototype was operational, Samsung had to master production. To meet its first order from J. C. Penney's, it had to improve its early rate of production from just 5 ovens a day to 50—a tenfold increase. In addition to long hours of employee dedication, Samsung's success was attributable to close attention to technical training and heavy investment in plant and equipment. Samsung soon employed more PhD engineers for microwave ovens than any American corporation and eventually produced nameplate microwaves for many former competitors—a part of the "hollowing" phenomenon we mentioned in an earlier chapter.[2]

For several decades—some say it started in the 1960s—American companies neglected technology in favor of marketing and financial issues. The decline in emphasis on production management in business schools and a rise in the weight of an MBA for promotions reflected this shift. The strategic importance of technology development is still often ignored in American corporations and is even sent outside the country to be done, while slick marketing and merger plans are hatched instead.

American managers were caught off guard as the Japanese not only copied but surpassed American products in quality, and foreign competitors conquered a widening range of domestic markets, replacing U.S. exporters abroad. We would argue that this was largely caused by lack of attention to quality; and more generally by management's failure to focus closely enough on technical mastery.

THE IMPORTANCE OF TECHNICAL MASTERY

As we discussed in Chapter 5, all four components of technical mastery link with profitability. Technical skills, performance, and productivity link with cash flow. Technical mastery and sales growth are intertwined, as is steadiness of growth. Smooth work flow, including both division of work and coordination of efforts, also links to technical mastery. Technical skills and productivity link most strongly to resource-allocation adequacy. Technical mastery is closely related to human relations and to the firm's public image. The weakest linkage is with resource acquisition. Ability to obtain supplies links to productivity, but that is all. All in all, technical mastery is a critical issue for the firm.

IMPROVING TECHNICAL MASTERY

Technical mastery is influenced by a wide variety of management practices and characteristics. As the Samsung example illustrated, employee skill development is critical to technical mastery. Hiring policy is another influence: Some places hire employees with more education and/or experience, even though the price is higher. Performance appraisal, incentive programs, work climate, and work methods also directly link to technical mastery. Let's look at these practices in more detail.

TABLE 13–2   Activities CEOs Participate in to Keep Abreast of Technical and Managerial Developments in their Industry: Comparison of Top Performers to the Remaining CEOs

	TOP PERFORMERS	REMAINING FIRMS
	$(n = 17)$[a]	$(n = 83)$
Ways in Which the CEO Keeps Up with Technology:		
Reads trade or other business magazines	82%	70%
Attends trade shows or conventions	71	65
Attends industry-related seminars	35	51
Networks with trade assoc. members	18	23
Serves on trade assoc. committees	41	45
Ways in Which the CEO Develops Management Skills:		
Listens to cassette tapes and reads books	39%	44%
Attends 1–3 day seminars	64	69
Attends executive training programs	25	22
Takes university courses	21	27
Acquires BBA or MBA	18	20

[a]This question was not asked of all CEOs. It was added part way through the study.

CEO Education and Development

How do CEOs stay abreast of relevant *technical* developments and management techniques? Table 13–2 provides some answers we got from our CEO interviews. Patterns for top-performing firms are very similar to those of the rest. In both groups, about 70 to 80 percent of CEOs read trade magazines and attend trade shows. Only half attend industry-related seminars (35 percent among top performers). About 20 percent of CEOs network with trade-association members to keep technically abreast. And almost 40 to 45 percent in both groups serve on trade-association committees.

How do CEOs keep up with new *management* techniques? Most popular, with two-thirds of all CEOs, is the one-to-three–day seminar. Forty percent read and/or use audiocassette tapes on their own. Twenty-two percent have taken executive management seminars or university business courses. About one in five have a BBA or an MBA—the same for both top performers and the rest.

Management Training and Development

So far, we've looked at the CEO. How do companies develop supervisory and technical skills for other employees? See Table 13–3 for our research results. For supervisory development, management meetings are most frequently used—by half of all managers, and two of three top performers. One-to-two–day outside seminars are in second place, taken by 25 percent of all managers and almost half of top-

TABLE 13–3   Typical Means for Developing Management and Technical Skills Among Managers

	TOP PERFORMERS	ALL FIRMS	REMAINING FIRMS
Ways to Develop Supervisory Skills			
Discuss management issues in meetings together	64%	51%	48%
Bring in invited speakers	9	9	9
Hold 1–2 day seminars inside the firm	14	11	11
Attend 1–2 day seminars outside the firm	46	28	25
Pay for tuition at area colleges	31	21	19
Invite consultants in to meet individually with managers	5	6	6
Ways to Develop Technical Skills			
On-the-job training: others show newcomer how to do the job	96	80	77
Distribute and review manuals	14	26	28
Hold training programs on special topics	27	21	20
Attend 1–2 day seminars outside the firm	23	30	31
Have groups meet as problem-solving teams	27	20	19
Pay for tuition at area colleges	14	22	24
Purchase training materials	14	15	15
Hire people with required skills	53	40	37

performing firm managers. Managers in one-third of top-performing firms and about 20 percent of remaining firms mention reimbursement for tuition of management and supervisory courses.

As for technical training, on-the-job training (OJT) is by far the most frequently mentioned (by 80 percent overall and almost all managers in top-performing firms). Managers in 27 percent of top-performing firms mention group problem-solving teams where employees learn from each other, compared with 19 percent in the rest. On the other hand, only 14 percent of managers among top-performers mention training manuals versus 28 percent of the rest. And tuition rebates for technical courses are offered by only 14 percent of top-performers compared with 24 percent of the rest.

Hiring Specialized Staff

Managers were asked the extent to which their firms hire specialized technical or professionally trained staff. Overall, 40 percent of the firms stress hiring of people with high skills—along with half of top performers. Not surprisingly, hiring trained staff boosts both employee technical skills and technical-performance levels. Hiring specially trained people also benefits coordination of efforts, especially in firms facing rapid growth or environmental predictability—although in rapid-growth firms, hiring specially trained people can cut profits.

Evaluating Costs and Profits—Not Sales

Performance systems tied to costs, profits, quality, and/or productivity may be more effective than garden-variety sales commissions in achieving technical and financial goals. On the one hand, although the sales commission is easier to compute and administer, it may backfire: Rewards based on raw sales correlate neither to sales growth nor to profitability and have an adverse effect on morale.

Companies that base performance evaluations and award incentives on cost control and profits, on the other hand, report better productivity, profitability, and cash flow. Our evidence suggests about a one-year lag in impact on these variables. Incentives to lower costs and generate higher profits link to profits even more strongly in the following year.

Job Definition and Work Division

Our research clearly showed that written job descriptions can have a negative impact on work flow, productivity, and cash flow, especially in larger outfits—but in many smaller firms, too. How can this be?

For one thing, writing accurate job descriptions requires an enormous amount of work—work that top managers often try to delegate. But when authorship of job definitions is decentralized, stated methods and goals often stray from the CEO's; and lower technical quality is likely to result. In our study, job descriptions have the most negative effect when first-level supervisors and employees author them.

Second, in growing firms, people's roles often change too quickly to be set down in a job description. By the time the ink is dry on the "properly" written description, roles may have changed two or three times. On the other hand, hastily drawn descriptions may have little to do with the person's actual job.

Third, by having job descriptions set "in stone" people are often less willing to handle problems related to their jobs but not written down. Job descriptions can be used as an excuse to let a problem slip through the cracks because dealing with it "isn't in my job description."

Not all job descriptions are bad, of course. Partly confounding the interpretation of research in this area is that firms vary so much in how they develop job descriptions. Descriptions that build in flexibility and that clearly reflect CEO priorities can be useful.

In sum, tread lightly with job descriptions. For many growing firms they may be worse than a waste of time. Although the degree to which employees are clear about their jobs is a strong, positive factor linked to productivity, the written job description is of doubtful value. There are other, more effective techniques to communicate job expectations.

Work-Flow Methods, Delegation, and Technical Mastery

Unlike the written job description, informal conversation, work-group meetings, the chain of command, and setting work standards to coordinate work efforts all result in better technical performance and company productivity.

The management team must be directly involved, so that everyone knows what is expected of them in order to meet goals. This does not necessarily mean the CEO should be involved, but the chain of command must be clear enough so that everyone gives the same message down the line.

Delegation is vital to successful growth; yet if too many people run the show, focus is lost and performance suffers. The more people a CEO delegates to, the worse technical performance and productivity are likely to be. Why? Perhaps management talent lacks depth. Or it may be only a few people are ever really able *and willing* to completely assimilate the CEO's point of view. After all, countervailing personal objectives will always be present. At JPI, a core of two or three top managers was responsible for training plant managers throughout the corporation. According to one former top manager, others hired to do this job never could understand and connect quite as well with the CEO's philosophy, objectives, and methods.

Finding these few managers is crucial, however. In a company past a certain size, a CEO needs to delegate through a chain of command. Bypassing the chain of command also lowers performance, productivity, and even quality.

Part-Time Staff and Technical Mastery

Whether staff are part or full-time can also affect technical mastery. Too heavy a reliance on part-time people, *year round*, links to lower overall technical performance and poorer quality. This does not apply to part-timers hired for peak periods. Recall that JPI avoided hiring part-time people throughout the corporation.

Corporate Climate and Technical Mastery

Several aspects of corporate climate are linked to technical mastery. Trust appears to be most important, linked with all four components of technical mastery.

In addition, where people are *less* afraid to rock the boat, technical skills and productivity are higher. Companies stressing quality report better productivity (though not necessarily higher quality). Where employees believe the CEO knows what is best, technical skills and performance are better, quality is better, and productivity is higher.

HOW TECHNICAL MASTERY WAS APPROACHED
AT J. P. INDUSTRIES

Co-author Dr. Psarouthakis describes how technical mastery was achieved at J. P. Industries (JPI) and the role he played:

"When JPI was started, I was familiar with the industry from my previous work at Masco. Masco had a culture of quality leadership. With a background in both engineering and management, I was sensitive to quality and technology issues in manufacturing and R&D—to the need for improving products and being sensitive to the role technology plays.

"Though it certainly helped me, all entrepreneurs do not have to be engineers to run a factory. One person can't do everything. If your product requires technical or engineering expertise, seek out help in that area.

"I wasn't closely involved with daily technical operations, anyway. That was delegated. My primary role was motivating people to strive for quality and their best performance. I concentrated on cultural 'atmospherics'—and on keeping current on technology and constantly improving know-how.

"My executive vice-president, Gary Reed, was assigned to the actual management of the technology issue, and each plant concentrated on relevant applications of technologies and procedures. But, in a smaller firm, more of these aspects would be concentrated in the CEO."

Volunteer Activities Keep You Current

Dr. Psarouthakis explains the importance of volunteer activities to stay abreast of technological advances: "In addition to reading on my own and attending occasional seminars, another way I also kept current was through volunteer activities with various technology-related institutes and universities. I served on the board of the Industrial Technology Institute (ITI), a research-and-development organization funded both publicly and privately in Michigan to develop improvements in manufacturer productivity and quality. This involvement routinely exposed me to new ideas. For instance, in our bearings group, ITI shared a methodology it developed using lasers in the inspection process to detect bugs and to reject damaged items from the line. I asked my engineers if there might be a relevant application. We never developed a system exactly like ITI's, but the review inspired us to modify and improve our own system. We concluded that we were actually doing pretty well without this level of sophisticated technology. For example, the bearings division was able to deliver 140 million bearings to Ford Motor Company with *no* returns. But at least the division was aware of the state-of-the-art technology and became satisfied that its current process was appropriate.

"At ITI, I also learned about computers for *self-running production*—a somewhat less automated system than a completely computer-controlled manufacturing process. We did implement this at our Grand Haven plant. ITI didn't design this but exposed us to technology that gave us the confidence to design it on our own. I was also active and remain involved with committees and boards of business schools and entrepreneurship programs at several universities.

"Volunteering needs to be done within reason. But I found working with people outside of JPI kept us on the cutting edge of new technologies and management approaches."

IMPROVING QUALITY AND PRODUCTIVITY AT *JPI*

Gary Reed, former executive VP at JPI, was one of the key managers who trained plant managers at acquired divisions. He adds insights about how quality and productivity were achieved at JPI:

How Managers Used to View Quality in the Automotive Industry

"Automobile industry owners and managers figure they have always provided high quality, in spite of historic defect rates that today are viewed as unacceptable. Among firms JPI acquired, this rosy perception prevailed. Everyone said they made high-quality parts. But while the parts worked, they were not without defects. When you asked the workers about quality, they would just laugh. If the manager said they had to meet a shipping schedule, those parts were shipped, defective or not. That used to be widespread in the industry and that undermined the psychology of quality among the hourly people.

"The old view was that you produce your product at any cost and then fix it after it goes off the line. This thinking is rapidly being replaced with the notion that you make your product right the first time. This requires an understanding of the process. That's a big jump for operators as well as for managers, especially if they have been brought up the old way, as was the case in most firms JPI acquired."

Mr. Reed continues: "Shortly after JPI bought a plant in Athens, Alabama, I had a conversation about quality with the plant manager. He thought he had accomplished a great deal by reducing the rejection rate from 5 percent to 1 percent. This probably would have been viewed as a great accomplishment ten years before. The manager couldn't comprehend the new way of thinking, which focuses on *zero* percent rejections by eliminating rejects at the source—not at the finished product stage."

Increased Demands for Quality

"If you don't have quality, you don't survive. At the time JPI acquired its Bellefontaine, Ohio plant, Ford Motor had just informed the plant it would be terminated as a supplier just as soon as a replacement could be found. This was due to an unacceptable defect rate. But rapid changes are possible, and they were made. Four years later, the plant held its account and won Ford's coveted Q1 rating—given only to suppliers with zero defects. The change was achieved with essentially the same personnel and with dramatic technical and organizational modifications of the manufacturing process at the floor level. A technical process must be in place that measures and even creates quality—mere inspection is not enough. The policy driving Ford is that regardless of functional need or cost-benefit analysis, all parts must meet precision specs. If exceptions are made for this part or that dimension because it doesn't seem to matter, then quality standards will again quickly deteriorate throughout the plant."

Turning Quality Around

"In underperforming companies, quality is often low, or mixed, at best. One of the first things to do is to check warranty returns and rejected shipments and to get other customer feedback. Next, institute an inspection process to determine whether and where a particular product is *not* meeting specifications. Then work backward through the production process to determine the source of quality problems. In this way, all faults and defects are recorded and traced. Sometimes as many as 30 defects can be detected for a single part.

"Once the sources of the defects are known, management and employees can work together to correct them. Each defect is tackled individually in order of prevalence until the problem is solved. Most changes are technical, involving machine changes, handling, tool maintenance, or other engineering changes. Acceptable tolerances are much smaller than in years past. Some problems are solved by operators themselves, others by managers, and still others through a team problem-solving effort.

"At JPI there was also a significant investment in equipment, manufacturing, design and inventory control, data processing, and information systems to maintain its edge."

Changes Mandated by the Big Three
to Improve Quality

Jim McAuliffe, former vice-president of human resources, describes other forces that triggered the need for change throughout the automotive-supply business:

"Requirements imposed by the Big Three car makers even went beyond zero defects. They mandated three other major changes in supplier-plant approaches to quality. Beginning in the late 1980s statistical process control was required, a technique requiring on-site education at all of our plants, since few if any of our employees had been trained in this area. Secondly, they mandated participation on the floor. It was no longer acceptable to have a quality system in which the operator would build a part and then an inspector would check for quality. Operators themselves were to participate in the quality assurance process—in short, a requirement by the Big Three to give more control directly to the operator. Inspection departments with 20 or 30 employees were eliminated completely. Now the operator is responsible for both their productivity and their quality.

"A third dramatic change related to quality checking. Previously automakers would go to the Quality Control Department. Now they go out and talk directly to an operator. If you have followed the traditional adversarial labor–management philosophy, having a customer talk directly to operators would have threatened both management and unions. And the employees themselves might have said things you wouldn't want your customer to hear.

"These three major changes—statistical process control, operator-controlled quality systems, and site visits where the Big Three speak directly to operators—began to force change throughout the automotive industry.

"Though implementing these requirements at each JPI plant was certainly a challenge, they were also consistent with Dr. Psarouthakis's basic philosophy described in his corporate handbook, *Better Makes Us Best:* Decisions should be made at all levels, so people have an opportunity to influence the process, and 'buy into the program.' "

Employee Involvement Programs at JPI

McAuliffe further describes the JPI approach to quality: "Quality needs to be present throughout production and can only be achieved if employees are engaged in problem solving. You need their full attention, skills, and know-how so that it takes place. Quality is not achieved through technological and statistical procedures alone but by the total goal orientation of all employees.

"Most JPI plants had about 400 employees, each responsible for achieving quality goals. But JPI did not devise a corporate-wide policy for quality, per se. As long as a plant met its goals, the philosophy was to let the plant pick the program it wanted to follow. But we did introduce plant managers to different concepts by sending them to special seminar programs. For instance, plant managers were sent to a seminar that described the *Scanlon Plan,* a profit-sharing and employee-involvement program. Three managers were so impressed they chose to adopt it.

"According to the plan adopted by JPI plants, a core group of 30 widely representative employees go through training that includes basic accounting, finance, and economics. They are taught that investors, customers, and employees all need to be treated equally and with respect in order to thrive. With guidance, education, and training, middle management and rank and file then develop their own program."

Challenges and Obstacles to Employee Involvement

"The fact that Scanlon worked at one JPI plant in a small town in Iowa does not mean it would work everywhere. The work ethic was deeply instilled among the nonunion employees. A very different climate persisted at another JPI facility in

Great Britain. That plant manager, an engineer by training, operated on a fairly structured and autocratic basis. Though required to hold quarterly plant meetings, he remained skeptical of employee involvement. One brief experiment in quality circles failed because workers were not allowed to discuss process or product issues—only working conditions—and they quickly ran out of things they were allowed to talk about.

"Even in Iowa, several obstacles had to be overcome before the Scanlon Plan was accepted and activated. Top-level staff had to rethink their quality roles, not previously perceived as a universally shared responsibility.

"It took six months for the core group to sign on, much longer than lower-level personnel later took. During that six-month period, managers finally began to really level with each other, agreeing that the plant was far from perfect. They then took the idea to foremen. When it was taken to employees, 98 percent approved it (only 90 percent are required under Scanlon guidelines). The steering committee named its plan *RPM*—for Real Participative Management.

"Some supervisors hesitated because they wondered whether they were competent to carry out the project. Others wondered if employees were willing to change and whether authoritarian managers were willing to become more participative. Economics courses and a 24-week supervisory training program in team leadership and problem solving were introduced in response to these concerns.

"Another obstacle to Scanlon implementation involved low employee skills, with the average plant employee functioning at a *seventh*-grade education level! A related obstacle was a *job-bidding* system that could put someone with more seniority but less skill or motivation at critical machines. In response to these obstacles, JPI tested and developed refresher algebra and reading courses on site, as well as statistics, computer, and problem-solving courses. As an incentive for training, the pay system was changed from seniority to *pay-for-knowledge,* which tied incremental raises to training.

"Pay-for-knowledge programs represent a major personnel change that greatly augmented employee technical skill levels. Pay-for-knowledge was developed by a team of plant and human-resource managers. First, employees were multifunctionally ranked. Second, there was literacy testing. Then, as skills improved, pay improved. Under the new program, employees could go from $6 at entry level to $12 at a multiskilled level. The differential compares with only $.50 for people of the same seniority before the new program was implemented. Pay-for-knowledge allowed plant managers to move people around the plant, as needed, in addition to motivating employees to improve their skills. At one unionized plant, employees eliminated all job classifications and were simply listed as 'team member.' "

Outcomes of the Scanlon Plan

"Iowa-plant Scanlon outcomes are noticeable. Employees began to contribute cost-saving ideas. At one economic education seminar, the scrap rate and its costs to the plant were discussed. A press operator asked, 'I scrapped out 10,000 bearings last month. How much do they cost at my operation?' The leader answered, 'A dollar a piece.' She responded, 'You mean I scrapped out $10,000? I know how to fix it. Come on.' And they went out and fixed it. People were not used to being asked for input. This episode occurred during the early phases when training had begun but the gain-sharing portion had not even been approved yet! This operator was just waiting to be asked. Now she was more knowledgeable about scrap and its impact—which managers and CEOs often take for granted.

"As changes from employee ideas and team efforts with management were introduced, the Iowa plant markedly improved quality, earning General Motors' Mark of Excellence and Ford's Q1 ratings. The plant eventually shipped parts that were put on the line without being inspected first (the ultimate compliment to a supplier of a quality-conscious firm!). Profits improved at both the Iowa plant and its client GM facility. Practical education levels dramatically improved. Of the 800 suggestions the plant received in Scanlon's first year, 80 percent were process and product oriented—ideas that reduce costs.

"Employee involvement reduces costs and improves productivity, as well. Shortly after the Scanlon Plan was introduced, we hit a business downturn. The employees saw profits falling and determined that 65 people would be laid off. This was nominally approved by the hourly committee. They knew that this was the right number. The plant manager, a 20-year veteran, noted at the time that this was the first time he could remember that layoffs meant *no* decline in remaining worker productivity. The employees disliked doing it, but they had a detailed understanding of what overstaffing meant to them and the company and knew that cutbacks had to be done.

"As sales rebounded, management figured it could bring back 30 people. But in keeping with the Scanlon process, they asked for employee input. At this point, many employees had already been through the economic literacy program and a gain-sharing program had been initiated. They looked at the full cost of bringing 30 people back and the workload and figured the company could get by with 4 people instead. Trust, open communication, and knowledge of costs brought this convergence of interest.

"Though not all plants chose Scanlon, almost every JPI plant adopted a training program for employee involvement—self-led and self-taught by employees and supervisors. Statistical process control was also introduced to all plants. Other changes were made throughout the plants: Lines were deliberately blurred between salaried and hourly workers; benefit inequities, such as time off for family illness and deaths, were made more comparable. Some other plants adopted other quality-improvement programs: the total quality-involvement program designed by Florida Power and Light; and Dr. Deming's program."[3]

Investment in Training and Development

McAuliffe further elaborates on the training done at JPI to maintain its competitive edge in technology:

"The investment in employee training at JPI was extensive. Elementary reading, mathematics, economics, and computer skills are important for workers to control machine tools numerically. Training in team collaborative efforts and formal management at upper levels is also necessary. Accounting people also need to keep up to speed in their areas. Subject to management approval, employees at JPI could sign up for technical seminars and workshops, encompassing computer design-applications, new machine-tool operations, product development, advanced materials, and advances in design.

"JPI plant managers were strongly advised, but not required, to take a formal management-training program. The plants picked which one they wanted and soon the word got around that the program was worthwhile.

"JPI also arranged periodic meetings between related plants to exchange ideas. Some acquisitions had been multiplant companies, where the same products were being made, yet no sharing was going on. In one instance, before their acquisition, a group of plants that had previously been part of the same multidivision firm had actually been forbidden by management from talking to one another. This included the discussing of solutions to commonly shared technical problems!"

Technical Mastery at JPI: Recap

Although JPI is much larger than those in our study, most firms it acquired were like our "small" to "medium" firm. Most failed to manage the issue of technical mastery prior to acquisition. Profits lagged, key customers threatened to pull out, and many would probably not have survived without JPI's changes. JPI invested in people—through training in problem solving, mathematics, economics, and technology. JPI followed through with computers, modern factory equipment, and a reorganization to bring employee involvement into daily operational decisions. Quality and productivity followed.

THE BUFFALO PROGRAM

Coastal Chem is a single-plant chemical-processing division with 150 employees. It was independent before being sold to Coastal Corporation, a FORTUNE 50 firm, but was still autonomously run by president Leo Smith. His efforts provide another example of how to use employee involvement to improve quality and reduce costs. Here is a first-hand account:

"Though I had looked into Scanlon, I developed my own employee involvement and gain-sharing program somewhat differently. I named it the *Buffalo Program,* inspired by a poster I saw of two buffalos fighting and the slogan underneath that read: 'Bring on the competition.' I bought 50 of these posters and put them up around the plant. Then I got a limited-edition belt buckle with a buffalo on it, and the same slogan. After I wore it around the plant for a few weeks, employees started asking where they could get one, too. I responded, 'Would you like one? Give me an idea to make this place run better. The ideas are worth a belt.' Then I switched to $18 gold-plated buffalo watches when almost everyone had a belt. I called this the 'buffalo' program and called the ideas 'buffalo ideas.' And the suggestion box?—the buffalo feed bin!"

Though the buffalo belts and watches gave the program its identity, a profit-sharing program didn't hurt acceptance. Leo Smith, like any other CEO, was under constant pressure to adjust wages up along with the cost of living. But no such automatic increase took place that year. Any increases would have to be earned, and on a teamwork basis. Two factors calculated profit-share: how well the plant met its budgeted materials for the month and how profitable the plant was (computed as a percentage of the monthly earnings budget). So it wasn't just the buffalo watches alone, although the buffalo was an appealing image to the employees in this Western town.

In 1985, prior to the plan, Coastal Chem lost a little money. At the start of the Buffalo Program, in 1986, the subsidiary earned about $50,000 (but on a half-billion–dollar investment!). But after four years on the Buffalo Program the company had broken all earnings records and was generating 20–25 percent return on assets, almost doubling revenues at the same time!

As with many change efforts, some employees are skeptical at first, often holding back ideas. Coastal Chem was no different. Smith describes his efforts to win Wally Daniels over to the program: "Several months into the program Wally still didn't have his watch and didn't seem particularly interested in getting one. I wanted to get everyone involved. One day, I went up and asked him to give me a Buffalo idea. Wally shrugged at first. He said no one wanted to listen to his ideas anyway. But I pushed him and he finally pointed to a corner where he worked. Some product was being lost from a remelt tank in the high-density ammonium nitrate plant. No one but Wally had noticed this before, and it turned out it was costing the plant $80,000 a year in waste. Wally allowed that this could be remedied. It would cost about $25,000 to fix the problem using Wally's solution of putting in a special heat exchanger.

"I immediately took the idea to the production manager. One of the important aspects of the program was quick response to ideas, and I wanted to get Wally his watch. The idea checked out. Even though the engineers eventually solved the problem without spending a dime, Wally got his watch! This group involvement of employees and engineers was typical. Suggestions were seldom received that could be acted upon without joint effort. This also built team spirit because people who may never have worked together before were solving problems together."

One hundred thousand dollars was saved by reducing scrap; another $100,000 from tapping unnoticed effluent. These employees at JPI and Coastal Chem had in some cases known about problems for months or even years. But before these programs were started, they felt that either the problems or their opinions were unimportant.

The really astounding part of these success stories is that most are within the firm's existing capabilities. Outside consultants might occasionally make sense, but often an enormous amount of know-how is just sitting there inside the firm, waiting to be tapped. In short, technical mastery is not just training on a new machine or introducing a new statistical technique but is also a management philosophy of total employee involvement in developing quality solutions.

MANAGING TECHNICAL MASTERY

Today technical mastery may be the biggest challenge. It is no longer satisfactory to produce "OK quality." In manufacturing, zero defects are required. In wholesale and services, the caliber of service given to each customer has an impact on the firm. The results from our interviews point to avenues for CEOs to take as the firm grows:

- Keep current in technological developments. Read trade magazines and attend trade shows.

- Find a one- or two-day seminar in your area on a relevant topic in management or technology.

- Hire people with the specialized technical or professional training needed, but weigh the costs and benefits.

- Evaluate performance and provide incentives for cost control and profits, rather than using sales revenues.

- Don't rely on written job descriptions to assure proper performance. If you use job descriptions, be involved yourself. When the immediate supervisor or an employee writes a job description, it may be worse than having no job description at all.

- Be sure, however, that employees are clear about their jobs and what they are expected to do. In larger firms especially, chain of command is effectively used to inform people about what work they are expected to perform when the CEO can no longer make the rounds.

- Be cautious about using part-time staff. This may hurt the quality of the overall services or goods you provide.

- Foster a positive climate of trust, collaboration, and innovation. This is likely to improve quality and productivity.

- Empower each employee to contribute to daily operations by introducing problem-solving meetings, employee-involvement programs, and profit-sharing or other incentive programs, and by instilling the underlying philosophy that each person's contributions are important.

As the firm gets larger, it often invests more in R&D and gets more specialized; but the supposed gain from such specialization—more collective know-how—can't be realized unless everyone works together as a team. Effective people management plays a surprisingly integral role in achieving technical mastery.

NOTES

[1]Ira C. Magaziner and Mark Patinkin, "Fast Heat: How Korea Won the Microwave War," *Harvard Business Review*, 67 (1989), 83–93. Also, Ira C. Magaziner and Mark Patinkin, *The Silent War: Inside the Global Business Battles Shaping America's Future* (New York: Random House, 1990).

For more background on Korea, see also T. W. Kang, *Is Korean the Next Japan?: Understanding the Structure, Strategy, and Tactics of America's Next Competitor* (New York: The Free Press, 1989). For further reading on strategic management of technology, see Rod F. Monger, *Mastering Technology: A Management Framework for Getting Results* (New York: The Free Press, 1988).

[2]Michael Umble and Mokshagundam L. Srikanth, *Synchronous Manufacturing: Principles for World-Class Excellence* (Cincinnati: South-Western Publishing Co., 1990).

[3]Rafael Aguayo, *Dr. Deming: The American Who Taught the Japanese About Quality* (New York: Lyle Stuart, Carol Publishing Group, 1990).

CHAPTER 14

Bringing About Change in a Growing Company

Your brakes are worn. So you fix them. Your cash is dwindling but receivables are growing. So you take out a loan. Easy enough: objective problems with simple solutions.

Now try improving productivity: Buy a new computer for accounting. But the bookkeeper is reluctant to learn either keyboard or software.

Set out a suggestion box. No entries appear after a week.

Work slips through cracks. Everyone knows it, but no one does anything about it.

Why are changes involving other people so difficult to make? Why does all change induce fear of loss, even when it's obviously intended to yield a *win-win* situation (one in which both sides gain)?

Changing behavior is both science and art. It is so challenging that a management-science specialty has emerged called *organization development* to address this very issue.[1] Organization development (OD) should not be confused with a growing outfit's unplanned evolution. OD deals primarily with *planned* change, the application of behavioral science to make changes effectively.

IT STARTS WITH THE *CEO*

What triggers a CEO to initiate change? The list includes:

- An old approach not working well
- A change in goals not due to existing problems
- A major change in structure or other internal circumstances
- An openness to change or experimentation—a willingness to try something new for its own sake.

You may want to come up with a personal example as we review each category.

An Old Approach Not Working Well

Sooner or later many CEOs recognize that an old approach has stopped working well—in human relations, work flow, or any other DSP issue. They see a tiresome pattern of crisis management replacing what was formerly a smooth road to profits. Some other CEOs realize they have lacked any type of system or plan all along, which has been stifling them. Declining sales quickly triggers calls for change. A climate of conflict and distrust can slowly build through normal operation of a grapevine, unless counteracted routinely by management's pro-employee initiatives. Other CEOs are ready for change when they notice that things are dropping through the cracks, that a formerly tight control is weakening, or that expenses are rising inordinately.

Some problems arise because of a change in external circumstances. Some CEOs mention government regulations as triggers for change. Others cite increasing competition, changing customer demands, changing applicant pools, and changes in customer paying habits. These changes often trigger a chain reaction that makes former management solutions outmoded.

A Change in Goals Not Due to Existing Problems

Among CEOs we interviewed, some emphasized positive goals to be achieved through change, including a desire to increase efficiency and control costs, gain more input from employees, or a need to professionalize. Others want "better communication," better quality, more clearly defined duties, reduced risk or better employee motivation. Of course, implicit in some of these cases is an attack on intractable problems. Differences between CEOs who "confront problems created by old approaches" and those "responding to opportunities to improve" reflect, mainly, differences in personality. Is the glass half empty or is it half full?

A Major Change in Structure or Other Internal Circumstances

Some changes from within spur other changes along. A new president or management group is guaranteed to provoke many alterations in style and substance; even if conditions don't demand it, the heat is on them to assert authority, and widespread change often results. Sheer growth (or rapid shrinkage) in numbers of employees is one of the most common triggers CEOs mention. The same is true for advancing company age and maturation of the staff. So, too, for a merger. As managers mature, they are ready to take on new duties. As a firm acquires a better cash position, it can then afford to tinker with its control systems and its distribution, etc. Sometimes the CEO has a change in attitude, perhaps because of a seminal personal experience. A change in the business mission, such as "diversification," is a powerful mutating force. So is new technology.

The Willingness to Try Something New for Its Own Sake

A new idea or suggestion from a consultant, a seminar, or even a social acquaintance can be powerful, despite lack of an observable impetus. Again, personality enters in. Some CEOs are more apt to change for change's sake, remaining on the cutting edge of managerial and technical innovation.

Summary of Triggers for Change

It should be clear from the many examples provided here that CEOs will find numerous reasons to rethink and modify past strategies.

MISTAKES *CEOs* MAKE DURING CHANGES

Successful planned change is possible, but it rarely goes smoothly. Many CEOs become frustrated because they underestimate the complexity of many alterations and the expertise required to bring them about. So beware of oversimplifying any change process. Management of the people involved is critical. Traditional management consultants do not always take people's natural resistance to change into account. A CPA or computer firm may recommend a new computer system or an accounting or cost-control structure to address a technical requirement. But the process of introducing change itself may be ignored. By oversimplifying or ignoring "process issues" altogether, CEOs run the risk of costly failure: a new computer that sits idle; a bonus system that in fact demotivates. Effective CEOs see any change as requiring careful study, comprehensive pretesting, and special choreography to maximize initial acceptance, understanding, and commitment of all employees affected. And on the heels of even the smoothest roll-outs comes the need to manage the new problems, vacuuming up good feedback, and taking bad feedback willingly, even *gratefully.* Let's look at typical mistakes CEOs make in introducing change.

Mistake #1: Ignore resistance to change.   Some CEOs tend to ignore people's built-in resistance to change: The resistance doesn't exist—or at least it shouldn't exist. Many CEOs have a take-charge attitude, allowing them to embrace change more quickly than the average adult. Simply making the decision to work for yourself takes a certain type of personality. Change is like taking a breath of fresh air. It is hard to understand and empathize with employees who actually fear change. After all, whose brainchild is it, usually, anyway? It's easy to get fond of your own ideas.

Badgering employees into acceptance of change is as ineffective as chiding a toddler for being afraid of the dark. Resistance based on fear is overcome through knowledge of and experience with the change; it's halfway overcome when an employee becomes convinced it won't cause their imminent termination. Other resistance may actually be warranted. Change is costly—emotionally, time-wise, and, often, even financially. And guess what—your employees might know something about the change that you don't. Their input and participation in planning and designing the change cannot only reduce resistance to change but often improves it, too. The alternative to involving them is to discredit yourself if a critical impediment thus remains in place.

Mistake #2: Inadequately diagnose the problem.   Another oversimplification is premature diagnosis. If you are not familiar with them already, it is helpful to review basic guidelines in the problem-solving process. Specialists in organization development agree that thorough diagnosis of many problems involves fact gathering from *all* levels, not just a CEO's immediate managerial circle. Involving more people is time consuming but assures more accurate determinations of the problem. There are many ways to do this, depending on the controversy, the size of your firm, and your budget. We return to this a little later.

Mistake #3: Define inappropriate solutions.   There are two ways to reduce one's chances of picking the wrong solution. Careful review of available resources is critical, including reviewing the knowledge, training, and motivation of employees who will implement the change. ''Experts'' can often help present an array of options that management and employees might not otherwise have considered. But solutions often need to be customized to fit a particular organization. Delegating the design of a change to an outsider can lead to plans that are wholly incompatible with a company's mission, culture, structure, or other aspect of the system. Frustration with past consultancy experiences was a surprisingly strong and fairly widespread sentiment among growth-company CEOs at the President's Forum (at Eastern Michigan University).

Leo Smith, president of Coastal Corp. is a good example of a CEO who took the time to design his own change effort without a lot of outside help. How did he do it? He boned up on the topic by reading on his own. He felt that his self-designed ''Buffalo Program'' fit his Wyoming-ites better than previously designed programs such as the more committee-oriented Scanlon Plan—even though both have elements of employee involvement and gainsharing (and the latter has been successfully applied elsewhere).

Mistake #4: Fail to evaluate the change.   Organizations have a way of repeating the same mistakes over and over. This comes about when they fail to evaluate the outcomes of changes already introduced. To maximize the return on time and money invested in diagnosis and execution of a particular plan, it is very helpful to measure its impact afterward.

Be sure to measure your *baseline* correctly (where you started from) and also where you end up.

OVERVIEW OF THE STEPS IN SUCCESSFUL CHANGE

The *action-research model* is a basic sequence to follow in designing change.[2] This model is difficult to implement when the corporate climate is one of distrust. It's predicated on CEO, manager, and employee openness to try new things. This convergence can happen in major crises or in times of good employee relations. To overcome pitfalls faced in this change process, the action-research model lays out these simple steps:

- Realization that a problem exists
- Development of commitment to change
- Diagnosis of the problem
- Development of an action plan
- Its implementation
- Evaluation and follow-up

Realization That a Problem Exists

No change is likely unless there is a general consensus that a significant problem or opportunity exists. Sometimes this simple step can take several months, as in an example from J. P. Industries (JPI) we'll look at shortly.

Development of the Commitment to Change

One big obstacle to change is distrust among employees. "Is this just some scheme to get more work out of us, or does management really care what we think?" "Is this going to result in layoffs or shorter hours?" "What about my own (vaunted) title?" Then there's the classic fear of all: "They're tinkering with my paycheck!" These common employee concerns reflect a lack of trust between managers and employees—a lack of trust often developed from previous mishandling of change. But without trust it will be difficult to change anything successfully. Building trust is a gradual process that continues before and during the change effort.

Along with simple trust, a certain level of commitment is needed foremost by the CEO, but also by affected managers and employees. Some programs are successful despite unilateral CEO design and implementation. Smith's program with nonunion employees is a good case in point. Others, such as the Scanlon Plan, require 100 percent consensus among top-level staff and 90 percent agreement among remaining employees, before going ahead. A formal vote is actually taken at plants that adopt Scanlon programs. This structured consensus approach can be especially helpful in unionized firms.

Diagnosis of the Current Situation

Once open to the notion that change is needed, you still need to plan what that change will look like. The next step in the action-research model is careful diagnosis.

The depth to which a diagnosis is made varies with the scope of the problem and the CEO's own orientation. In small companies the CEO already sees and hears nearly everything that goes on. Sophisticated diagnostic tools may not be necessary there. However, even in groups of five or ten, if the CEO is not an experienced communicator, problems can bubble below the surface. Employees are afraid to bring these up or figure they have petitioned before to no avail. Above 20 employees, it's hard on a daily basis for CEOs to keep up with day-to-day activity and to spot problems in every sector. A pattern of gradual decay in information quality often emerges, because of filtering through middle managers. (''Concerns of employees are too petty to bother with.'') Or managers may fear employee problems reflect badly on their management acumen. The informal means that the CEO used in the past to stay in touch with employees—seeing and hearing everything by wandering around and talking to people—is no longer quite adequate. To offset information decay, specific diagnostic approaches are used to say in touch overall and to explore more narrow issues: anonymous surveys (advised *only* if the CEO is prepared to follow up with feedback to employees about which of their concerns will be acted upon); informal group meetings at which the CEO can meet face to face with the rank-and-file; one-on-one conversations and interviews with individual employees; direct observation, either informally by the CEO or by someone formally trained to collect observational data; and finally, systematic review of records for patterns of defects, absenteeism, turnover, sales, special orders, costs or any other information that can be reviewed in tabular form. In larger firms, employees and middle managers can assist with this data gathering. Each CEO must decide which combination needs to be used to stay in touch. What kinds of questions should be asked in a survey? The Dynamic System Planning Model provides a framework for quickly inventorying and targeting areas of greatest concern. We'll cover this in more detail.

Developing an Action Plan

The diagnosis lays the foundation. Now determine the area in most need of change and the way to go about it. Although approaches of other firms provide some direction, take into account your unique employee personalities, the age and size of your firm, and the nature of your industry.

Have both management and rank-and-file brainstorm different ideas. Be open. No idea ''is bad.'' Better put—any creative thinking is welcome. Don't analyze ideas at first: Log them in without criticism or comment. Then you have a wider universe to choose from. Often, this process works even better if everyone writes their ideas down first before sharing them. This process, referred to before as the *Nominal Group Technique,* equalizes power and ''air time'' more effectively than typical brainstorming.[3] Whatever technique you use, make sure the problem-identification phase is completed before solutions are identified.

Evaluating Changes

Change programs often have one or more of the following goals: increased productivity, increased sales, increased profits, improved employee trust, lower absenteeism and turnover. To evaluate the results of a change program, certain guidelines should be followed:

  a. Decide on what you hope to accomplish *before* you introduce the change.
  b. Then come up with some way of measuring whether you reached your target (higher profit or sales, lower absenteeism or turnover, more quality-improvement ideas).

c. Be sure to take baseline measures—how good were you doing before you changed anything. (Even for objective measures, try not to do this retrospectively).

d. If it makes sense to do so, take *control* measurements before the change, also. (More on this in a minute).

e. Make the change.

f. Once the change has been made, determine whether the change actually got implemented to specification (hoped-for consequences aside).

g. Take your follow-up measurements. You might want to do this over time, especially if you see dramatic improvement. Some changes bring short-term improvement, which drops off sharply over time. Other changes linger.

Suppose that you set up a management-by-objectives program for your sales force in which each rep sets his or her own target. You want to decide whether delegating the target to the individual rep is a good idea—in particular, if it will boost sales.

Now you institute the program. Sales climb. Was it due to the program or some other cause? How can you know? If you introduced the change to the whole sales force at once and lack a good comparison group, you probably won't be able to uncover the answers to these questions. What can you do to be sure next time that it's really your program and not just an up-tic in the economy that is boosting sales? Traditional evaluation calls for a *control*—comparison with a similar division or department not influenced by the change. But most growing firms lack a suitable internal control—they are too small. Sometimes you might be able to compare your firm's performance to industry standards. If sales are increasing while most competitors' sales decline, this might suggest that the change helped. Of course, this allows comparison on only readily published information for your industry.

Even if your firm is large enough to define a separate control group—a group that is similar to the *experimental* group but that will not be introduced to the change—you are still faced with difficulties. People talk to each other or hear through the grapevine what some other department is doing. ("Why don't we get to set *our* goals?") Jealousy may occur and an actual performance decline can follow!

One alternative is a *phased-control approach.* Even if you don't have different sales departments, perhaps you have enough sales reps to divide into teams or groups. Phase in change for each group. The first group will serve as the *experimental* group the first go-round; the others will be temporary *controls.* One by one, as each group is introduced to the change, it acts as an experimental group, in turn. Eventually, everyone has had a chance to try the new program. If you see spikes of improvement after each group has been introduced to the change (but not before), then you can be reasonably sure your plan is working.

Of course, depending on the type of change, a drawback to the phased-control approach is its potential expense. You're committed to the change for everyone. It might be worth piloting a program, first, to test whether a change is workable and well received, before fully introducing it to everyone. But don't abandon evaluation on a larger scale. Otherwise, as is often the case, you may simply end up with a "pleasant" program that everyone "enjoyed" but never see any bottom-line or sales results.

Evaluation doesn't really cost much. It requires discipline to plan and gather data at certain intervals and to look at that data later to see whether you got your anticipated results. But if you forget to collect data before the program begins, it is often too late to go back and get all the information you want, retroactively. A little planning will go a long way.

Evaluation sounds like a lot of bother. But why spend far more time and money on training programs, new policies, and new equipment—without knowing whether it was really worth the effort? Evaluation can provide added proofs of success, giving confidence that the change is worth the investment. This helps make your future change efforts more productive and cost effective. Evaluation often suggests a modified action plan to resolve thoroughly some remaining elements of the problem—whether it means installing a new computer system or an employee-involvement program.[4]

GATHERING DATA

To find out what is really going on within your firm, try:

- Direct visual inspection
- Review and analysis of records
- Informal individual or group discussions
- More formally designed interviews for the individual or group
- The questionnaire

Direct Visual Inspection

Observation is the simplest and most commonly used data-gathering device. Simply wandering through the work area can be eye-opening. Is the workplace clean or dirty? Are people alert? Do obvious safety problems persist? Are assemblers tripping over excess inventory instead of taking the time to notify their comrades upstream?

Develop a mental or written checklist to gather observations on the same issues in a consistent, trackable way. Direct observation is very powerful, but a lot of CEOs don't venture out of offices they themselves rendered too "cushy." They may be missing more than they know.

Review and Analysis of Records

All firms keep records. But to provide insight into nagging problems, existing data can often be recompiled to reveal new insights. Payroll information is seemingly mundane. Attendance, for example, is recorded to determine use of sick days or unexcused absences. But the *overall* rate of absence, or the rate of absence for different departments should be examined for trends. High departmental absenteeism is often a symptom of poor morale, which in turn reflects some other problem you need to probe for. Turnover rate is also important to track by department. Absenteeism and turnover should be compared against rates for your industry. Seventy percent turnover may be terrible in the lumber business, but terrific in the fast-food industry. A rate that is out of line in one area of your firm suggests problems that require further diagnosis—is the problem a poor supervisor, or improper hiring practices? Look at what kind of employee is leaving. Is it low performers (suggesting that perhaps they shouldn't have been hired in the first place) or your top performers (suggesting that you may want to examine how you differentially reward good and poor performers)?

Sales and production records can also reveal useful trends. A solar-panel manufacturer sold product more or less by the size and shape each customer needed. Overzealous, commission-only sales reps wanted to squeeze as much square footage on the side of the house as possible, even if it meant cutting odd-shaped pieces around windows and doorways. The net result was an enormous assortment of sizes and shapes—and scrap from the process—as well as lost money when an order was cancelled after a custom-sized panel had already been put into production.

After months of debate, an assistant to the CEO finally took all the production data and made a chart. She found through a simple tabulation that about 80 percent of the panels were made in about 20 percent of the sizes. That convinced the CEO he could accommodate most orders with about five standard sizes of panels—and simply not accept odd, money-losing orders.

Much progress in quality improvement comes from study of records. Rates of defect are measured for every step in the production process. Look at which production steps account for the greatest number of defects. Tackle those first. Analyze the types of defects, also. Armed with this information, employees and managers can work jointly to come up with ways to eliminate them.

Informal Discussions and Group Interviews

Interviews occur either casually or more formally, and with individuals or groups.

The most common is the informal conversation. Successful CEOs go right to employees in their regular workplace settings—it's less intimidating than having the employee "called on the carpet." In their book *In Search of Excellence*, Peters and Waterman discuss this technique of "walking around."[5] This technique requires minimal advance preparation. But be aware of risks that comments will be misinterpreted as mandates or directives. Emphatically do not bypass middle managers while doing this. This doesn't mean you can't talk directly to employees, but that you be aware of the *implied* and actual messages given in such a tour. Control misinterpretations by simply telling people that your queries and comments should not be interpreted as orders and that any changes will come directly from their immediate supervisor.

Meetings with groups are another diagnostic tool. They can be totally unstructured, with perhaps a few initial questions such as: "What do you see as areas for improvement right now?" "Are there any aspects of operations that hamper your ability to perform as well as you might like?" More focused questions then can follow on narrower issues.

Group settings can save time, and for some issues, they are more effective problem solvers than individual conversations: Employees can build on others' ideas. But if the current climate is one of high distrust and conflict, such meetings can degenerate into counterproductive blaming sessions, or worse. Employees may be afraid to say anything at all, for fear of repercussions. Although a desired long-term goal is to build trust and openness of communication, that groundwork may need to be laid before group problem solving is implemented.

An alternative is private one-on-one meetings. If you need a focused, accurate picture, design a structured interview. These assure that the same issues are discussed with people one after the other. Yet talking allows more nonverbal cues, flexibility, and follow-up than any questionnaire. Unique comments can emerge that provide important insights.

We have suggested a number of questions throughout the book that can be used in such an interview with your managers. Appendix B notes additional questions you can use.[6]

The Questionnaire

The questionnaire is often routinely used in larger firms to measure the employee and customer pulse. Small and medium-sized companies use them to explore opinions employees have about their jobs, their supervisors, and the firm in a confidential, but inexpensive, manner. Properly administered, a questionnaire can provide you with insights on obstacles to effective operation, which you may have no other way of obtaining.

One of its major advantages is efficiency: Large numbers of employees can be surveyed at relatively low cost. But this must be weighed against pitfalls such as inflexibility in what can be asked. You can't effectively counteract this with global introductory or closing questions: "Do you have anything else to add?" or "What do you see as areas of improvement?" Most respondents ignore such questions or answer them in such specific terms that it is difficult to determine more general trends among employees. Another drawback is the lack of "richness" inherent in the questionnaire item, which often makes interpretation of data difficult. The survey may detect a climate of distrust but follow-up questions (i.e., what is causing the distrust? What changes need to be made?) don't fit well into questionnaire format and are not likely to be answered, even when they are asked.

Questionnaires also fail to convey empathy or emotion. Talking with a manager face to face, the employee feels their opinion is important, that the manager is taking time out of his or her busy day to listen and show concern. A piece of paper accomplishes none of this, even with the vaunted personalized cover letter from the CEO. (Everyone *knows* the signature is rubber-stamped.)

The most appropriate way to use the survey is in a feedback effort: Employees jointly participate in survey design. Once data is collected, groups of employees, usually organized by department, discuss results and implications. Surveys are completed anonymously and only aggregate or combined responses for groups of five or more people are shared, to assure confidentiality. The questionnaire can thus be used as a tool in a group problem-solving session, as described in the previous section. Be cautioned that a group leader usually requires a certain level of training and expertise to run such a meeting productively. Without appropriate training, feedback sessions have been known to backfire—leaving a defensive, frustrated supervisor who swears he will never get put in this awkward position again and equally disappointed employees disillusioned and distrustful of management.

Writing good survey questions seems simple but also requires a fair degree of sophistication and experience. If the firm does not have access to someone trained in survey techniques, it can still improve overall survey quality by following these general guidelines:

1. Avoid asking for respondent names. Confidentiality is essential to honest answers.

2. Avoid asking other identity-revealing questions. In a small firm, just one or two demographic questions can pinpoint a specific person. Questions such as age, seniority, and job title aren't usually needed and destroy confidentiality in a small firm.

3. Pay attention to every detail—even the way in which employees turn in their surveys. One manager set out a cardboard box with a slot. Employees did the survey in their free time, rather than in one large group. As each individual turned it in, the manager reached in the box to pull the survey out obviously destroying the intended confidentiality. Three alternatives are better: a) Have all employees complete and turn in the survey in groups of five or more people; b) use an outside firm (however, this can be costly); or c) have a stamped envelope so that the employee can mail the response back directly to the CEO's office.

4. Use a cover letter. Explain who is doing the survey, how the information will be combined, what the information will be used for, and who will receive the results.

5. "Feed back" results. A survey feedback approach provides a report to all participants and is strongly advised. Surveys without feedback may actually *harm* the firm. Employees pour out their innermost thoughts, expecting *some* response or results. When none is given, strong resentment can result.

6. Act on results. From the employee perspective, at least before, employees could excuse a particular problem because they assumed that management didn't know about it. Now management knows and it's still doing nothing. Unless you plan to commit to a full diagnostic program in which you respond to survey results, better skip this approach and wait until you can carry out the whole feedback process.

7. Keep surveys short. Length depends a lot on whether you will provide time during the work day to complete the survey and on the reading level of the typical respondent. Even good high-school students typically read at *half* the speed of college juniors. A seventh-grade reading level is typical among blue-collar workers. Others may not be able to read at all. A "simple, short" survey could take someone an hour or more to complete. A good rule of thumb for a paper-and-pencil questionnaire is that it should be able to be completed in less than 20 minutes. After that, most respondents tend to lose interest. If more in-depth information is needed, combine interview and questionnaire formats. To keep a survey short, be very hard-nosed about what to include. Every question should have a reason for being there or should be tossed out!

8. *Avoid building bias in as you write questions*. Don't imply how you would like a question answered by writing leading questions.

9. *Avoid ambiguity*. It is amazing how many words in the English language carry multiple and conflicting meanings. Even a word such as "supervisor," straightforward enough in most settings, can become a source of confusion if you use rotating shifts, or have a floor supervisor as well as a shift supervisor. Keep in mind usage common in your firm, especially if you are borrowing questions from somebody else's survey or off some boilerplate a consultant gave you.

10. *If English is a second language to many employees, translate the survey*. If they don't understand the questions properly, their answers will be meaningless.

11. *Have specific answers to choose from*. This greatly increases the speed with which results can be tabulated and also gives comparable data across employees on the same issues. You've seen examples of the Likert scale throughout the book: A range of answers in which specific words are provided for each answer choice. This is much better than the "ten-point scale," which only anchors the two ends of the scale with words such as beautiful and ugly. Even if you invent your own questions, try to adapt a scale someone else has used.

12. *Include all possible answer choices*. Even for a simple question such as "marital status," remember to include separated, widowed, and divorced, along with married and single. Omitting categories leads to confusion, less interest in the survey ("they left out *my* title, did they!"), and reduced accuracy.

13. *Pretest your questions*. It is hard to write surveys perfectly the first time. So pretest your survey before giving it to all employees: Simply ask some people to take the survey and let you know if any questions are not clear or can be interpreted more than one way. Ideally, locate people with similar education and jobs to take the survey. Use your spouse and kids if you have to! If you have no one to try it out on but your own employees, give it to a very limited group, first, and work out the bugs that way. For the pretest, ask them not to turn in their answers, to preserve confidentiality. Instead have them let you know if any questions are unclear. (If you're lucky, you can talk them into retaking the revised survey with the rest of the employees—important if you are dealing with small numbers).

Following these simple tips should greatly improve the quality of any written forms you might develop, as well—even job application forms, performance-evaluation forms, and customer-response survey forms. By having a questionnaire written in-house, you can save money and avoid some glaring errors with respect to job titles or other terminology foreign to your situation. It also provides you with flexibility to focus on questions most important to your own needs.

Surveys at J. P. Industries: A Word of Caution

Jim McAuliffe, former vice-president of human resources at JPI, comments on the use of surveys at JPI: "At one point, JPI administered a short survey on employee satisfaction, covering pensions, fringe benefits, wages, and supervisory relations. It gave a thumbnail sketch of each plant, including several recently acquired. But it also created unwelcome side effects. JPI's exerience illustrates challenges related to surveys, even when feedback of results is designed in.

"The design was simple. Employees at each plant completed surveys, results were tabulated at corporate headquarters, with appropriate results *fed back,* or returned, to each plant. Supervisors in each area were expected to discuss results with their own employees.

"Three major problems surfaced. First, many supervisors were not prepared to run a feedback session and were given little, if any, support for doing so. They became defensive in their effort to respond to the sometimes critical information about their performance.

"Second, not all information was shared openly, especially ratings for the firm as a whole, which could provide a comparison for each work group and plant. Thus there was the feeling that corporate headquarters had received a "report card" on each plant that it wasn't willing to share.

"Finally, provisions were not in place to respond to all the issues that surfaced. As often happens with the survey approach, so much information was gathered, it was almost impossible to respond to all concerns raised—either immediately or in even the long term. This lack of response can undermine trust and open communication.

"The survey worked well in some plants—especially where supervisors were better trained in management skills and where there was already more trust built between employees and management.

"Surveys can also backfire when employees are asked to make ratings with incomplete information, at best. The questions about wages are a good example. Employees often have only part of the picture when asked to rate their satisfaction with pay. They are not always aware of the true costs of their wages with the benefit burden. Nor are they familiar with comparable salaries, what others in the firm make (from CEO on down) or the general economics of running a business. This information is useful in providing a less-distorted view, especially when employees hear about eight-figure salaries of Fortune 500 CEOs."

HOW CHANGES WERE INTRODUCED AT J. P. INDUSTRIES

Fortunately, other change efforts at J. P. Industries (JPI) were usually more successful.

The Role of Change at JPI

The whole success of JPI rested upon its ability to locate problems at the firms it acquired and bring about effective change. JPI targeted firms for acquisition that were underperformers—companies with a solid market niche but because of mismanagement were not as profitable as they should be. JPI was consistently able (with few exceptions) to move its own management team into these firms and turn them around. Its success hinged largely on understanding the change process and how employees were an integral part of this success.

The Gradual Introduction of Change

A company is an ongoing system. Change must be gradual and orderly. Otherwise, change may jeopardize ongoing activities already established as part of the firm's routine. At JPI, top management educated personnel about the change from the start. Why was JPI going to make the change? What would the benefits be? How did JPI managers hope this would be accomplished? Only then was change introduced.

For example, a common change at JPI dealt with taking accounting and order processing from an almost completely manual method to a fully computerized system. In many firms, a consultant is hired to develop the new system and then, abruptly, the old system is shut off and the new system is put in—even before it is debugged. Instead, at JPI, employees would run the new system *parallel* with the old system for awhile. That way, if the new system had bugs in it—which is usually the case—they still had the old system, and the information everyone needed during the transition period. This parallel system also allowed personnel time to get trained and to feel comfortable using the new system. In introducing change, management thoroughly considered the types of motivational changes and skill training employees might require to handle the new systems effectively. A complete shift occurred only when everything was in place; all the bugs were out, and people were trained and comfortable with the new system.

Any change needs to be thoroughly thought through and planned out. The same approach applied at JPI whether management was introducing an award program or a total quality-management program.

Documentation on Japanese-style management would suggest that Japanese managers tend to think things out more thoroughly and involve input from more levels than managers in many American firms before they try to persuade people to adopt change. One notable American exception, and one that influenced the JPI management style, is the approach taken by the United States Space Program at the National Aeronautics and Space Administration (NASA). As in Japanese-style management, at NASA everything was totally planned out and thought through from the perspective of the entire team. This approach is sometimes called *total-system management*. This means you do everything on paper, first—planning everything out in the tiniest detail. Then you develop timetables, pert charts, and critical paths. Only after that do you begin. Of course, the business cannot be planned as tightly as the space program. But the basic concept that pervaded the JPI culture was that nothing is unimportant. As long as it has a function, it is not unimportant. The person on the manufacturing floor is not unimportant because if he does not clean up well, someone could fall and slip and break his neck or leg. We don't emphasize this total problem-solving perspective enough in business schools. Courses are divided into functional areas that train you to think too narrowly.

Reducing Resistance to Change

Managers reduced resistance to change at JPI by letting people know as much as possible about the change ahead of time and by stressing the benefits of the change. What causes resistance to change is the fear of the unknown. Once employees were informed about what JPI was trying to do, they began to consider themselves as players or participants. It still wasn't as familiar as the old method they had used for five years, of course—but the change no longer felt to them as if they were stepping into a blackened room with no light.

This concept applies to any type of change, managerial or technical. When you want people to use some new technological equipment, they will go back to the equipment they know how to use unless you take all these factors into account and plan properly.

Building Trust and Commitment to Change at JPI

When changes are made, what are the reasons? Explaining how the change fits into the organization's goals and objectives and benefits employees accelerates acceptance and reduces resistance. Why is the firm going through this expense? What is it going to do for the firm? Will any jobs be eliminated as a result of the change? These are questions that should be answered up front. To deal with this, JPI managers explained the goals, objectives, and the expected return on the investment. If a change eliminated certain functions, JPI would introduce a retraining program. This way, employees knew they would be retrained for other activities. Or if a reduction in personnel was anticipated, then JPI coupled the change with development of an outplacement program. The company worked with community colleges frequently to develop courses for retraining. JPI also worked with the city, county, or other appropriate groups for outplacement assistance. The company would often pay to participate and would sometimes also hire a private consultant if needed. Top management, and especially the CEO, felt a strong social obligation to help with such placements if JPI had to reduce staff, even temporarily.

JPI was guided by the CEO's philosophy that you don't have any choi~ ـ.t to take these steps if you want to succeed. This also benefits the firm directly because the change is smoother and the overall company benefits, rather than creating fear and distrust every time changes are introduced. It turns out not to be that expensive, either. The alternative is more expensive—discontinuities such as strikes are the most obvious. But the more subtle damage created by developing long-term distrust in employees is the more fundamental and costly issue. Trust is critical to the smooth flow of work and effective human relations. In addition, it is an important influence on product quality and the level of technical performance of employees.

Building commitment is more complicated than sitting everyone down, presenting a plan, and asking them all to agree. You never get 100 percent consensus; but before you go ahead, you should have a majority of the people feeling this is the thing to do. JPI management accomplished this by involving people in the process.

At most JPI plants, plans were well communicated. Sitting in a lecture hall to explain changes and asking everyone to say "yea" or "nay" does not induce commitment. It requires bringing employees in from the beginning to help plan the change. JPI modeled its decision making after the Japanese: The Japanese process is not really bottom-up. The top management has a clear idea about the overall direction for a particular change. However, the change is not pushed down the throats of the lower-level people as in many traditionally run American firms. Even lower-level employees have a chance to review and modify the plan until the two ends meet in the middle. Thus, it is more appropriate to think of this Japanese-style process as a "top-down, bottom-up" approach. Eventually the two ends meet, after modifications are made along the way.

The Relationship Between Participation and the Formal Structure

Do not confuse the decision making and implementation that takes place in the formal structure with the brainstorming and idea generation in the informal structure. Though JPI managers didn't have to move off premises after work, as in many Japanese firms, to get employees to open up, the distinction of formal and informal structure was important at JPI. Within the formal structure, authority and responsibility were clearly defined. If a manager wanted to make changes, he or she had to make it through that structure. But employees and management exchanged views and ideas outside that structure in brainstorming sessions and problem-solving meetings, as well as in informal conversations. That was the most productive way at JPI. But JPI managers didn't make actual changes through the informal structure, or the company would have ended up in disorganization.

To make this dual structure work, managers including the CEO, clarified specifically whether a particular conversation or meeting was part of the formal planning process or an informal discussion. This way, the CEO could go directly to employees in the plant to find out what was going on, without bypassing the chain of command. For this to work, JPI managers also had to build trust in the idea that people could feel free to communicate their views. The classic "suggestion box" is a waste of time, because employees expect some sort of positive response to their ideas. They would like to sit down and discuss these ideas, not just place them in a box. The formality of the written message becomes an impediment to open discussion. If an employee brings up the idea in person, however, the manager and employee can build on the idea together and decide that perhaps the foreman should be included in the planning and discussion, as well.

Viewing the Firm as an Open System

JPI took the concept of the "dynamic" or "open system" out of theory and into practice. This was not just theory at JPI, but the day-to-day philosophy upon which business decisions were based. You can't manage within the walls of your firm and think of it as self-contained, because it's not. People flow in and out of that system—people who come with influences, political power, environmental concerns, and other thoughts.

JPI was successful, in the end, because of the recognition of how everyone would be affected and would benefit from the changes management introduced. These benefits ranged from more jobs and/or more secure jobs for those inside the firm to economic, social, and even ecological improvements for the investor and the community.

SUMMARY OF CHANGE EFFORTS
WITHIN GROWING FIRMS

Firms change for many reasons. Common triggers in small firms are growth and a desire to function more effectively in many different areas. In spite of this obvious need, change is often very difficult to bring about and requires thorough understanding of human behavior, of the natural tendency to resist change, and the need to plan for the new and less well known. The steps in the action-research model provide a useful guide: 1) Obtain commitment to change; 2) diagnose the problem carefully; 3) develop solutions; 4) carry out the action according to a carefully developed plan; and 5) evaluate the change so that you know whether you want to do it again in the same way.

Commitment requires trust between employees and managers. This does not occur overnight, but the way in which the change process itself is carried out can contribute to or undermine trust among employees.

At JPI change didn't just happen. It was carefully planned and managed. This was a key to JPI's profitable growth to almost $500 million in sales within one short decade.

NOTES

[1]For a good overview of the field of organization development, you might look at Thomas G. Cummings and Edgar F. Huse, *Organization Development and Change,* 4th ed. (St. Paul: West Publishing Company, 1989).

[2]See Cummings and Huse, *Organization Development and Change,* Chapter 3, for discussion of action-research models. For further reading see William Foote Whyte, *Participation Action Research* (Newbury Park, CA: Sage Foundation, 1991).

[3]The Nominal Group Technique is most thoroughly described in Andre L. Delbecq, Andrew H. Van de Ven, and David H. Gustafson, *Group Techniques for Program Planning: A Guide to Nominal Group and Delphi Processes* (Glenview, IL: Scott, Foresman, 1975). The discussion here is based on this work and one of the author's own extensive experiences with the approach. See also, Chapter 7.

[4]You can find further discussion on the merits of evaluation in an article by Barry Macy and Phil Mirvis, "Organization Change Efforts: Methodologies for Assessing Organizational Effectiveness and Program Costs Versus Benefits," *Evaluation Review,* 6 (1982), 301–72.

[5]Thomas J. Peters and Robert H. Waterman, Jr., *In Search of Excellence* (York, NY: Warner Books, 1982).

[6]An excellent source for validated employee-attitude survey materials is Stanley Seashore and others, eds., *Assessing Organizational Change: A Guide to Methods, Measures, and Practices* (New York: Wiley-Interscience, 1983).

CHAPTER 15

Rethinking Our Approach to Strategic Planning

Running a successful growing firm takes hard work—and good planning. It's harder than many management books make it sound, but it's not rocket science. We have argued in this book that successful management of the growing firm comes from a strategic-planning approach especially suited to turbulent times. It is a relatively simple process: Clarify your vision and assure that all eight issues in the DSP Model support that vision.

THE 1980s: WHAT WORKED AND WHAT DIDN'T

The 1980s will most likely be remembered as the decade of mergers and acquisitions, of a time when many solid small to medium-sized companies cautiously had to hide their cash, lest some larger conglomerate implement a hostile takeover. Temporary growth was often fueled by number-crunching passive investors lacking a vision for their conglomerates, collecting smaller companies as one would collect a set of rare baseball cards. As these investors gutted the cash, the talent, and the spirit of scores of America's top businesses, the result left not only those failed conglomerates but the entire banking system that supported this spending binge in a sea of red ink by the early 1990s.

But in the midst of such tales rises another story, in which a combination of vision and thorough attention to detailed planning resulted in quite a different ending. While it was eventually merged with T&N plc, itself, in late 1990, J. P. Industries provided an alternate model of how companies could be managed profitably— even so-called ''rustbelt'' companies that had been floundering in a declining automobile industry.

J. P. Industries is an exceptional story, not just because it grew rapidly and successfully through acquiring other companies, but because of how it grew.

Guided by a clear vision, and with careful, exhaustive planning and thorough attention to detail, JPI substantially increased the earnings of 12 of its 14 acquisitions (encompassing 32 production facilities worldwide). Even the other 2—very small acquisitions, by JPI's standards, of between one and three million dollars in revenues—were divested without loss to the company.

JPI's success was due to a few simple factors:

1. A clear strategic objective of buying companies in the two industries it was in: plumbing and engine components. JPI purchased only companies that were synergistic with its other companies in either of these two industries. Unlike many other acquisition-oriented firms, it sought companies producing good products with a solid customer base that fit into the mix of products JPI already offered.

2. An action plan based on this synergy was developed and carried out. Every detail of the business was reviewed prior to acquisition, and plans were developed and begun even before each acquisition was finalized.

3. In developing a plan, JPI planners gave full attention to the human factor from the beginning. JPI recognized that the culture and the attitudes of the acquired companies were different from JPI's. Therefore, the action plan prior to acquisition included programs and activities needed for gradual cultural change without losing the talent and the productivity that was already there. This resulted in a gain in both excitement and in productivity.

4. JPI was careful to retain continuity of leadership during the entire acquisition process. Each JPI team charged with developing the action plan for the acquisition during the evaluation, negotiation, and buying process continued for some time afterward as the managers of that plant. Only gradually was this team phased out, well after the acquisition process was completed.

The keys are simple, though carrying them out requires a lot of work: A clear vision and thorough planning that extends well beyond attention to financial and marketing details, and places the human factor at the top of the list.

THOROUGHNESS: YOUR "SECRET" FOR SUCCESS

If we had to pick one word to describe the basis of sustained, profitable growth, it might be the word *thorough*. You might get by for awhile—ignoring team development or group morale, or doing your books by hand. But the most really successful companies that continue to grow past a limited size and age—companies like J. P. Industries—eventually develop a plan to address all eight of the issues we have summarized in the Dynamic System Planning Model, guided by an overall vision, monitored and re-evaluated on an ongoing basis. None can be ignored. In our interviews, we found that even among many of the small to medium-sized companies, top performers paid attention to a broad range of issues at any particular time.

Many entrepreneurs are so preoccupied with sales growth, and with becoming part of the INC. 500 or the FORTUNE 500, that they lose sight of other parts of the business. They overlook the investment that needs to be made to sustain growth— developing a good accounting information system (probably computer-based), or the changes that must be made to maintain a strong, healthy corporate culture. This overemphasis on marketing and finances is in part a bias reinforced by current treatments of strategic planning.

REVIEW OF THE DYNAMIC SYSTEM
PLANNING MODEL

We have identified seven key organizational issues that must be managed effectively. By analyzing how effectively you manage each of these seven issues, and by considering your strategy for each issue, you can improve your firm's performance on the eighth issue, financial viability. Financial viability—meaning cash and profits in the short term and survival in the long run—is really a yardstick of how well you have mastered the first seven issues. We agree with Peter Drucker in that profits cannot be managed per se, but come as a result of how effectively the rest of the firm is managed.[1]

Although each of the seven organizational DSP issues rarely requires your exclusive attention, you need an action plan at all times for addressing each issue and a feedback loop that will alert you if changes in the plan are required.

Strategic planning according to the DSP model can be summarized in the following seven steps:

1. Clarify your company vision. No company, no matter how well managed on a daily basis, thrives without a clear overall direction.

2. Track each of the seven organizational DSP issues using the DSP Grid. Consider for each issue how effectively it is managed, what strategies you now use to manage it, and what new strategies you need to introduce to remain effective in each area. These seven issues include resource acquisition, market strategy, work flow, human relations, resource allocation, mastery of technology, and public relations and are derived from viewing companies as open, dynamic systems.

3. Watch your financials closely—especially cash flow. It is your firm's pulse. Learn how to read your financial statements as well as your statement of cash flow. Be alert not only to dips in profit but to drains in cash. Although financial viability cannot be directly managed, it is your barometer of success. If profits or cash decline, it is time to analyze and seriously rethink your overall vision, as well as your approach to management of the other seven DSP issues.

4. Constantly re-assess your strategy in each area and take action as needed to modify strategy to fit new conditions. Throughout the book, we have shared the approaches that other CEOs have used for each issue. But in the end, you will find a strategy that works best, given the unique context of your own firm.

5. In making changes, plan for the people side, not just the technical side. Anticipate resistance to change and take steps to prevent it. J. P. Industries and other successful firms pay close attention to the dynamics of change. Changing people in order to keep up with your changing organization is one of the biggest challenges faced by the CEO of a growing company.

6. Create feedback loops so that you can evaluate progress for every issue. Some of these feedback loops are computer-driven, quantitative measuring tools. Other loops are as simple as tours of the shop floor or the responses employees may have in a confidential questionnaire. Use both the subjective and the quantitative approaches to track your company's progress.

7. Repeat steps 1 through 6 as often as needed to stay on course. Strategic planning, if done right, should be thought of as a daily guide to running your growing business more profitably, not some textbook exercise you do with hired consultants and stick on a bookshelf once you're done. It's a problem-solving way of thinking about your business—with a relatively finite number of problems or issues that you monitor continually. You don't even have to write the plan down—if you can keep it all in your head. Most successful CEOs have their plans memorized anyway.

THE *DSP* APPROACH VERSUS CONVENTIONAL PLANNING

Though similar in some respects to conventional strategic planning, our approach differs from most conventional strategic-planning approaches in several key aspects. In particular, according to the DSP approach:

- You analyze company strengths and weaknesses based on issues that are problem based, not on functions such as marketing, human resources, and production.

- Market strategy is only one of several key issues, not the "leading" issue, as most conventional strategic-planning models assume.[2]

- The CEO is central to development of the overall plan. This is the only way to assure that each individual part of the plan contributes to the CEO's overall vision.

- Strategic planning is a daily exercise, not an annual event. This is one of the most critical differences from conventional planning. Strategic planning becomes more of an attitude, of constantly monitoring your feedback loops for strategies that need minor calibration or even dramatic redesign. Growing firms change far too quickly to wait an entire year to review each issue.

GUIDELINES FOR MANAGING EACH ISSUE

Each company is unique. The strategy that works for one firm may not work for another. This said, it is still always tempting to review the data to look for trends and patterns. Indeed for each of the seven organizational issues, we do find certain trends that hint at possible directions to consider. But please be cautious in adopting any particular strategy without careful consideration of the unique context of your own firm. For every pattern, there is the exception—a company that goes counter to the common wisdom—and is quite successful. The key to success is not in mimicking the strategies in any specific DSP issue, but of an ongoing careful consideration of all seven issues within your own unique setting. Keeping this in mind, we'll summarize some of the key trends supported by our research.

Managing Market Strategy

Though the actual direction set by the firms in our study is almost as diverse as the number of firms themselves, certain market strategies are most apt to be found in the more profitable, higher-performing firms:

- Quality and increased market share are linked to higher profits, although their impact may take a year or two to be felt.

- Discounting rarely if ever proves to be a profitable strategy for small firms. It is possible to be profitable in a price-competitive environment using strategies other than discounting.

- Diversification is a hazardous avenue, especially for smaller firms. Even among firms with more than 80 employees, diversification should probably be along complementary lines of the existing services or products.

- The CEO should not be afraid to set direction based on his or her experience, instincts, and intuition. A success track is not always quantifiable into neat formulas. Many successful firms in our sample—large or small—are driven by CEO intuition.

- Counter to some popularly held beliefs, it may be more effective for small-firm CEOs to set strategy by themselves. Firms ruled by committee do not perform as well as those with a strong visionary leader.

Some of these findings are consistent with current popular teachings, including the emphasis on quality. Others showing the greater importance of CEO leadership and intuition over formal business planning may fly in the face of convention. They are all backed by our findings and recent research. With a firm's growth, many decisions need to be delegated, but direction setting does not appear to be one of them.

Managing Work Flow

Over half the firms in our study had changed their approach to managing work flow since start up. Optimizing work flow may be one of the hardest exercises a CEO faces. There are no set formulas. And change in size is only one of several design contingencies that need to be taken into account. However, certain designs also stand out as effective for the firms as a whole: Coordination of efforts appears to be best achieved "people-to-people," rather than "paper-to-people". Informal conversations and meetings are more effective than written guidelines and written job descriptions. With growth, people-to-people strategies must be coupled with carefully developed tracking systems. These should leave paper trails—often computer assisted—of how well goals are being met, rather than spelling out what jobs are to be done in advance. These feedback systems provide a way for CEOs to rely on chain of command without relinquishing too much operating authority.

Conversation forms the backbone of work flow coordination in the majority of firms, large or small. But as a firm grows, it faces pressure to adopt a more bureaucratic approach, with more written rules and procedures and less reliance on informal discussion. However, larger top-performing firms in our interviews *resist* this trend. Consistent with findings in our research, J. P. Industries (JPI) relied on chain of command, monitoring systems, and informal conversations and meetings, but not on written rules or job descriptions. The former approaches help CEOs digest a greater amount of information and continue to control operations without stifling the vital creativity and flexibility of their employees.

Delegation of authority is one of the most controversial and difficult parts of growth. A CEO cannot possibly do everything, but delegating wrongly can hurt. CEOs in top-performing firms are likely to share decisions about day-to-day operations, but insist on a clear set of standards and a well-developed monitoring system. Top-performing CEOs keep up with every aspect of the firm. Overdelegating appears to be the greater risk to profitability. Even so, underdelegating can lead to stress and even to serious health problems, as several of the CEOs reported. Delegation is best done through a clear, monitored chain of command.

Small-firm CEOs have more latitude: They can control through direct contact and observation of work or via monitoring systems. But even in small firms, CEOs notice that a monitoring system frees up valuable time.

Managing Acquisition of Resources

We focus most attention on obtaining personnel. In contrast to work flow, this appears to be one of the *least* dynamic organization issues—few companies change strategy over time. This may be a function of size: Compared with our company median of just over $3 million, at the Presidents' Forum sponsored by Eastern Michigan University's Center for Entrepreneurship, CEOs of growth firms averaging over $50 million a year frequently complained about keeping positions filled. In our own group, employees are usually hired from within. Among the firms participating at the Center for Entrepreneurship, several hire top-caliber people who can grow with the firm, even though younger or less experienced than those company veterans not as capable of improvement. At JPI promoting from within was preferred because this gave top management the opportunity to observe candidates closely in an actual work setting.

When people are brought in from the outside, networking is preferred over recruitment agencies and advertising. Its advantage? Networking often provides at least secondhand observation of someone's work by a trusted friend or colleague.

Managing Human Relations

Resolving "people" issues is a great challenge. Many start-up entrepreneurs focus primarily on product and customer needs. In short, the focus is outside the firm. But internal climate and culture cannot be ignored. Whereas work flow can reach a crisis point at 20 to 50 employees, human relations issues crop up a little later, usually at about 70 or 80 employees.

We uncover many ways human relations can be improved. Several work-flow practices affect employee morale and commitment. The CEO needs to be clear about chain of command and reporting structure. The CEO should not bypass managers by giving orders directly to employees but instead should work through managers if change is needed. This doesn't mean you cannot talk to employees. Just make it crystal clear that your conversation does not include a command.

To improve and maintain morale, clear performance standards often help, too. Let employees at all levels know how well they are achieving those standards. Jobs and supervisory duties should be structured so that employees are provided with positive and negative feedback. The "cell" concept at JPI and performance-evaluation systems were both geared to this. Employees need clear role definition: It should be easy for both you and the employee to know when the employee is doing well.

Certain internal climates are clearly linked to better morale. Trust, cooperation, and innovation breed profit. Political intrigue breeds the opposite. At JPI, trust depended upon the CEO's familiarity with events outside the firm and inside the minds of employees. In successful firms, employees have confidence in the CEO: Employees feel the CEO knows what is best.

Certain practices for sharing values and the firm's mission also contribute to better human relations. Meetings can be an effective means, especially meetings whose primary purpose is to explain the CEO's values or the firm's goals. The CEO should also take time to talk to employees one-on-one—to find out what is going on and to share the CEO's philosophy and mission.

Managing Resource Allocation

Start-up firms may get by without a formal budget and computer to manage it, but past 60 or 70 employees, these steps are essential for profitable growth. Computer-based formal budgeting allows delegation of mid-range spending decisions to managers without jeopardizing cash or time.

Few if any CEOs in our interviews mentioned use of a budget explicitly linked to the firm's overall strategic business plan. But capital spending plans assure that all the money spent helps accomplish top objectives. Otherwise, spending is hit or miss. With a clear plan, it's easier to delegate up to specific dollar amounts to managers while still meeting goals. Never lose sight of the cash. Routinely review spending to assure that the plan is on track.

It's never too early to start budgeting. In addition to our top-performing large firms, many small ones budget too. Educate managers so they understand its use. Don't wait until costs have already gone out of control and are difficult to track.

The squeaky-wheel approach—giving out funds for what appears to be the most pressing need—is acceptable in small firms, but may skew priorities once the firm hits 60 to 70 employees. At that size, "squeaks" are increasingly politically driven, not objectives-driven.

The results of this section echo those of work flow. Monitoring systems, once in place, greatly improve CEO ability to control expenses and activities without having to be everywhere at once. Even CEOs with fewer than 20 employees enjoy the added free time to attend to other aspects of the firm's operation.

Managing Public Relations

To maintain image and public reputation, the CEO should consider educational, environmental, safety, and affirmative-action issues. A "good neighbor" policy—encouraging volunteerism in the community—is also important.

Not all problems can be thwarted, but careful attention can reduce risk. Otherwise, major disruption can result, even if the firm is guiltless. Lack of funds was never accepted as an adequate excuse at JPI for allowing environmental and safety problems to remain unresolved.

Managing Technical Mastery

In the early 1990s, the United States continued to lag behind other industrialized nations in new technology investment. Customers will switch to those who deliver quality. Growth doesn't happen on its own. It requires ongoing investment in equipment and direct management of your technology.

One percent (1%) defect rates no longer satisfy the customer. The new norm in manufacturing is *zero defects*. In other sectors, the quality of customer service is of increasing importance. Employee involvement is a key to achieving high standards, as at JPI and Coastal Chem. Successful employee involvement may require special training programs. Though expensive, costs can often be kept down by using self-led seminar formats. In smaller firms, technical mastery begins with the CEO. Keep current by reading trade or other business magazines, attending trade shows, and, for specialized topics, attending an occasional seminar.

Hiring people with specialized training is more costly but in some types of businesses, a necessity. Weigh the costs of training versus the benefits of experience. Do you have the expertise and time available to train green recruits? This answer varies across firms but for more complex technologies, it's usually better to hire the expertise.

To improve productivity, measure and reward productivity. Evaluate performance and provide incentives based on costs and profits, rather than on raw sales. And be wary of relying on written job descriptions to assure proper performance.

Be sure that employees are clear about their jobs and what they are expected to do—directly or via chain of command. Don't rely too heavily on part-time staff, especially in key positions. This complicates the communication of roles and work flow, which in turn has an impact on quality.

Good morale, fostered by a positive climate of trust, collaborativeness, and innovativeness in the firm, is likely to improve quality and productivity.

The approach you take to flow of work also affects technical mastery. Empower each employee to contribute to daily operations by way of problem-solving meetings, employee-involvement programs, profit-sharing plans, or other incentive programs, coupled with an underlying philosophy that each person's contributions are important.

Top-performing firms generally value quality more highly. JPI's success was based on a combined technical quality/employee involvement strategy that included low and mid-level staff—the majority of whom had worked at the same companies for their previous underperforming owners!

FUTURE DEVELOPMENT OF THE *DSP* MODEL

We started this book with the premise that all eight DSP issues are equally important, and each is linked with the other. As the results of Part II present, we did not find full support for this premise in our interviews. Indeed, the throughput issues, including work flow, resource allocation, and human relations, are linked with each other and most of the other issues. And profit, as we measured it, is linked strongly to six of the seven other issues—only resource acquisition being the exception. But resource acquisition, the one input issue, is only linked with the three throughput issues. Sometimes these effects lag over time, also, meaning that you may not see an immediate effect of one issue on the other.

Of course, these are results from a certain slice of companies—in particular, relatively small companies. Some issues, as we have seen, do not surface as major challenges until a company has grown significantly in size. Further work in this area would shed light on the relative importance of issues for different sized firms and for different kinds of companies.

LEADING YOUR OWN FIRM THROUGH TURBULENT TIMES

This book provides you with a new strategic-planning approach to chart your best course for managing growth. We identify issues all firms face, but the way in which each issue is managed varies and is ultimately the choice of each CEO. We have presented not only theory but also examples of actual choices, and how well they have worked for individual CEOs and for the group as a whole.

Many managers want a simple summary—a quick fix—but we believe there really is no shortcut to careful analysis and review of your firm's own situation. The set of issues we have identified here are quite comprehensive but clearly defined. They should reduce the number of mystery problems you may experience in your firm—those unanticipated jolts that lurk around the next bend as you experience growth. When you know what problems to look for, half your battle is won.

NOTES

[1] Peter F. Drucker, *Management: Tasks, Responsibilities, Practices* (New York: Harper & Row, 1974).

[2] Porter's work has had a very strong influence on the strategy field. A substantial part of current strategy texts are devoted to a summary of his approach to market-strategy analysis. See for instance, Arthur A.

Thompson and A. J. Strickland III, *Strategic Management: Concepts and Cases,* 6th ed. (Homewood, IL: Irwin, 1992).

  Porter has presented his model in several books and articles, including: Michael E. Porter, "How Competitive Forces Shape Strategy." *Harvard Business Review,* 57, no. 2 (March–April 1979), 137–45.

———, *Competitive Strategy: Techniques for Analyzing Industries and Competitors* (New York: The Free Press, 1980).

———, *Competitive Advantage* (New York: The Free Press, 1985), Chapter 2.

Overview of Research Methods for "Managing the Growing Firm"

The DSP Model is backed by data collected and analyzed by co-author Dr. Lorraine Uhlaner Hendrickson from almost two-hundred companies while she was Director of Research and Program Development at the Center for Entrepreneurship at Eastern Michigan University. Appendix A provides a brief overview of the research methods used to draw many of the conclusions we report on.

METHOD FOR PHASE I

The project, Managing the Growing Firm, spanned two phases. Phase I consisted of personal interviews with 28 CEOs and two additional managers selected randomly from the 1986 Dun and Bradstreet *Million Dollar Directory* from manufacturing, wholesale, and construction. Respondents were interviewed for about an hour using the Critical Incident Technique to bring to the surface the typical problems and situations that CEOs of growing firms face. These responses helped in the formulation of the Dynamic System Planning Model used in Phase II of the project.

METHOD FOR PHASE II

Sampling Procedure

For Phase II, firms were drawn randomly from the Dun and Bradstreet "Market Identifiers' Index," a computerized database of businesses and locations that is more complete than the *Million Dollar Directory*. This source was ideally suited to allow us to sample according to several criteria: size of the firm (10–500 employees), geographic location (portions of an 11-county region within a one-hour drive from the research site, as determined by zip code), rate of growth (at least at the rate of inflation—10 percent over the three-year period from 1983–86), industry (manufacturing, construction, wholesale, and business services). Finally, the firms had to be at least three years of age and at or above $500,000 in sales. In the natural population, smaller firms and those in certain industries are disproportionately represented. To assure an adequate subgroup by size and industry, stratified sampling procedures were used. The one drawback of this source was that the youngest firm on record was five years old. Since we were not looking at start-up firms, per se, this was not a major problem but could present an obstacle for other studies aimed at that group.

Twelve cells were created based on three size categories and four industry types, with firms identified and randomly sampled within each cell. A goal was set to obtain at least 13 firms within each cell, to allow for sufficient subsamples for further analysis by size and industry. In order to do this, substitute firms were selected for replacement if firms initially drawn refused to participate.

These parameters were chosen in an attempt to eliminate most firms still in start-up mode and to obtain a sufficiently large sample of high-growth firms, a factor in the original research design. The minimum of 10–19 employees was chosen also because, based on research by Flamholtz, it was thought to be a size just below the point at which the first managerial problems tended to emerge.[1] Both the research literature and popular opinion seem to suggest that as companies exceed 20 employees, the management problems of the founding owner begin to increase very rapidly. In addition, subsidiaries or divisions of larger firms were excluded because their management is usually embodied within the culture and management style of the parent firm.

The one-hour distance was a parameter included for practical reasons. To provide sufficient depth, face-to-face interviews were desirable. The one-hour radius provided a wide range of locales—from a major metropolitan area with a population exceeding one million residents, to rural areas, to a medium-sized university town.

Response Rate and Descriptive Statistics

The research team contacted 382 firms, of which 168 participated in the study, for a company completion rate of about 44 percent; 168 presidents and 294 managers were interviewed, with separate interview schedules designed for each group.

Firms averaged 68 employees (counting part-time employees as .5 employee) in 1988, the year of data collection, with median sales of $3.25 million. Average sales in 1987 were $12.7 million (the median being $3.5 million), growing from an average of $4.3 million in 1982. Although most firms continued to grow through 1988, not all did, and not all did profitably. In 1988, average aftertax net profit among the firms was 4.4 percent, with a median of 3.0 percent. At the extremes, one firm reported an 18 percent net loss, while another reported a 35 percent net gain. About 80 percent of the firms reported a profit of at least 1 percent.

Almost 60 percent of the firms report steady growth over the five-year period prior to the study. This is higher than average because we tried to sample growth firms. However, our selection of firms was based on previous performance and about one in four had leveled off or even declined at the point of the interview. Since our firms were selected for growth rate, the average growth was fairly high: a median of 18 percent annual growth over a five-year period, but ranging between 20 percent annual decline and 700 percent annual growth.

Other characteristics of the firms are described throughout the book.

Types of Data Collected

A combination of structured (those with specific response choices) and unstructured (those that are open ended) questions were used in both the managers' and CEOs' forms. In addition, six pages of survey material were imbedded in the manager's form, which managers were asked to complete during the interview. The self-assessment questions throughout the book and Appendix B provide more specific examples of the questions used.

Data-Analysis Techniques Used to Test for Main Effects

The majority of bivariate linkages—those linking two variables—mentioned in this book are based on Spearman Rho correlation coefficients, a nonparametric correlational statistic suitable with ordinal data. For findings reported in Chapter 8, multiple regression techniques were also used together with Pedhazur's approach to test for interactions.

Data-Analysis Techniques Used to Test for Contingency Effects

Chapter 8, in particular, reports on a number of contingency effects. Two approaches were used to test for interaction or contingency effects, depending on whether the contingency variable was ordinal or not. First, for the industry variable, the only nominal variable in this study, the significance of the difference in the Spearman Rho correlation coefficients was tested by a V-statistic described by Hayes.[2]

For the other contingency variables, significance of an interaction was tested using the approach recommended by Pedhazur.[3] First, an interaction term was constructed by multiplying the value of the contingency variable by the value of the independent variable. Then a multiple regression was carried out, with the independent variable, contingency variable, and interaction term regressed onto the dependent variable. According to Pedhazur, significance of the beta-weight of the interaction terms is evidence of the interaction. To ascertain the likely nature and direction of the significant interactions, the overall sample was then broken into subsamples based on the contingency variable involved in that particular analysis. Contingency effects in Chapter 8 were reported when these beta-weights of the interaction terms of the regression equations described above were significant at the $p<.05$ level, or better.

Though perhaps not considered by some as a direct test of interaction effects, a second approach was also used to explore the relative importance of the various contingency variables. For each contingency variable, firms were divided into subgroups based on the value of that particular variable (e.g., by four size subgroups, three diversification subgroups, etc.). For each subgroup defined in this way, a separate multiple regression was carried out with the coordination strategies as independent variables and each of the organization-effectiveness variables—coordination, profit, and liquidity—in turn, treated as dependent variables. For each multiple regression, the forward entry procedure was used with an entry criterion of $p<.05$. Results of multiple regressions significant at the $p<.01$ level or below are also reported as "linkages" in Appendix C.

ROS VS. *ROA*

Selecting ROS (return on sales) rather than ROA (return on assets) or ROI (return on investment) was a very pragmatic one for our study. Most CEOs we interviewed weren't sure how to compute the latter two, did not track them routinely, and were not necessarily willing to hand over all their financial statements for us to do so. Some other studies that purport to measure ROA simply ask CEOs to report it in mail-in questionnaires. Our information, as gathered in face-to-face interviews, raises the question about what figures CEOs are actually using when they do this. We are satisfied that by using the measures we did—percentage return on sales, subjective ratings of profitability, and subjective ratings of liquidity (each for a two year period)—that we had, at least, a fairly consistently understood way of assessing the financial viability of each firm.

NOTES

[1]Eric G. Flamholtz, *How to Make the Transition from an Entrepreneurship to a Professionally Managed Firm* (San Francisco: Jossey-Bass, 1986).

[2]William L. Hays, *Statistics for the Social Sciences,* 2nd ed. (New York: Holt, Rinehart and Winston, 1973), p. 663.

[3]E. J. Pedhazur, *Multiple Regression in Behavioral Research,* 2nd ed. (New York: Holt, Rinehart and Winston, 1982).

APPENDIX B

Guide to Assessing Your Firm

A key part of any planning process is a thorough review of your own company. In Chapter 3, we presented the DSP Grid as a tool to analyze the organizational DSP issues, including the effectiveness of each issue, the current strategy used, and the context for that issue. Appendix B is aimed at further helping you to assess your company strengths and weaknesses and to pinpoint those areas that may require further work. Sections are organized according to the eight issues of the DSP Model.

Questions previously presented are only referred to by number here. The first of the two numbers always refers to the chapter in which it can be found (e.g., question 6-6 is first presented in Chapter 6). We also point out which questions are suited for inclusion in an employee survey vs. interview. Be sure to ask questions anonymously, especially regarding effectiveness ratings. Chapter 14 provides more guidance on survey design and implementation.

ASSESSING FINANCIAL VIABILITY

There are many alternative ratios that can be calculated using the information your accountant provides you on your income and expense statement and balance sheet. You can compare your figures by referring to Dun and Bradstreet and Robert Morris Associates reports, available in most libraries. These reports also have a helpful section in the front, explaining the way each ratio is calculated and why it is important. Refer to question 5-6.

Here are a few other ratios you might want to consider:

FV-1: Return on stockholder's equity. Divide your net income (after taxes) by the average stockholders' equity for one year ago and the year to date (found on your balance sheet). This is sometimes also referred to as your return on net worth.

FV-2: Return on assets. Divide after-tax net income by the total assets shown on your balance sheet. Again, some books suggest you use the average of assets from one year ago and year to date, rather than your current figures, in the denominator of the ratio.

FV-3: Quick ratio. Our measure of liquidity was most rudimentary. A more accepted measure is the ratio of your cash, marketable securities, and receivables, added together, divided by your current liabilities. A quick ratio of one or greater is usually considered acceptable. But again, you can refer to figures specific to your industry.

See also questions 5-1 through 5-5.

ASSESSING MARKET STRATEGY

Assessing Market-Strategy Effectiveness

Refer to questions 6-4 through 6-8.

Assessing Market-Strategy Approaches

Refer to questions 6-1, 6-2, 6-3, 6-9, 6-10, 6-11, and 6-12. (The last two are ideal to ask of your managers). Review also your answer to question 8-19.

Assessing the Market-Strategy Context

We spend little time on this but extensive resource materials are available to assess the nature of the general environment, your industry, and your competition.[1]

ASSESSING WORK FLOW

Assessing Work-Flow Effectiveness

Recall that work flow includes two components: division of work and coordination of effort. To assess how effectively you structure or divide work, review questions 7-1, 7-4, 7-11, 7-12, and 7-13. To assess coordination of efforts, review questions 8-9, 8-10, and 8-11. Ask your managers these questions, too—preferably in a confidential survey format (see Chapter 14).

Here are two more questions you might also consider:

Question WF-1: Clarity of structure. List the job titles or one-sentence job descriptions for each of the managers reporting to you (question 7-5). How easily were you able to answer this question? If you struggled with your answer, this may reflect the lack of a clear reporting structure in your firm.

Question WF-2: Work clarity. (To be asked of employees and managers.) How clear are you about how you are supposed to do your job?

[1] Extremely clear
[2] Very clear
[3] Fairly clear
[4] Not so clear
[5] Not clear at all

Assessing Work-Flow Strategies

To assess the actual practices or strategies used to divide work, review the following questions: 7-2, 7-3, 7-5, 7-7 through 7-10b, and 7-14. To measure or assess coordination strategies, consider questions 8-1 through 8-8, and 8-12 through 8-14. Questions 7-2, 7-3, 7-8, 7-9, 7-14, and all the coordination questions are appropriate to ask of managers (in an interview or survey format). Consider also question WF-3 below, which is actually an expanded, reformatted version of question 7-10:

Question WF-3: Distribution of authority (expanded version). Look over the list of functions in the following table. Who is closely involved with each of these functions in your own firm? Consider the following groups:

[1] The CEO
[2] Top management other than the CEO
[3] Middle management or supervisors
[4] Nonsupervisory employees
[5] Board of Directors
[6] Others

You may indicate more than one group in your answer.

	CHECK ALL THAT APPLY:					
Market Strategy						
Setting the direction of the firm	[1]	[2]	[3]	[4]	[5]	[6]
Selling the products or services that you offer	[1]	[2]	[3]	[4]	[5]	[6]
Selecting physical facilities to purchase or lease—how, when, and where to expand or locate	[1]	[2]	[3]	[4]	[5]	[6]
Work Flow:						
Defining specific job positions below the level of top management	[1]	[2]	[3]	[4]	[5]	[6]
Making sure activities among staff flow smoothly	[1]	[2]	[3]	[4]	[5]	[6]
Resource Acquisition						
Recruiting personnel	[1]	[2]	[3]	[4]	[5]	[6]
Tracking information about products or services (what competitors are doing, new developments in the industry)	[1]	[2]	[3]	[4]	[5]	[6]
Obtaining financing for the firm (outside investments, bank loans, etc.)	[1]	[2]	[3]	[4]	[5]	[6]

	CHECK ALL THAT APPLY:

Resource Acquisition (cont.)

	[1]	[2]	[3]	[4]	[5]	[6]
Obtaining materials, equipment, supplies, and services (e.g., subcontracting), including fulfilling unusual needs or providing scarce resources	[1]	[2]	[3]	[4]	[5]	[6]

Human Relations

	[1]	[2]	[3]	[4]	[5]	[6]
Motivating employees	[1]	[2]	[3]	[4]	[5]	[6]

Resource Allocation

	[1]	[2]	[3]	[4]	[5]	[6]
Monitoring and controlling costs	[1]	[2]	[3]	[4]	[5]	[6]

Public Relations

	[1]	[2]	[3]	[4]	[5]	[6]
Developing relations with community	[1]	[2]	[3]	[4]	[5]	[6]
Dealing with the government—regulations, unemployment–compensation problems (other than routine payments), tax issues, workman's compensation, etc.	[1]	[2]	[3]	[4]	[5]	[6]
Developing relations with others in your industry (competitors, joint ventures)	[1]	[2]	[3]	[4]	[5]	[6]

Technical Mastery

	[1]	[2]	[3]	[4]	[5]	[6]
Developing and training personnel	[1]	[2]	[3]	[4]	[5]	[6]
Monitoring quality	[1]	[2]	[3]	[4]	[5]	[6]
Selecting or designing products or services that you sell	[1]	[2]	[3]	[4]	[5]	[6]
Actually producing the products or services that you offer	[1]	[2]	[3]	[4]	[5]	[6]

Note: Per our terminology, you *delegate* authority in a particular function if you did not check off [1]. You decide *participatively* in a particular area if you checked off [1] as well as [2], [3], and/or [4].

Assessing the Context of the Work-Flow Issue

Review questions 8-15 through 8-19 to measure the context of the work-flow issue. Consider also questions 6-7, 6-8, and 6-9. The rate of growth, size, and type of industry may all affect the nature of the work-flow solutions you choose.

ASSESSING RESOURCE ACQUISITION

Assessing Resource-Acquisition Effectiveness

For this, review questions 9-1 through 9-6, 9-8, and 9-9. You might ask your key managers these same questions, again, preferably in a confidential survey format.

Assessing Resource-Acquisition Strategies

Review question 9-7. You might also consider the resource-acquisition section in question WF-3 above. In addition, with minor rephrasing, you can adapt question 9-7 to the other resource areas. For instance, do you have a particular way of obtaining your supplies? Your capital? Your subcontractors? And so forth.

ASSESSING HUMAN RELATIONS

Assessing Human-Relations Effectiveness

There are literally thousands of questions on employee attitudes. We tried to select those we thought most accurately reflected our definition of human-relations effectiveness. Questions 10-1 through 10-5, 10-6, 10-7, 10-9, and 10-10 focus on the components we feel are most relevant. These can all be asked independently of your managers. Consider, in addition, the following cluster of questions HR-1 through HR-9, which describe the work climate in your firm.

To what extent do each of the following phrases describe your firm?

[1] To a very great extent
[2] To a great extent
[3] To some extent
[4] To a small extent
[5] To a slight extent or not at all

Question HR-1: There is a spirit of cooperation.

Question HR-2: There is a climate of trust.

Question HR-3: Conflicts are dealt with head on.

Question HR-4: The most productive people are highly respected by their peers.

Question HR-5: If a problem comes up, people are confident the management will deal with it in the best possible manner.

Question HR-6: New ideas are encouraged.

Question HR-7: The most productive people are distrusted and ostracized by their peers.

Question HR-8: You get further ahead if you don't rock the boat.

Question HR-9: A spirit of competition and rivalry exists among groups within the firm.

(HR-1 through HR-6 are signs of a positive climate. HR-7 through HR-9 are usually seen as signs of a negative climate.)

Assessing Human-Relations Strategies

Consider question 10-8. There are also many other aspects here, including the degree of employee involvement, team-building activities, supervisory training, and other actions that overlap both the work-flow and human-relations areas. In addition, the following questions were found in our study to be specifically related to both work-flow effectiveness and morale. For questions HR-10 to HR-17, use one of the following answer choices:

[1] To a great extent
[2] To a moderate extent

[3] To a small extent
[4] To a slight extent
[5] To a very slight extent, or not at all

Question HR-10: To what extent does the CEO (or president) interfere with the authority relationships you have with your subordinates—for instance, allowing subordinates to bypass you without your input.

Question HR-11: Employees get specific feedback about the areas in which they need to improve.

Question HR-12: Employees, in general, feel or believe that the CEO knows what is best for the firm.

Question HR-13: People around here would do almost anything the CEO (president) asked, without question.

Question HR-14: Training programs are planned out, based on a specific assessment of what is needed.

Question HR-15: Better performers here tend to be more highly paid than those in similar jobs doing just average work.

Question HR-16: Employees here get feedback about the areas in which they have done particularly well.

Question HR-17: Due to the nature of the work at your firm, in general, how easy is it for people *below* the level of top management to know whether they are doing their work correctly?

ASSESSING RESOURCE ALLOCATION

Assessing Resource-Allocation Effectiveness

Questions 11-2 through 11-6 are a rudimentary assessment tool to assess your firm's ability to allocate resources. You may devise more sophisticated or specific tools for your own setting. Once again, you might want to get the confidential opinions of your managers.

Assessing Resource-Allocation Strategy

Here again, question 11-1 is only a rudimentary introduction to this area. Budgeting is a complex subject and you may want to refer to other sources to get an idea of the approach you might want to take. In addition, consider the following questions:

Question RL-1: Financial indicators. What are the few most important financial indicators you track to know whether or not your business is doing well?

Question RL-2: Use of CPA. Do you use a CPA firm? If so, what do you use it for—financial statements, tax work, auditing, general business advice, or for some other purposes?

ASSESSING PUBLIC RELATIONS

Assessing Public-Relations Effectiveness

Our treatment of this issue in the research study was quite limited, simply due to time limitations for the overall study. Refer to question 12-1, and consider having not only your managers respond, but also your customers, suppliers, members of your community, and so forth. Further, consider whether you have experienced litigation or regulation problems in any of the areas discussed in Chapter 12, such as affirmative action, and environmental or safety issues affecting workers or the public. You may also want to devise your own measures unique to your company or your industry.

Assessing Public-Relations Strategy

We included nothing specific in this area, except for the related section in question WF-3 above. Consider the following questions, too:

Question PR-1: Affirmative-action strategy. Do you have a particular way to assure that you and your managers comply with federal, state, and/or local guidelines on hiring practices and that you hire, evaluate, and promote without prejudice? If so, what do you do?

Question PR-2: Environment and safety strategy. Do you have a particular way to assure that your firm complies with or exceeds federal, state, and local environmental and safety standards, set forth by the Occupational Safety and Health Administration (OSHA) or other agency affecting your company? If so, what?

Question PR-3: Community-relations strategy. Do you have a particular way to assure that you maintain good relations with members of your community, other than customers and suppliers? If so, what?

ASSESSING TECHNICAL MASTERY

Assessing Technical-Mastery Effectiveness

This was another issue, due to limited scope of the study, that was measured on a very rudimentary level. Review questions 13-1 through 13-4 and ask your managers the same questions, again, preferably in a confidential survey format. You are very likely to want to develop more specific indicators (or perhaps already have) for each of these questions.

Assessing Technical-Mastery Strategies

Review question 13-5. In addition, you might consider asking your managers the following questions, TM1 through TM8, some of which may also be helpful in the human-relations and work-flow areas:

Question TM-1: Ways in which employees acquire technical skills. Which of the following describes your firm's approach to developing the technical skills of its employees? Indicate all that are appropriate to your firm.

——*a.* On-the-job training: The newcomer is shown how to do the job and then practices these tasks on the job.

——*b.* Manuals (operator's manuals, specification manuals) are distributed and reviewed.

——*c.* Training programs are planned just for your own employees on technical topics.

——*d.* Employees are sent to outside-sponsored one- or two-day seminars (ones that are offered the same way to lots of different firms).

——*e.* Groups of employees meet or work together in problem-solving teams, committees, or in some other group-learning device in which members can learn from one another.

——*f.* Employees are offered tuition rebates for taking relevant classes at area colleges or community colleges.

——*g.* The firm purchases training materials that employees are encouraged to go through on their own (e.g., audio cassette/training binder).

——*h.* The firm hires people with the required skills to begin with (e.g., master carpenters).

Question TM-2: Ways in which CEO develops managerial skills. Have you used any of these to keep up with management ideas and information other than the technically related information for your specific industry?

——*a.* Audiocassette tapes; books; in home, self-teaching program (e.g. from AMA)

——*b.* One- to three-day seminar

——*c.* More extensive executive-training program

——*d.* Courses from a college or university in business administration

——*e.* Degree in business (BBA or MBA)

Question TM-3: Ways in which employees acquire supervisory skills. Which of the following activities take place in your organization on a *planned* basis (as opposed to people choosing to do any of these activities on their own time and initiative) to develop leadership and supervisory skills of your employees?

——*a.* Discuss management issues in meetings together

——*b.* Invite speakers to talk on management issues

——*c.* Set up 1–2 day seminars inside the firm for employees

——*d.* Send managers to 1–2 day seminars outside the firm

——*e.* Pay for tuition at area colleges and universities

——*f.* Invite consultant to meet individually with managers to develop their management skills.

Question TM-4: Frequency of performance review. How frequently are you reviewed?

[1] monthly
[2] quarterly
[3] annually
[4] on some *other* basis.

Question TM-5: Areas of performance evaluation. Even if not done formally, in checking on your own work, in which of the following areas does the CEO pay the closest attention?

——*a.* How well you keep costs in line in your own area

——*b.* How profitable the firm is, overall (net profit)

——*c.* How profitable your own area is (e.g., as a profit center)

——*d.* Quality standards

——*e.* Productivity standards (how much or how quickly services and products are produced)

——*f.* How well you are able to recruit

——*g.* Sales

——*h.* General attitudes

Question TM-6: Specific incentive. In most companies, if the firm does well, it can afford to pay its employees a bit better or give them a little bonus at the end of the year. We are not interested in this but in specific incentives your firm may give for reaching specific performance targets. Does your firm tend to set up specific incentives for doing well?

Question TM-7: Performance rewarded. (If answered *yes* to question TM-6.) Who does the system apply to and how does it work? Which performance area or areas determine the size of the incentive or whether or not it is given?

——*a.* How well you keep costs in line in your own area

——*b.* How profitable the firm is, overall (net profit)

——*c.* How profitable your own area is (e.g., as a profit center)

——*d.* Quality standards

——*e.* Productivity standards (how much or how quickly services and products are produced)

——*f.* How well you are able to recruit

——*g.* Sales

——*h.* General attitudes

Question TM-8: Hiring practices (HP). To what extent are people with specialized technical or professional training hired?

[1] To a very great extent

[2] To a great extent

[3] To some extent

[4] To a small extent

[5] To a very slight extent, or not at all

(See also OP-6 and OP-7 in the Human Relations section)

NOTES

[1]Arthur A. Thompson and A. J. Strickland III, *Strategic Management: Concepts and Cases,* 6th ed. (Homewood, IL: Irwin, 1992).

Linkages Supported by the Research Study "Managing the Growing Firm"

The following linkages are supported by analysis of the research data collected for the study, "Managing the Growing Firm." In most cases, linkages are based upon simple statistical procedures such as the Spearman Rho correlation coefficient or analysis of variance. Because statistical techniques test for probabilities but not certainties, the wordings are stated in terms of likelihoods. (In most cases, linkages are supported at the $p < .01$ level of significance.) Actual discussions of these linkages are included in the respective chapters being referenced.

LINKAGES FOR CHAPTER 5: FINANCIAL VIABILITY

Linkage 5-1: The greater the firm size (relative to others in the same industry), the higher profits are likely to be.

Linkage 5-2: The steadier the sales growth, the higher profits and the better cash flow are likely to be (the latter lags in time).

Linkage 5-3: The more rapid the sales growth, the higher profits are likely to be.

Linkage 5-4: The more effective the direction-setting strategy, the better cash flow and profits are likely to be.

Linkage 5-5: The more effective the work-division strategy, the higher profits are likely to be.

Linkage 5-6: The more effective the coordination strategy, the higher and better cash flow and profits are likely to be.

Linkage 5-7: The greater the firm's ability to obtain needed capital, the higher profits are likely to be (causal direction may be in reverse).

Linkage 5-8: The greater the firm's ability to obtain needed capital, the better cash flow is likely to be (same year and lagged effects).

Linkage 5-9: The higher the employee morale, the higher profits are likely to be.

Linkage 5-10: The higher the employee morale, the better cash flow is likely to be (same year, only).

Linkage 5-11: The more similar the views of the company mission among CEO and managers, the higher profits are likely to be (lagged effect).

Linkage 5-12: The more effective the strategy for communicating values, the higher profits are likely to be.

Linkage 5-13: The more effective the resource-allocation strategy, the higher profits are likely to be.

Linkage 5-14: The greater the firm's ability to allocate people correctly across the firm, the higher profits are likely to be.

Linkage 5-15: The greater the firm's ability to allocate nonpersonnel resources correctly, the better cash flow is likely to be.

Linkage 5-16: The better the community image, the better cash flow is likely to be.

Linkage 5-17: The better the community image, the higher profits are likely to be.

Linkage 5-18: The better the technical skills and performance of employees, the higher profits are likely to be (same year, only).

Linkage 5-19: The better the technical skills and performance of employees, the better cash flow is likely to be (lagged effect).

Linkage 5-20: The higher the quality of output, the higher profits are likely to be (same year, only).

Linkage 5-21: The higher the productivity, the better profits and the cash flow are likely to be.

LINKAGES FOR CHAPTER 6: MARKET STRATEGY

Linkage 6-1: More effective work assignments and work coordination link to growth rates, steadier growth, and a more effective direction-setting strategy.

Linkage 6-2: Neither relative- nor absolute-sales size links to work-flow effectiveness.

Linkage 6-3: The firm's ability to obtain managers and capital links to greater sales.

Linkage 6-4: The better able a firm is to obtain supplies, the smaller sales are likely to be.

Linkage 6-5: The better able a firm is to recruit and to obtain capital, the faster the rate of growth is likely to be and the more effective the direction-setting strategy is likely to be.

Linkage 6-6: Steadier sales growth and a common sense of mission link to effective value-sharing strategy.

Linkage 6-7: Faster growth is linked to a more effective value-sharing strategy.

Linkage 6-8: Faster growth links to employee goal integration (lagged).

Linkage 6-9: Steadier growth, faster growth, and a more effective direction-setting strategy link to better community image and reputation.

Linkage 6-10: Steadier growth links to quality of product or service, better productivity, and a better skill level.

Linkage 6-11: Faster growth links to better product or service quality and better employee technical skills.

Linkage 6-12: Firms whose primary mission is to expand market share are likely to be more profitable.

Linkage 6-13: Firms whose primary mission is quality are likely to be more profitable.

Linkage 6-14: Firms whose CEOs emphasize product or service uniqueness are likely to report higher profits.

Linkage 6-15: Among "mini-firms" (10–20 employees), those offering a full range of services are likely to be less profitable.

Linkage 6-16: Among "medium-sized firms" (20–80 employees), those with diversification as a primary goal tend to be less profitable. But in the largest firms (above 80 employees), the pattern is reversed.

Linkage 6-17: Intense competition, with respect to both customers and technical know-how, links to a poor rating of direction-setting strategy.

Linkage 6-18: Firms that serve customers demanding quality tend to rate their direction-setting strategy more highly.

Linkage 6-19: In "micro-firms" (10–20 employees), the more customers expect discount prices—even if it means lower quality—the slower the growth rate is likely to be and the less profitable the firm is likely to be.

Linkage 6-20: In firms of 80 to 500 employees, the more customers expect discount prices—even if it means lower quality—the *more* profitable the firm is likely to be.

Linkage 6-21: Companies that select or design products and services and/or set direction participatively tend to report less steady growth, a poorer rating of direction-setting strategy, and lower profits.

LINKAGES FOR CHAPTER 7: DIVISION OF WORK (WORK FLOW)

Linkage 7-1: The more adequate the information that a CEO obtains from inside the firm, the more adequately authority is distributed, and the more effectively roles are assigned, then the more profitable the firm is likely to be.

Linkage 7-2: The more widely information is shared among employees and the more effectively roles are assigned, the more rapid sales growth is likely to be.

Linkage 7-3: The more adequate is the information obtained by the CEO inside the firm and the more effectively roles are assigned, then the more effective direction-setting strategy is likely to be.

Linkage 7-4: The more widely information is shared inside the firm, then the more able the firm is likely to be to obtain needed outside information, recruits, suppliers, subcontractors, and capital and the more effective the CEO's recruitment strategy is likely to be.

Linkage 7-5: The more adequate is the information obtained by the CEO and the more effectively roles are assigned, the more effective the management-recruitment strategy is likely to be and the more adequate outside information is likely to be.

Linkage 7-6: The more widely information is shared and the more effectively roles are assigned, the better the morale and commitment is likely to be and the more integrated individual and organizational goals are likely to be.

Linkage 7-7: The more widely information is shared, the more likely the CEO and managers are to share the same sense of mission.

Linkage 7-8: The more the CEO delegates responsibility to managers, the less consistent the CEO's values are likely to be with managers.

Linkage 7-9: The more managers perceive they are given authority, the better integrated are employee and organizational goals.

Linkage 7-10: The more widely information is shared, the better people and supplies are allocated across departments.

Linkage 7-11: CEOs getting adequate inside information and assigning roles effectively are likely to have (a) more effective resource allocation and (b) better people and supply allocations across departments.

Linkage 7-12: The more effectively roles are assigned, then the better technical performance, technical skill, quality, and productivity are likely to be.

Linkage 7-13: The more widely information is shared, the higher technical performance is likely to be.

Linkage 7-14: The more authority managers have to do their work, the higher the firm's productivity level is likely to be.

Linkage 7-15: The more able the CEO is to get adequate information from within the firm, the higher the levels of technical skills and performance of employees are likely to be.

LINKAGES FOR CHAPTER 8: COORDINATION
ADEQUACY (WORK FLOW)

Linkage 8-1: The more able the firm is to obtain needed managers, capital, and information from outside the firm, then the more effective coordination strategy is likely to be, the less likely are things to slip through cracks, and the less often are unnecessary work delays likely to occur.

Linkage 8-2: The more closely employee goals integrate with company goals, the better are employee morale and commitment likely to be. And the more effective is the CEO's value-sharing strategy, the more effective is coordination strategy likely to be.

Linkage 8-3: The more closely employee goals integrate with company goals, the better employee commitment and morale are, and the more effective the CEO's value-sharing strategy is, the less are unnecessary work delays likely to occur.

Linkage 8-4: The more closely employee goals integrate with company goals and the more consistent managers' perceptions of values are with the CEO's, the less likely are things to slip through the cracks.

Linkage 8-5: The better a firm is able to allocate equipment, supplies, and people, the more effective coordination strategy is likely to be.

Linkage 8-6: The better a firm is able to allocate equipment, supplies, and people, the less likely are things to slip through the cracks.

Linkage 8-7: The better able the firm is to allocate people, the less are unnecessary work delays likely to occur.

Linkage 8-8: The fewer the unnecessary work delays, the less the CEO must wait to receive financial reports.

Linkage 8-9: The fewer the unnecessary work delays and the less likely things are to slip through cracks, the better the firm's reputation.

Linkage 8-10: The more effective the coordination strategy is, the better product (or service) quality, technical skills, and productivity are likely to be.

Linkage 8-11: The more that things slip through the cracks, the worse technical performance is likely to be.

Linkage 8-12: The reliance of business-service firms on monitoring systems is significantly greater than that of construction, manufacturing, and wholesale.

Linkage 8-13: Construction firms and manufacturers rely significantly more on daily plans to coordinate efforts than do wholesalers or business-service firms.

Linkage 8-14: Construction firms rely significantly more on work standards than do business services, manufacturers or wholesalers.

Linkage 8-15: The larger the employment size, then the less directly involved the CEO is likely to be, the more he or she is likely to rely on chain of command, and the more managers he or she is likely to delegate to.

Linkage 8-16: The larger the employment size, then the more likely it is that written guidelines, job descriptions, and meetings will be used to coordinate efforts.

Linkage 8-17: The larger the employment size, then the less often is informal conversation likely to be used to coordinate efforts.

Linkage 8-18: The larger the employment size, the greater the number of monitoring systems a firm is likely to have.

Linkage 8-19: The more a CEO relies on work standards to coordinate efforts, the better are profitability and cash flow likely to be.

Linkage 8-20: The more monitoring systems a firm sets up, the greater the reliance on employee judgments, the greater the use of meetings, and the fewer managers delegated to, then the more effective is coordination likely to be.

Linkage 8-21: The larger or older a company is, the better the cash flow (same year and previous year) is likely to be.

Linkage 8-22: The more predictable the firm's environment is and the less diversified the firm is, the more effective coordination is likely to be.

Linkage 8-23: In firms with fewer than 20 employees, the greater the reliance on chain of command, the greater the reliance on employee judgments, the fewer managers a CEO delegates to, and the greater reliance on work standards to coordinate efforts, then the more effective coordination is likely to be.

Linkage 8-24: In firms with fewer than 20 employees, the fewer managers a CEO delegates to, the higher profits are likely to be.

Linkage 8-25: In firms of 80 to 500 employees, the fewer the written job descriptions and the greater the use of meetings, the more effective coordination is likely to be.

Linkage 8-26: In firms of 80 to 500 employees, the less reliance there is on written job descriptions, and the more on informal conversation to coordinate efforts, the better cash flow is likely to be.

Linkage 8-27: In industries with low predictability, the more reliance there is on work standards to coordinate efforts, the more effective coordination is likely to be.

Linkage 8-28: In industries with low predictability, the less directly involved the CEO is in work flow and the greater the reliance on work standards to coordinate efforts, the higher profits are likely to be.

Linkage 8-29: In industries with high predictability, the more directly involved the CEO is in work flow, the higher profits are likely to be.

Linkage 8-30: In industries with high predictability, the more daily planning that takes place, the worse cash flow is likely to be.

Linkage 8-31: In single product or services outfits, the fewer CEO "total delegations" and the more monitoring systems there are in place, the more effective coordination is likely to be.

Linkage 8-32: In single product or services firms, the more directly involved the CEO is with work flow, the higher profits are likely to be.

Linkage 8-33: In firms with several related products or services, the more informal conversation is used to coordinate efforts, the better cash flow is likely to be.

Linkage 8-34: In firms 5 to 10 years of age, the more the CEO relies on employee judgments, work standards, and monitoring systems to coordinate efforts, the more effective coordination is likely to be.

Linkage 8-35: In firms 5 to 10 years of age, the fewer the written guidelines to coordinate efforts, the better cash flow is likely to be.

Linkage 8-36: In firms 11 to 20 years of age, the more work standards are used to coordinate efforts, the more effective coordination is likely to be.

Linkage 8-37: In firms older than 39 years, the more the CEO relies on chain of command to coordinate efforts, the higher profits are likely to be.

Linkage 8-38: In slower growing firms, the fewer the managers the CEO delegates to and the more work standards are used to coordinate efforts, the more effective coordination is likely to be.

Linkage 8-39: In slower growing firms, the less often written job descriptions are used and the more work standards are used to coordinate efforts, the better cash flow is likely to be.

Linkage 8-40: In manufacturing firms, the more monitoring systems are used, the more effective coordination strategy is likely to be.

Linkage 8-41: In manufacturing firms, the less involved the CEO is with work flow and the more informal conversation is used to coordinate efforts, the better cash flow is likely to be.

Linkage 8-42: In wholesale firms, the less often meetings and the more often work standards are used to coordinate efforts, the higher profits are likely to be.

Linkage 8-43: In construction firms, the more often meetings are used, then the better profits and cash flow are likely to be.

LINKAGES FOR CHAPTER 9: RESOURCE ACQUISITION

Linkage 9-1: The greater the firm's annual revenues, the better the profits, and the more liquid the firm, then the better the firm's ability to obtain capital is likely to be.

Linkage 9-2: The better able the firm is to recruit, the more rapid the sales growth of the firm is likely to be.

Linkage 9-3: The more able the firm is to recruit needed management and technical personnel and to obtain the subcontracts, the capital, and the information it needs, the more effectively is work likely to be divided and efforts coordinated.

Linkage 9-4: The more able the firm is to obtain personnel—management and technical people, as well as subcontractors—the better the allocation of people across departments is likely to be.

Linkage 9-5: The more able the firm is to obtain the information it needs, then the more effective overall allocation strategy is likely to be and the better the allocation of people across departments is also likely to be.

Linkage 9-6: The more able a firm is to recruit both management and technical personnel, the higher the morale of employees is likely to be and the better integrated employee goals with overall firm objectives are likely to be.

Linkage 9-7: The more effective the CEO's management-recruitment strategy is, the better integrated employee goals are likely to be, the higher the morale is likely to be, and the more effective the CEO's value-sharing is likely to be.

Linkage 9-8: The better able the firm is to obtain supplies and capital, then the better integrated employee goals are likely to be and the higher morale is likely to be.

Linkage 9-9: The better able the firm is to obtain supplies, the better team climate is likely to be.

Linkage 9-10: The better able the firm is to obtain capital and outside information, the better the firm's image is likely to be.

Linkage 9-11: The better able the firm is to obtain needed supplies, the higher productivity is likely to be.

Linkage 9-12: The better able the firm is to recruit nonmanagement personnel, the higher technical-skill levels are likely to be.

Linkage 9-13: Firms basing incentives on seniority and salary rather than on performance are more able to recruit technical personnel.

Linkage 9-14: Firms hiring more specialized help have an easier time recruiting.

Linkage 9-15: Firms using written job descriptions and firms in which employee roles are clear are more able to recruit nonmanagement personnel.

Linkage 9-16: The more a CEO values quality, the more able a firm is to recruit nonmanagement personnel.

Linkage 9-17: Firms monitoring productivity have more trouble recruiting than those that do not.

LINKAGES FOR CHAPTER 10: HUMAN RELATIONS

Linkage 10-1: The higher the morale, the more consistently values between CEO and managers are understood, and the more effective the value-sharing strategy, the higher profits are likely to be.

Linkage 10-2: The more clearly the firm's mission is understood, the higher profit is likely to be, on a lagging basis.

Linkage 10-3: The more integrated employee and company goals are, the higher the morale, and the more consistent values and mission are between CEO and managers, the better the public image is likely to be.

Linkage 10-4: The more integrated company and employee goals are and the more consistent values between managers and CEO are, the higher productivity is likely to be.

Linkage 10-5: The higher morale is, then the better technical performance and overall quality are likely to be.

Linkage 10-6: The more appropriate staff allocations are and the more accurate budgets are, the more integrated company and employee goals are likely to be.

Linkage 10-7: The more appropriate staff allocations are and the speedier financial reporting is, the higher morale is likely to be.

Linkage 10-8: The clearer the reporting structure and the less frequently the CEO bypasses managers, the higher morale and goal integration are likely to be.

Linkage 10-9: The clearer the standards, the more chain of command and meetings are used for work flow, the more positive and negative feedback are given, and the clearer roles are, the higher morale is likely to be and the more integrated goals are likely to be.

Linkage 10-10: The more informal conversation is used to coordinate work and share values, the higher morale is likely to be and the more integrated goals are likely to be.

Linkage 10-11: The more positive the company climate (i.e., the more trust, cooperation, and innovativeness and the less politics) and the more confidence employees have in the CEO, the higher morale is likely to be and more integrated goals are likely to be.

Linkage 10-12: The more training programs are based on formal assessment of needs and the more rewards are based on performance, the clearer employees are likely to be about the firm's overall objectives.

LINKAGES FOR CHAPTER 11: RESOURCE ALLOCATION

Linkage 11-1: The fewer the number of days the CEO must wait after the end of a fiscal period to receive financial reports, the higher employee morale is likely to be.

Linkage 11-2: The more satisfied the CEO is with his or her resource allocation strategy, the better morale among employees is likely to be.

Linkage 11-3: Firms in which employees have a better understanding of the firm's objectives are also likely to allocate equipment and supplies more adequately across people and departments.

Linkage 11-4: The better the image and reputation of the firm relative to others in its industry, the more effective the resource-allocation strategy.

Linkage 11-5: The better the image and reputation of the firm relative to others in its industry, the fewer the number of days after the end of the fiscal period is the CEO likely to receive his or her financial report.

Linkage 11-6: The more effective the resource-allocation strategy, the better are quality and productivity likely to be.

Linkage 11-7: The more appropriately equipment and supplies are distributed in the firm, the better are the technical performance and technical skills of employees likely to be.

Linkage 11-8: The more appropriately employees are allocated in various assignments across the firm, the better the overall level of technical skill among employees is likely to be.

Linkage 11-9: The fewer the number of days after the end of the fiscal period until the CEO receives his or her financial report, the higher the overall productivity of the firm is likely to be.

Linkage 11-10: CEOs who track sales as a key financial indicator are likely to experience higher sales growth over a five-year period than those who do not.

Linkage 11-11: CEOs who track gross profits are more likely than those who do not to head larger firms (as measured by annual revenues).

Linkage 11-12: CEOs who track cash flow are more likely than those who do not to have a higher level of profitability in the subsequent year (relatively weak effect).

Linkage 11-13: CEOs who track their budget are more likely than those who do not to have a more adequate allocation of material across groups and departments.

Linkage 11-14: The more diversified the firm, then the less effective is the strategy for allocating resources likely to be.

Linkage 11-15: The clearer the CEO seems to be about his or her reporting structure, the more effective is the strategy for allocating resources likely to be.

Linkage 11-16: Firms in which authority is delegated by the CEO to a larger number of managers, in which the CEO is less involved, generally, and in which managers below the CEO are more involved with monitoring and controlling costs, are firms in which reports tend to be delayed a greater number of days.

Linkage 11-17: The more decentralized the cost-control function is, the less accurate budgets are likely to be.

Linkage 11-18: The more the firm relies on the chain of command, meetings, and standards to coordinate efforts, the more adequate the allocation of people is likely to be.

Linkage 11-19: In firms in which employees receive a greater amount of positive feedback for work done well and in which corporate climate in general is more positive, the more adequate is the allocation of people across departments likely to be.

Linkage 11-20: The clearer a CEO is about his or her reporting structure, the more adequately is a firm likely to distribute equipment and supplies across projects and departments.

Linkage 11-21: Companies that use a CPA firm are likely to distribute equipment and supplies more appropriately across projects and departments than those who do not use CPA firms.

LINKAGES FOR CHAPTER 12: PUBLIC RELATIONS

Linkage 12-1: Firms with a higher public image also report higher technical performance, quality, productivity, and skill.

Linkage 12-2: Firms relying on informal conversation and the use of standards also report a better image, relative to competitors.

Linkage 12-3: Firms in which the CEO delegates the government-relations function have lower ratings of image and reputation.

Linkage 12-4: Firms relying more heavily on chain of command (in which the CEO is less likely to bypass managers) have better reputations.

Linkage 12-5: Managers tend to rate role clarity and employee understanding of organizational goals more highly in firms with a higher reputation.

Linkage 12-6: Firms whose CEOs share specific values with managers, regardless of what those values are, have a better reputation or image.

Linkage 12-7: Firms in which middle managers see quality as more highly valued have a higher reputation.

Linkage 12-8: Firms with better reputations tend to be those where profits and costs are monitored, with a feedback system that compares actual performance to set standards.

LINKAGES FOR CHAPTER 13: TECHNICAL MASTERY

Linkage 13-1: The more specialized the technical and professional hires, the better the firm's technical performance is likely to be.

Linkage 13-2: Companies that base performance evaluation and incentives on costs and profits are more likely than those that do not to achieve better profits and cash flow.

Linkage 13-3: Companies that base performance evaluation and incentives on cost control and profits are more likely than those who do not to achieve better productivity.

Linkage 13-4: Companies that use incentive programs based on raw sales are more likely than those who do not to achieve lower levels of morale.

Linkage 13-5: For small to medium-sized firms, the more a firm uses written job descriptions, the lower the productivity.

Linkage 13-6: When lower-level personnel write job descriptions, a poorer quality of output is likely than when lower-level personnel are not involved in writing them.

Linkage 13-7: The clearer employees are about their jobs, the better productivity is likely to be.

Linkage 13-8: The more a company relies on informal conversation, a chain of command, and setting work standards to coordinate work efforts, the better technical performance and company productivity are likely to be.

Linkage 13-9: The more managers a CEO delegates authority to, the worse the technical performance and productivity are likely to be.

Linkage 13-10: The more a CEO bypasses managers in the chain of command, the lower the technical performance of employees and the poorer the quality of goods or services are likely to be.

Linkage 13-11: The more part-time people are used year round, the lower the technical performance of employees and the poorer the quality of goods or services are likely to be.

Linkage 13-12: The greater the climate of trust, then the better the technical skill and performance of employees, the better the quality of goods or services, and the higher the productivity of employees are all likely to be.

Linkage 13-13: The less afraid people are to rock the boat, the higher the productivity is likely to be and the better technical skills are likely to be.

Linkage 13-14: Companies that stress quality as a value are likely to report higher productivity.

Index

More About the Authors

Dr. Lorraine Uhlaner Hendrickson currently serves as Professor of Management at Eastern Michigan University, teaching courses in entrepreneurship, strategic planning, organizational behavior, and organization design. In addition to consulting with industry, she served as a company officer, board member, and investor in former INC 500 company StarPak Solar Systems Corporation between 1976 and 1986. She holds a BA in psychology from Radcliffe College, Harvard University; a doctorandus from the University of Leiden in the Netherlands; and an MA and Ph.D. in organization psychology from the University of Michigan, Ann Arbor. She has published articles on management topics in the *Journal of Organization Change Management, Productivity Review,* and proceedings of several management associations, including the Academy of Management and the International Council for Small Business. Dr. Hendrickson served as founding director of the Center for Entrepreneurship at Eastern Michigan University and, while there, directed the study "Managing the Growing Firm."

Dr. John Psarouthakis was born on the island of Crete. He holds a BSC and MSC in mechanical engineering from the Massachusetts Institute of Technology and a Ph.D. in mechanical engineering from the University of Maryland. After holding several engineering and executive positions, in 1979 he founded his first entrepreneurial venture, J. P. Industries, Inc. (JPI). JPI specialized in turning underperforming, "rustbelt" small businesses around. As JPI president and chairman, he parlayed a modest initial investment into a FORTUNE 500 firm with sales of over $500 million. In 1990 he was able to merge JPI into T&N plc, a large British industrial corporation, for $376 million. His accomplishments have been described repeatedly in *Forbes, Fortune,* the *Wall Street Journal,* and other national media, though none provides the detail and depth included in this book. In 1991 Dr. Psarouthakis founded a new acquisition-based company, JPE Inc., targeting somewhat larger companies for turnaround. Dr. Psarouthakis also serves as Adjunct Professor at the School of Business Administration at the University of Michigan, Ann Arbor. Dr. Psarouthakis's first book, *Better Makes Us Best,* published by Productivity Press, describes the culture of continual improvement practiced at JPI. The recipient of honorary doctoral degrees from Eastern Michigan University and Cleary College, Dr. Psarouthakis has received numerous awards for his entrepreneurial and civic achievements, among them the MIT Corporate Leadership Award, the Entrepreneur of the Year Award twice from *INC Magazine,* and the Medallion for Entrepreneurship from Beta Gamma Sigma National Honor Society of Schools of Business. In his early career he received the Distinguished Young Scientist Award from the Maryland Academy of Science. Dr. Psarouthakis served as founding Chairman of the Advisory Board to the Center for Entrepreneurship at EMU, also serving as an advisor to the research project "Managing the Growing Firm."